D1129986

This Book
Belongs
to:
Peggy Lusk

THREE WAYS OF LOVE

THREE WAYS OF LOVE

by
Frances Parkinson Keyes

ST. PAUL EDITIONS

Library of Congress Catalogue Card Number: 63-16770.
Suggested decimal classification: 922.

FIRST EDITION: *November, 1963*

Reprinted by arrangement with
Hawthorn Books, Inc.

NIHIL OBSTAT

Daniel V. Flynn, J.C.D.
Censor Librorum

IMPRIMATUR

✠ Francis Cardinal Spellman
Archbishop of New York

New York, August 22, 1963

The nihil obstat and the imprimatur are official declarations that a book or pamphlet is free of doctrinal or moral error. No implication is contained therein that those who have granted the nihil obstat and imprimatur agree with the contents, opinions or statements expressed.

Printed by Daughters of St. Paul, 50 St. Paul's Ave., Boston, Ma. 02130

Permission to quote from the following works is gratefully acknowledged.

Avignon Au Temps des Papes by Robert Brun. Copyright 1928 by Librairie Armand Colin, Paris.

Catherine of Siena by Sigrid Undset. Translated by Kate Austin-Lund. Copyright 1954 by Sheed and Ward, Inc., New York.

Catherine of Siena—Fire and Blood by Igino Giordani. Translated from the Italian by Thomas J. Tobin. Copyright 1959 by The Bruce Publishing Company, Milwaukee.

Caesars and Saints by Stewart Perowne. Copyright 1962 by Hodder and Stoughton, Ltd., London.

Daily Life in Florence in the Time of the Medici by J. Lucas-Dubreton. Translated from the French by A. Lytton Sells. Copyright 1960 by The Macmillan Company, New York.

The Life of St. Catherine of Siena by Blessed Raymond of Capua. Translated from the Italian by George Lamb. Copyright 1960 by P. J. Kenedy and Sons, New York.

The Life of St. Frances of Rome by Lady Georgiana Fullerton. Copyright 1885 by D. J. Sadlier & Co., New York. Reprinted by permission of William H. Sadlier, Inc.

More Saints for Six O'Clock by Joan Windham. Copyright 1935 by Sheed and Ward, Ltd., London.

The Mystics of Siena by Piero Misciattelli, English version by M. Peters-Roberts. Copyright 1929 by W. Heffer and Sons, Ltd., London.

Pageant of the Popes by John Farrow. Copyright revised edition 1950 by Sheed and Ward, Inc., New York.

Roman Women—Their History and Habits by J.P.V.D. Balsdon. Copyright © 1962 by John Day Company, New York.

Saint Françoise Romaine et Son Temps by Berthem-Bontoux. Copyright 1931 by Bloud and Gay, Paris.

The Story of the Church by Domènico Grandi and Antonio Galli. Translated into English and edited by John Chapin. Copyright © by Doubleday & Company, Inc. Reprinted by permission of the publisher.

The Sublime City by Igino Cecchetti. Published for the Catholic War Veterans of the United States of America by Edizioni Arte e Scienza, Rome.

A Traveller in Rome by H. V. Morton. Published 1957 by Methuen & Company, Ltd., London. Reprinted by permission of H. V. Morton.

To
Dorothy Good
—a learned and lovely lady—
with gratitude and affection

TABLE OF CONTENTS

LIST OF ILLUSTRATIONS

FOREWORD

THE CREDIT for the title and subject matter of *Three Ways of Love* belongs to Kenneth Seeman Giniger, the President of Hawthorn Books, Inc. The research, traveling, writing and editing were my contribution.

Mr. Giniger burst like a bomb upon my consciousness, which is his highly effective way of approaching an author who has not previously worked for him. He suddenly appeared at the Sulgrave Club in Washington, where I was then almost up to my neck in another writing project, and asked me if there were not any more saints about whom I would like to write. (Up to that point, I had already written about seven, besides Juan Diego, the Indian to whom was vouchsafed the grace of Guadalupe; and the Venerable María Vela, the third mystic of Avila.) With some hesitation, I admitted that, for thirty years, I had wanted to write a brief biography of Santa Rosa de Lima and, for nearly ten years, a similar one about Santa Mariana, designated in Ecuador as the Lily of Quito. There was no hesitation on the part of my caller. The words were hardly out of my mouth when he said, "Fine! We will put the two biographies into the same book and call it *The Rose and the Lily*. I do not think there will be any problem about financial arrangements." To prove his point, he drew his checkbook from his pocket and, before I had recovered from my shock, went on, conversationally, "And next? Aren't there still some more saints?"

I hesitated longer this time, but eventually I made a second confession: I had never been able to understand why Santa Francesca Romana had not achieved a more prominent place in the annals of the saints. She embodied so much that was an integral part of the Eternal City that her very name was inseparably linked with it; she had lived during one of the thrilling periods in history, when the Great Western Schism was raging and when the Middle Ages were merging into the Renaissance; and she was that rarest of all types of holy women, a great lady who had achieved sanctity despite the distractions and responsibilities of her social position, her marriage and her motherhood. Her ideal was another Roman patrician, who had lived one thousand years earlier, but also during a most thrilling period of history, when Christianity had begun to triumph over paganism.

"And this was?"

"St. Agnes, the child martyr, whose name has become synonymous with innocence. She was slaughtered before she was old enough to surmount any of the obstacles which usually block the path to holiness, but her purity had such a shining quality that it has illuminated the centuries. Only seven female saints have found a place in the Canon, but she is one of them."

"And you feel there is a definite tie between her and Francesca?"

"I do indeed. Francesca was baptized and confirmed in the Church of St. Agnes. She named her only daughter Agnes. Her devotion to this saint was lifelong. She, too, yearned for martyrdom. It would have made her very happy if she could have died as Agnes did, to avoid being forced into an unwelcome marriage. The story of the one seems to complement the other, for Agnes achieved sanctity, through her death, before she achieved womanhood; and Francesca, very completely a woman, achieved it through her life. . . . And then, of course, there is that greatest of all female Italian saints, Catherine of Siena, whose sanctity transcends womanhood, because she was primarily a mystic and a politician and these remarkable qualities have nothing to do with sex."

"So why," inquired Kenneth Giniger briskly, "couldn't you write another book about those three saints—Agnes—Francesca—Catherine? Yes, that's the idea. We will call it *Three Ways of Love,* which is what these women personified, isn't it?"

I said I believed it was and that was practically the end of the conference. In fact, there was nothing left to settle, except details.

Work on *Three Ways of Love* was begun in 1959, when I visited all the major and several of the minor cities of Italy, in search of persons and places, as well as paintings, documents and books that would help me to interpret the lives of St. Agnes of Rome, St. Frances of Rome, better known as Santa Francesca Romana, and St. Catherine of Siena. This research was interrupted in 1960, because of work in South America on *The Rose and the Lily;* but it was resumed and expanded in 1961; and that same summer the actual writing was not only begun, but well under way, as far as St. Agnes was concerned, and also well under way as far as St. Catherine was concerned. However, I felt that, in order to do the latter justice, I should not only return to Italy, but go to Avignon, which I had not previously visited in some years and never when mindful of its important connection with St. Catherine. I also felt that I should spend more time in Genoa, to check and recheck on what seemed to me one of the most dramatic episodes in her life, and that I should somehow make time for a brief visit to Montepulciano, where her story was interwoven with that of another St. Agnes, and where I had hitherto never been.

When all this was done, I felt I had familiarized myself, as thoroughly as it was possible for me to do, with every city associated with the life and works of St. Catherine, since, in addition to spending months in Siena and its environs, I had studied and searched for further enlightenment in Florence, Pisa, Lucca and Rome. But I still was not sufficiently acquainted with the Eternal City, as personified by Agnes and Frances, though I went there for the first time nearly seventy years ago and have been revisiting it at frequent intervals ever since. So once more I spent a golden autumn there, finding it more wonderful than ever before, both as the setting for the stories of the two Roman patricians who were such an integral part of it, and as the scene for the opening sessions of the Ecumenical Council. And when I finally came home, early in November, it was with the satisfaction of knowing that all research and practically all writing on the book had been done *sur place,* without haste or hindrance, and that it was therefore as authentic as it was humanly possible for me to make it.

As I have said, I sought out persons, as well as places, who could and would help explain the three ways of love which I was trying to interpret. Foremost among these I must mention Miss Dorothy Good, to whom this book is dedicated. A resident of Italy for most of her long life and a recognized authority on its art, letters and history, she has been privileged to spend her later years in the house built for Catherine by the saint's very good friends, the Soderini, on the outskirts of Florence. Originally, the property corresponded to the biblical description of a tower and a vineyard; in time the tower was enlarged to become a more modern dwelling place and the vineyard is now the charming residential Costa San Giorgio; but St. Catherine's oratory and study-bedroom are still not only intact, but structurally unchanged, and there she seems very close, both to the present occupant of her quarters and to those who come there seeking to know her better. The search is richly rewarding.

Besides receiving me so quickly at St. Catherine's house in Florence—thanks to the kind offices of my friends the Honorable Edmond Howard, then British Consul General in Florence, and his lovely and talented wife Cécile—Miss Good visited me at length in both Siena and Rome, accompanied me on my fact-finding excursions, recommended books that she thought would be useful to me and went over large portions of my script with me, making suggestions and corrections. But for her, I doubt whether I should ever have braved the trip to Vallombrosa or come to recognize the important part played by the loggia in medieval history or located some of the pictures and books which have proved most valuable to me for illustrations and reference. I am indeed deeply indebted to her.

Next on my list should come Igino Giordani, a former librarian of the Vatican and an author of many books, among them the most reliable of the modern biographies of St. Catherine. I had leaned heavily on the biography by Raymond of Capua, Catherine's confessor, because I felt the comments of her contemporary so peculiarly suitable for quoting; but I wanted the viewpoint of *my* distinguished contemporary, too. The privilege of conferring with him was arranged through the good offices of Michael Barjansky, Cultural Attaché of the American Embassy in Rome, to whom I am indebted for this opportunity. Signor Giordani clarified many points which were obscure to me and brought up others which, without his helpful suggestions, I would not have thought it necessary to introduce.

Others who have been most helpful to me, as far as the story of St. Catherine is concerned, are Dr. Arnaldo Luvini, Dr. Diego

Castruccio and Dr. Roberto Prando of Remington Rand Italia, in both Rome and Genoa; Miss Caroline Bonzi of Genoa; and Signor and Signora Stoppini, my kind and cooperative host and hostess during my protracted stays at the Hotel Excelsior in Siena.

Signor Luigi Coppe of the Italian State Tourist Bureau was most helpful in making appointments, securing photographs and acting as interpreter in connection with both the stories of St. Agnes and Santa Francesca Romana. In the line of research I should not fail to add the names of Miss Katherine Andrews, research assistant to the Honorable Norris Cotton, Senator from New Hampshire; Mrs. Ellen Taylor, Assistant Cultural Attaché in Rome; the Marchesa Dottoressa Olga Campanari, who was recommended to me by Mrs. Taylor; and Miss Elizabeth J. Bunner.

In connection with the biography of Santa Francesca Romana, I am indebted to the Reverend L. G. O'Connor, S. J., of Loyola University in New Orleans, who gave me a letter of introduction to the Reverend Ernest J. Burrus, S. J., in Rome, who, in turn, introduced me to the Misses Esther, Carola and Francesca MacMurrough, who make their home in a splendid old building, once the hostel of the Genoese Guild of John the Baptist, which has its own chapel and one of the most beautiful patios I have ever seen. They were kind enough to lend me their own copy of Lady Georgiana Fullerton's life of St. Frances of Rome, an extremely valuable book published a century ago and now out of print and very difficult to come by. I was keenly aware of the responsibility this entailed and personally carried the book in my briefcase in the course of all my travels until the time came when I could restore it to its owners. As Lady Georgiana based her material on that contained in the biography by Dom Giovanni Matteotti, Francesca's confessor, I have drawn on it heavily in quoting—for the same reasons that I did in connection with Raymond of Capua's life of Catherine.

Among those who have been generally helpful with the entire script are the Very Reverend Monsignor William A. Carew of the Vatican Secretariat of State; George Whittinghill, our Consul General in Rome, and his wife Sandy; the Countess Piella and the Countess Gravina-Ramacca, respectively the aunt and cousin of the Edmond Howards whom I have already mentioned, and the latters' son John; and Mr. Francis Rosett, now located in Washington, but long a resident of Italy and, like Miss Good, a veritable mine of information. I owe the pleasure of his acquaintance and, also, my acquaintance with one of the most valuable works of reference I have found—*Sainte Françoise Romaine et Son Temps* (1384-1440) by Berthem-Bontoux—to my friend, Mrs. Robert Walsh, President of the Guild of Santa Francesca Romana in Washington, who, more than anyone else I know in the United States, has shown great devotion to this saint and a firm determination to make her better known. Mrs. Walsh feels that Santa Francesca Romana has suffered, rather than benefited, by her social position and quotes this humorous little poem from *Iolanthe* by Gilbert and Sullivan as expressing what she would like to say herself:

> Spurn not the nobly born
> With love affected,
> Nor treat with virtuous scorn
> The well connected.
> High rank involves no shame—
> We boast an equal claim
> With him of humble name
> To be respected!

The list would be incomplete without mentioning Dr. S. Levet, the genial director of the Grand Hotel, where I have frequently and joyfully made my headquarters when in the Eternal City; Dr. Levet's capable assistant, Mr. Luigi Scianda; Lorenzo, the hotel's incomparable concierge and Tommaso Tomassi, the resourceful driver who has often acted as my chauffeur.

In the case of persons and places presumably less familiar to the average reader, I have used the English spelling of their names—it would not seem natural to most of us, for instance, to refer to St. Francis of Assisi as Francesco or to St. Catherine of Siena as Caterina or to our little martyr St. Agnes as Agnese. On the other hand, it seems equally unnatural to refer to Santa Francesca Romana in any other way; and the same is true about the members of her family, the Christian and family names of popes before they were elevated to the throne, and to certain churches, streets and localities. If this procedure seems inconsistent, at least it has been undertaken with the best of motives.

Frances Parkinson Keyes

SAINT AGNES OF ROME

1

THE BENEDICTINE nuns of St. Cecilia yearn for a late Easter. For, at Easter, their most cherished visitors leave them.

These visitors are two little lambs which are brought to their convent every year after these have been blessed at the end of the Pontifical Mass, which is celebrated in the Basilica of St. Agnes by the Abbot General of the Canons Regular of the Lateran. This Mass marks the beginning of a time-honored sequence of ceremonies which commemorates, touchingly and picturesquely, the story of St. Agnes —that beautiful child who, early in the fourth century, suffered death for love of Christ, and "whose name blossoms like a flower in the long illustrious martyrology." [1]

Originally, two such lambs formed the annual tribute from the Basilica of St. Agnes to the Basilica of St. John Lateran; and the nature of this chosen offering was prompted by the fact that, in sacred and legendary art, Agnes is nearly always depicted with a lamb—the appropriate symbol of both her purity and her sacrifice. Since the symbolism is as effective as ever, it is considered fitting that lambs should have a part in the celebration of her feast, which falls on January 21. They are provided by the Trappist Fathers of the Monastery of Tre Fontane, which is located near St. Paul's Basilica and which has its own sheepfold; and when they arrive at St. Agnes' Basilica they are wearing crowns on their heads and are lying in baskets decorated with red and white flowers and red and white ribbons—red for martyrdom, white for purity.

The Church of St. Agnes, built by Constantine, the first Christian emperor, in the fourth century, over the grave of the young martyr, is one of the most beautiful in Rome and on her feast day it is invested with additional splendor. Soft red and gold velvet is festively draped over the balconies between the slender antique columns of the *matroneum*—upper galleries on both sides of the aisle, formerly reserved exclusively for the use of women. The ornate stone vases at each corner of the canopy are filled with enormous bouquets of red and white carnations and garlands of roses are hung from each supporting pillar. To the left of the high altar an exquisite gold and jeweled chalice and paten are exposed. Nuns belonging to various Orders are ensconced in the embrasures of the *matroneum,* where the antique marble forms a framework for their beautiful white coifs and dignified black habits.

The Titular Head of the Church arrives, escorted by a bishop and the three celebrant priests of the High Mass. The vestments are dazzling—rich red, heavily embossed with gold embroidery, which catches and reflects the light from the candelabra, giving the effect of a thousand miniature rainbows. The cardinal is escorted to the canopied episcopal throne behind the altar, on each side of which hang crimson and gilt tapestries depicting the cardinal's hat with tassels, keys and the heraldic coat of arms.

As the Mass begins, St. Agnes gazes down in her stylized Byzantine robes from the mosaic in the tribune between Symmachus, the Sardinian Pope whose election was unsuccessfully challenged, and Honorius I, who holds a model of the early Church in his hands. The mosaic is in subdued tones of brown and muted gold against a blue background and is noteworthy for representing a transition period in the art of the time, as the saint and the two pontiffs here take the place hitherto assigned to Christ and his apostles. Clouds of incense rise and the ancient sacrifice of the Mass proceeds in solemnity and grandeur. Just before the last gospel, a further procession comes up the aisle—little girls veiled, and dressed in white lace with pale blue ribbons and sashes. Following are four splendid *carabinieri* with cockaded hats and smart blue and red uniforms, carrying on their shoulders two garlanded, rustic straw baskets, in each of which reposes a baby lamb. They, too, are garlanded—one with a wreath of miniature red roses, the other with white. A basket is placed on either side of the altar and the lambs are duly blessed and incensed. At this point, one little fellow sometimes becomes restless, no doubt disturbed at his unaccustomed surroundings and attention. He makes determined attempts to leap out of the basket and look for grass and has to be forcibly restrained by the combined efforts of the three celebrant priests and the cardinal. When this happens, a delighted ripple of amusement echoes through the church.

Still crowned and ensconced in their baskets, the lambs are next taken to the Vatican, where they are presented to His Holiness by the Dean of the Sacred Roman Rota, a Consistorial Advocate, the Treasurer of the Canons of St. John Lateran and a Papal Master of Ceremonies. The Pope himself blesses them and entrusts them to the Master of Ceremonies, who carries them carefully to the Benedictine nuns of St. Cecilia, whose convent adjoins her church. There the nuns are eagerly waiting to receive them. A little shelter has been prepared for them in a corner of the patio, and semolina and beetroot provided to supplement the garden grass and assure them of an ample and well-balanced diet. They become not only the charges but the pets of the fifteen nuns who make up the community. They are not named, but that is because they are always addressed as "darling" and therefore names seem superfluous.

The length of the lambs' sojourn with the nuns depends on the date of Easter. If this is early, it may be over on March 19; if this is late, it can last until April 23. It is easy to understand why the nuns yearn for a late Easter. For, on Maundy Thursday, the little lambs are shorn and, on Good Friday, they are "sacrificed." This is the only expression the nuns consent to use in talking of them and represents not only their reluctance to speak more realistically, but their conviction that the lambs share their symbolism with the Savior. As the nuns do the shearing, their eyes are already overflowing with tears; the next day the lambs are gone to their fate and the nuns are weeping without restraint. The little shelter is empty; the grass in the patio goes uncropped.

But that is not the end of the story. The wool from the shorn lambs is carefully cleaned and dried by the nuns; then it is woven into the pallium, which is the special insignia of an Archbishop who is also a Metropolitan—that is, an Archbishop with a residential Archdiocese. It consists of a narrow strip of white wool, marked with six black crosses and weighted at either end with lead encased in black silk, and is worn around the neck and over the chasuble in such a way that one strip falls in front and one behind. Approximately twelve pallia are made each year and these are kept in a golden box in the crypt directly below the High Altar of St. Peter's. When they are taken out, the Benedictine nuns of St. Cecilia proudly share from afar in the accolades which they call forth.

In early days, only the Pope was entitled to wear the pallium and, even today, though Metropolitans—and in some rare instances, Bishops—share this honor, only he can wear it on all occasions. As a badge of office it is even older than the Papal Tiara "and the moment when the Pope is invested with the pallium at his coronation is the most solemn in the ceremony; perhaps one might compare it with the unction of a lay coronation. 'Receive the pallium,' are the words used as it is placed in position, 'To the Glory of God and of the Most Glorious Virgin, His Mother, and of the Blessed Apostles, Saint Peter and Saint Paul and of the Holy Roman Church.' As the strip of lambswool descends on the shoulders of the Pope, he becomes the Shepherd of Christ's Flock; at least this is the meaning which later ages gave to this investment." [2]

No wonder the nuns are immensely proud of the prerogative which permits them to make the pallium! But their real joy—and their real sorrow—lies in the lambs themselves.

Personally, I found my visit to their convent one of the most delightful experiences of a long stay in Rome. The Sister who received me in the parlor, Donna Maria Teresa,[3] chatted on and on, in the friendliest fashion imaginable, part of the time in rather rudimentary French, part of the time in Italian, which one of the friends who was with me interpreted as she went along, since my command of that language is as inadequate as Donna Maria Teresa's is of French. She brought a newly finished pallium for me to see and passed it through the grille so that I could feel it; and she gave me an envelope filled with the wool that had been blessed by the Pope. When I asked her if I could see the patio where the lambs were kept, she shook her head regretfully; it was part of the *clausura*. Yes, she had understood that I had sometimes been admitted to cloisters, even those of very strict Orders, when my work required it; but she was sure this time the Superior would not permit it. However, she said, suddenly brightening, they had a great treasure in their choir, a thirteenth-century fresco, "The Last Judgment," by Cavallini; official permission was sometimes granted for outsiders to view that. If I could secure permission, I would inevitably see the patio as I walked through the corridors and ascended the stairs on my way to the choir. . . .

St. Cecilia's has always been one of my favorite churches, ever since I first came to Rome, which is nearly seventy years ago, and I welcome every opportunity of revisiting it. It has a beautiful courtyard that seems doubly spacious and serene after leaving the crowded noisy street through the beckoning archway that leads to it. Children are always playing around its charming central fountain, young girls walking arm in arm, priests reading their breviaries. It is a pleasant place in which to linger before entering the church. The interior is adorned by numerous imposing monuments; but somehow these seem to lose importance as you walk toward the main altar which enshrines the statue of the saint, representing her as she appeared to those who first visited her tomb. This lovely recumbent figure, carved from pure white marble, is irresistibly appealing. Nothing about it suggests the horrors of death; it is surely one of the most touching and graceful representations of martyrdom in the whole world.

The church stands on the site of St. Cecilia's home, and what is now the crypt was originally the pillared and vaulted mansion of a royal Roman family. Beyond a small chapel with gleaming golden walls, dedicated to St. Agnes, which is located at the foot of a short stairway, can still be seen the living quarters, including the bath; and these, scarcely less than the church overhead, have always been an object of great interest. Now another had been added.

I acted promptly on Donna Maria Teresa's suggestion and the day after she made it I was back again, the official permit safely in hand. This time there was a considerable wait before the massive bolts were drawn back from the heavy door at the left of the courtyard, and it swung open to admit my two companions and myself. Even when this happened, we did not immediately see our newfound friend. This was not only because the light in the corridor was so dim; it was also because Donna Maria Teresa was so tiny! When we had seen her before, seated on the further side of the grille, we did not realize that she must have been sitting on a very high stool, for we saw only the upper part of her figure. Now she was disclosed almost as a Lilliputian. But she was as merry and as friendly as ever and chattered away in her mixture of French and Italian while she trotted along ahead of us, ringing the little bell that proclaimed the presence of outsiders in the convent and warning the other nuns to remain in seclusion. Reaching the choir involved an arduous climb, rather hard on a large lame lady like myself, but Donna Maria Teresa kept urging me forward, telling me that the Lord—and the fresco—would reward me. The early dusk of autumn prevented us from seeing the fresco to best advantage, but the twilit glimpses of the patio *were* rewarding. We saw the famous shelter for the lambs, and we also saw a small, shaggy, white animal which, for one startled moment, I thought must be a lamb, though this was September. Then I realized that it was a little white dog.

"So you have a pet still?" I asked, glad that this appeared to be so. She began to speak volubly in Italian, and the friendly interpreter explained in English.

"On account of the mice. A cat, if they fed her at all, would not catch mice for them. She would be too lazy. But their dog, he is not lazy. He takes pleasure in chasing them." And, at that moment, as if to justify himself, the dog bounded off in the direction of a suspicious looking corner, barking joyously.

As he disappeared, Donna Maria Teresa dismissed the subject of pets for a more practical one and, this time, her French was wholly equal to the occasion. "I know that yesterday you gave an offering of your own accord, before I asked for one," she said. "But it is customary, when permission is granted to see the fresco, to make one in recognition of that opportunity. So, if you feel inclined to give us another. . . ."

I already had it in my hand, waiting for a propitious moment to present it, so she need not have worried. But nuns have very little to come and go on; therefore, they can take no chances about such things. In that, she was wholly in character, and I understood and sympathized with her, as I did when she said she had learned I was a writer, and she hoped that, if I wrote about the lambs and the pallia, I would make it very clear that it was the Benedictine nuns of St. Cecilia who cared for the first and made the second. It seems that on the radio, just this last year, some announcer had given another Order the credit for both. I promised I would be very careful and told her I would be the last to rob the Benedictines of any glory which should be coming to them, considering how much time I had spent among them in Lisieux, and how happily. I should, however, like to ask her a question.

"All the Benedictines I know wear black," I said. "With only the wimple white. But you are all in white except for your cloak—like Dominicans. Is there a special reason for this?"

"Yes," she said, and her eyes twinkled more than ever as she answered. "It was the will of the Pope."

"The will of the Pope?"

"Yes. This building was once a monastery. The nuns of our Order took it over four hundred years ago. And when Pope Clement VII [4] gave us our patent and our instructions, he said, in passing, 'I prefer doves to ravens.' So we have tried to be doves ever since."

We left her, feeling that the point was well taken and delighted to have such a pleasing sidelight on this cultured and personable Pope, who belonged to the powerful Florentine family of the Medicis. He was, in fact, a nephew of Lorenzo the Magnificent and a cousin of Leo X (Giovanni di Medici), and was endowed with all the charm and grace which such a background and such connections could help to give him. He is chiefly famous for having conferred upon Henry VIII the title, "Defender of the Faith," as a mark of gratitude because the English King had written a treatise, called "A Defense of the Seven Sacraments Against Martin Luther," and the firm stand Clement afterward took against Henry's repudiation of Catherine of Aragon and his marriage to Anne Boleyn. This was all the more to his credit, since momentous decisions came hard to him and, in many ways, his neutrality and procrastination were disastrous, both to his personal dignity and to that of the Church. However, his pontificate is notable not only for the tragic defection of Luther and Henry, but for a great revival within the Church itself. "The Lateran Council had been warned that 'men must be transformed by religion, not religion by men' and these words typified the new spirit. A unity of belief might have been lost but the faith that remained was to be the sturdier because of surviving the storms of doubt and oppression. Spontaneously the new mood invigorated both the secular clergy and the ancient Orders and also caused the formation of other groups of devoted men and women who were moved to unselfish service of God and mankind." [5]

Unquestionably, the Benedictines of St. Cecilia were among those invigorated by this new mood. It is fitting that they should have been entrusted, as a mark of special favor, with the making of the pallia from the wool of the little lambs who have been their charges: lambs with crowns on their heads, who have received the Papal blessing after having been previously blessed at a Canonical Mass, celebrating the Feast Day of the little martyred saint whose name —Agnes—is a symbol of innocence and purity.

2

LESS GRAPHICALLY, if indirectly, Clement VII is connected with the story of St. Agnes. A much earlier pope is connected with her story quite as graphically and much more directly.

This is Damasus I, whose pontificate (366-384), we are told, was "studded with achievement. In his person were combined the talents of theologian and administrator, and in the warmth of his zeal and the fertility of his wisdom the power of the papacy became nurtured to a larger and well-consolidated strength. In all fields his energy was manifested. Ardent missionaries journeyed to distant places. Eloquent legates harangued Councils and Synods. Churches were restored and built. And masons and architects, spurred by the papal patronage, labored diligently to preserve the catacombs. It was Damasus who fixed the canon of the Old and New Testaments and it was with his encouragement that St. Jerome, for a while his secretary, revised the earlier Latin version of the Bible. Schismatics were outmaneuvered and heresies were stemmed. . . . Two years before Damasus died and in the sixteenth year of his jurisdiction splendid triumph came to him in the form of the famous Imperial Edict *De fide Catholica,* issued by Theodosius, which declared the official religion of the Roman State to be 'that doctrine which St. Peter had preached and of which Damasus was supreme head.' He was the first pope to refer to Rome as the 'Apostolic See.' "[5]

All this is so interesting and so significant that it seems to me worth quoting at length; but it was Damasus' zeal in restoring and building churches and preserving catacombs that makes him especially important to us. For the Church of St. Agnes Outside-the-Walls, built by Constantine in A.D. 324, was one of those that arrested the Pope's attention; and though, fortunately, it was not one of those that needed repair, it seemed to him worthy not only of enlargement and greater ornamentation, but of some special indication of his devotion to the little martyr. So he wrote an inscription to surmount the steps leading to her tomb, and it is still there for all to see:

Fama refert sanctas dudum retulisse parentes
Agnen, cum lugubres cantus tuba concrepuisset,
Nutricis gremium subito liquisse puellam,
Sponte trucis calcasse minas rabiemq(ue) tyranni
Urere cum flammis voluisset nobile corpus,
Virib(us) inmensum parvis superasse timorem
Nudaque profusum crinem per membra dedisse,
Ne Domini templum facies peritura videret.
O veneranda mihi, sanctum decus, alma, pudoris,
Ut Damasi precib(us) favcas, precor, inclyta martyr.[6]

This heartfelt tribute, paid so soon after Agnes' martyrdom, seems indicative of two things: first, that she was very early regarded officially as a saint, despite the fact that canonization in the early days of the Church did not take its present elaborate form; and, second, that one of the most famous stories which has come down to us about her is founded on fact, though it is not entirely factual. Even if it were, that would give us no sound reason to misprize it. I have quoted before, and probably shall quote many times again, because it is so wise and true, the statement of the great Cardinal Merry del Val to the effect that "tradition, wisely controlled, even in the absence of written documents, gives us manifest proofs of the truths of our beliefs." I do not know of any instance where this is more applicable than to the life of St. Agnes. Besides, the established facts are of such a nature that we can use them as a framework.

We know, for instance, that she came of a noble Roman family—probably the Clodia Crescentiana—and there are abundant records of how noble Roman families of the third and fourth centuries lived—what they wore, how they occupied themselves, how they were housed. We are so accustomed to studying this era through statues that we are apt to visualize its people as being clad exclusively in white; and readers of *Fabiola,* dazzled by Cardinal Wiseman's descriptions of Agnes' glittering and snowy garments, are inclined to think of her as always so clothed, especially since white, as a color, is so closely associated with purity as a symbol. As a matter of fact, Roman girls and women generally wore quite brilliant colors and, therefore, we may safely assume that Agnes and her mother did so. Since the family was a wealthy one and cost not a major consideration, we may also assume that probably some of their best clothes were made of silk, which was then imported from China, the price being a pound of gold for a pound of silk; but their long loose garments, covering them almost completely from head to foot, were generally made of wool, thin for summer and thick for winter; and the style of these, though not ungraceful, was not distinctive and it did not change much from year to year, or even from decade to decade. It was color that made them attractive. "Purple, with gold, was traditionally the epitome of extravagance in dress, as the debate on the repeal of the Oppian law well indicates. This word was applied to a wide range of colours, from blue and red to purple itself. Among the fancied colours were dark rose (*nigrantis rosae color*), hard and brilliant scarlet (*nimiae eius nigritiae austeritas illa nitorque*), amethyst and 'the colour of congealed blood, blackish at first glance, but gleaming when held up to the light.' These were, in the main, shell-fish dyes from the *murex,* the remarkable nature of whose secretions was first discovered and put to commercial use in the eastern Mediterranean at Tyre. The elder Pliny describes the process with his accustomed thoroughness. The Romans also used vegetable and mineral dyes, and these produced a wide variety of colours: sea-green (*cumatile*), saffron, Paphian myrtle, amethyst, pale rose, Thracian crane, acorn, almond, according to Ovid's list." [7]

Personally, I like to think of Agnes as dressed in pale rose or sea-green most of the time and wearing her dazzling white only for special occasions, exactly as a girl of her age would now wear a white dress for parties and for her First Holy Communion.

Though Agnes would have worn only simple jewelry, if any—again, like a little girl of today—her mother would have worn a great deal. The daughter would eventually have inherited gold jewelry and, also, many precious stones, the same ones that we have today, if she had lived to grow up. Pearls were a prime favorite, so Agnes probably would have had a necklace of tiny pearls. She would have been taught from babyhood to keep herself exquisitely neat and clean, and to make sure that her hair was carefully parted and becomingly waved, though dressed in a simpler fashion than her mother's. She had her lessons at home and, indeed, she spent most of her time there; for the ladies, both young and old, of a patrician household moved about much less freely and frequently than their modern counterparts. But, after all, home was a very spacious and pleasant place. The exterior was plain and bare, with few windows, but the interior was adorned with mosaics and paintings which gave it color and mitigated the cold severity of its statues. The rooms were more sparsely furnished than we would have considered comfortable, and it was probably Agnes' father, rather than her mother, who was tempted by such expensive rarities as tables made of citrus wood with ivory legs and sofas inlaid with tortoise shell, for Roman women were generally more interested in jewelry than interior decoration. However, what furniture there was would have been in excellent taste and attractively arranged. As to the general plan of the house, a vestibule and a corridor led from the entrance—which was guarded by a porter—to the *atrium,* a large rectangular open court with rooms leading from it on either side. At the very end of the *atrium* was the *tablinum,* a combination study and office, where Agnes' father kept his money and his books; he wrote with a style on wax-coated wooden tablets, which were bound together with metal rings. Some of his books were in the form of scrolls, others were bound sheets of parchment.

At the rear of the *tablinum* was a second court, called the *peristyle,* which was surrounded by a portico; the bedrooms and the dining room opened out of this; and beyond was still another court, the *oecus,* which was the main living room. The bedrooms were small and simple, but there were mattresses, cushions and blankets—though no sheets—for the narrow beds. In the dining room, cushions surrounded three sides of the table, the fourth side being left free for service, and the family and the guests reclined as they ate. They had earthenware dishes, but their goblets, though generally of clay, were sometimes made of metal or glass.

Since we know all these details and many besides about the way wealthy and aristocratic Romans lived in the fourth century, the statement, so often made, that we have only legend on which to build, in retelling the story of Agnes, is, on the face of it, incorrect.

We also know that, at the age of ten or thereabouts, Agnes consecrated herself to Christ and that this must have been done with at least the tacit consent of her parents; for, according to Roman law, a father could force his daughter to marry and to marry the man of his choice. This actually happened in the case of at least two saints whose lives are well authenticated—Cecilia and Francesca Romana; and it almost certainly would have been done in the case of Agnes as well, if her father had not respected her vow, which he would hardly have been likely to do unless he himself were secretly a Christian. We know that two or three years after she had taken this vow she was asked in marriage by a young man of high official status—probably the son of the Prefect who, at that time, was Maximum Herculeus, and that she declined with the words, "The one to whom I am betrothed is Christ whom the angels serve." For this act of insubordination she was condemned to death and, even then, her father did not resort to the legal measures which might have saved her life—a further indication that he himself was a follower of Christ. She was seized by soldiers, dragged from her home and forcibly thrust into a brothel. Obviously, the evil plan of her abductors was that she should be violated and thus deprived of the virginity which she had sworn to preserve. But she was spared profanation. Something about the quality of her purity was probably in itself a shield against attack by those who recognized it and respected it, however base they may otherwise have been. Although nobody touched her, one legend states that a young man who "looked at her with lustful eyes" was immediately blinded. Being interpreted, the meaning seems clear: he was so stricken with a sense of shame that he could not face the dazzling light of complete innocence and averted his gaze. There is also a legend to the effect that her golden hair, when unbound, covered her so completely that she needed nothing else for a protective garment. Personally, I have always loved this story, perhaps because one inevitably becomes tired of hearing how certain saints ruthlessly chopped off their beautiful long hair, so that their main attraction in the marriage mart would be gone, and they could keep their vows of chastity unmolested by their matchmaking mothers. It is rather refreshing, for once, to hear of a saint whose hair helped her, instead of hindering her, in her consecrated life!

The story of the brothel, in one form or another, is certainly entitled to acceptance, as I have already stated; otherwise, so scholarly a man as Pope Damasus would not have incorporated it in his inscription. This erstwhile brothel was located under an arch in the Stadium of Domitian, the Roman Emperor who succeeded his elder brother Titus (A.D. 81) and whose reign, at first devoted to the interests of order and public welfare, became gradually more and more despotic and, toward the last, was drenched with blood. This former brothel, in what is now the Piazza Navona, like many other parts of the stadium, is still in a state of almost perfect preservation. It forms the crypt in the Church of St. Agnes in Agone and, quite understandably, has been converted into a shrine, though structurally it remains unchanged. The church itself has undergone many transformations and, historically, has an unique claim to distinction: Prince Battista Pamphili, who became Pope Innocent X, having built his palace, one of the most magnificent in Rome, at the site of the church, desired to transform this into a more important one. He committed its construction to Borromini and the two Rainaldi and the little basilica took the form of a Greek Cross, the same that Bramante and Michelangelo had thought of giving St. Peter's. The result of their labors was marvelous. In every way the church turned out to be a monument worthy of St. Agnes: for its superb façade, made of *travertino,* and, above all, for the amount of marble and gold profusely used for the decoration of its interior. In the Bull dated February 7, 1653, Pope Innocent X bestowed on it the patronage of his family and made it independent from all other jurisdiction, except for that of the Cardinal Protector. This unique independence has survived the centuries.

The story of the courageous child's martyrdom is harder to authenticate than that of her ordeal in the brothel. There is one touching detail, oft repeated, to the effect that she went to her doom unshackled because there were no handcuffs small enough to fit "such tender limbs"; but one early writer speaks of death by fire, another of decapitation and another of strangulation. Still a different version of the story tells us that fire was tried first, but to no avail, because the fagots on the funeral pyre would not ignite. The statue above the main altar in St. Agnes of Agone shows her rising above simulated flames which, inevitably, are not very realistic, since white marble is not a convincing medium for representing a raging fire; and one famous painting shows Agnes standing unscathed beside a low ineffectual pile of logs. Still other paintings show a soldier plunging his sword into her breast and thus giving the fatal thrust, which I have not found elsewhere presented in this manner. Most paintings of the death scene show decapitation and the faithful little lamb is almost always at the victim's side.

Whatever form her martyrdom took, there is no doubt that Agnes paid for her faith with her life, in some horrible way, early in the fourth century, during the so-called Persecution of Diocletian. We are told that present in this emperor's character was "every trait that we associate with the word 'Roman'—the organizing ability, the sense of discipline, the love of hard work, of erecting magnificent public monuments, of military glory. . . . Only in the realm of religion was he to show himself the enemy of all reform, even enlarging upon the cleverness and violence with which his predecessors had assailed Christianity. His thoroughly reactionary attitude would find its sanction in this principle: that it was not permissible to claim that a new religion could reform the old religion. To desire, in that sphere, to change ancestral institutions was the greatest of crimes. Although he was astute enough to lay on the shoulders of his colleagues the odium of certain enactments, Diocletian has bequeathed his name to the most savage of the persecutions." [8]

It was the most savage, but it was likewise almost the last. "With Constantine's reign came the two great changes: the transference of the capital [of the Roman Empire] to the new city by the Bosporos [Constantinople]; the recognition of Christianity as the official religion of the Empire. The two singularly offset each other: one seemed to destroy Rome; the other gave the great, old, dishonoured city the vital principle of a new life." [9] Thus Agnes, like Francesca a thousand years later (when the Middle Ages merged into the Renaissance), lived in one of the most portentous periods of history; in that way, though in no other, the two were alike. When Christ triumphed over Caesar, pagan Rome was indeed destroyed. And Agnes was one of those who contributed most vitally to this destruction. "The death of this brave child made a profound impression, and she became among the best known and most widely honored of the Roman martyrs." [10]

Among her relatives must have been someone having enough influence with the authorities to prevent a final desecration of her mutilated body; it was not thrown into the river, as was customary after the execution of a Christian, but buried in the "Domestic Cemetery" belonging to Agnes' parents, which formed part of the catacombs that now bear her name and that adjoin the church, also dedicated to her, on the Via Nomentana.

The twenty-first of January is very generally accepted as the date when this execution took place; hence it became the feast and the "official" birthday of Agnes for, in the case of saints, it is a day when they are born into the Eternal Glory of Paradise that is celebrated as such. However, the twenty-eighth was actually her birthday, and on that day her parents went to pray at her tomb. There they were granted a vision in which they saw her surrounded by a bevy of virgins, resplendent with light; and on her right hand was seen a lamb whiter than snow.

Happy in the consolation they had received, her parents made this vision known, and "the second feast day of St. Agnes," which coincides with her Octave, was the result. Like the ceremonial presentation of the lambs, this celebration has been taking place for a long, long while—just how long we do not know, but certainly throughout centuries. For, almost immediately after her death, a little chapel was built over her grave; and, though the entrance to this was carefully concealed, because Diocletian had ordered the seizure of all properties, including cemeteries and the records concerning them, the faithful managed to reach her tomb by some underground passage. And when the need for secrecy had passed, the little chapel was enlarged and transformed by order of Constantine, who had succeeded Diocletian as emperor. Afterward, a long succession of popes continued the work of enlargement and transformation. The present magnificent basilica is the result.

And is this all we can say with conviction about St. Agnes? Certainly not. With no more to go by she might, understandably, still have become a favorite subject for painters and sculptors, since there always has been and probably always will be something irresistibly appealing in the representation of such a young and innocent girl, so tragically fated. According to Anna Jameson's *Sacred and Legendary Art,* a standard work of reference, there is no saint, except the apostles and evangelists, whose effigies are older than those of Agnes; and modern artists continue to give us their interpretation of her. In like measure, she might easily have been the inspiration not only for such songs of praise as those written by holy men like

Ambrose and Prudentius, but for more modern writers like Keats and Tennyson,[11] for innocence and beauty appeal to poets quite as strongly as they do to painters. But these attributes must be combined with sterner qualities if they are to survive the centuries and have a universal appeal through the ages.

And this is what happened. "Every people, whatever their tongue, praise the name of St. Agnes," St. Girolamus declared in a letter written near the end of the fourth century; and this is as true now as it was when it was first written. That she should be a favorite saint of Roman women, that her name should be kept alive through their local associations, that her church and even the steps leading to it should often be so crowded with milling worshipers that it is almost impossible to make one's way among them—all this is not surprising. That Mother Cabrini, herself an embryonic saint, should instinctively couple the name of Agnes with those of Rosa de Lima and Mariana de Quito, when writing about the Virgins in Paradise to her spiritual daughters, during the course of her voyage to South America, is somewhat more surprising: it plainly shows that the little martyr was never absent from the great missionary's thoughts, no matter how far she herself might be from Rome; and what is true of her is true of countless others.

Agnes' name is one of only seven, borne by canonized maids and matrons, which is commemorated every day in the Canon of the Mass—the most ancient of all the liturgical prayers of the Catholic Church. True, this selection was made a long time ago—certainly before the year 600—and there were not then as many saints in the calendar as there are now. Still, there were many times seven and most of them had died in the defense of their faith, for those first centuries after the time of Christ were stained and sanctified by the blood of martyrs. But the choice was characterized by a high degree of selectivity even then and the Church has not seen fit to make any changes in it, as far as female saints are concerned, though its Register has since been enriched by saints who have been great historical figures, like Catherine of Siena and Joan of Arc, for instance; by reformers and founders, like Scolastica and Teresa of Avila, for instance; and by some who have introduced new forms of devotion, like Margaret Mary, for instance. There must, therefore, be some very sound reason why the original seven names have been allowed to stand. It is worth our while to consider what these reasons are—briefly in the case of six, more at length in the case of the one with whom we are most concerned at the moment.

Even the names of these seven maids and matrons seem significant, for all but one—Cecilia, which comes from an old Roman family name—are symbolic. Felicitas means happiness; Perpetua, steadfastness; Agatha, goodness; Lucia, light; Agnes, purity; and Anastasia, that which pertains to the Resurrection. Felicitas and Perpetua were both natives of Carthage, married women with children at the time of their martyrdom; Anastasia, a Roman, was a widow at the time of hers; Agatha and Lucia, both Sicilians, Agnes and Cecilia, both Romans, were all virgins.[12] Felicitas was a slave; the others represented various classes of society, from those in moderately comfortable circumstances to those of great wealth and high rank. In age, they differed as much as they did in degree. Felicitas, Perpetua and Agatha were mature women, Agnes hardly more than a child; but they shared the sterling qualities of steadfastness and courage. They were all faithful unto death—a terrible death. They knew the truth of the biblical saying, "Greater love than this no man hath, that a man lay down his life for his friends"; and they knew that a still greater truth lay in something which had not yet been said, but which they were ready to prove, "Greater love for Christ no man hath than he who is ready to lay down his life for his faith."

It was in their deaths, even more than in their holy lives, that these seven female saints of the Canon made their greatest contribution to Christianity; and Agnes is outstanding among them because of her extreme youth. Ordinarily, a child of twelve is not sufficiently developed, in a mental sense, to know her own mind about matters of slight consequence, much less to remain steadfast in the defense of a principle. She is not capable, in a physical sense, of enduring hardships, much less cruelty, without flinching. "At such a tender age a young girl has scarcely enough courage to bear the angry looks of her father," St. Ambrose reminds us, "and a tiny puncture from a needle makes her cry as if it were a wound. And still this little girl had enough courage to face the sword. She was fearless in the bloody hands of the executioner. She prayed, she bowed her head. Behold in one victim the twofold martyrdom of chastity and faith." In a spiritual sense she was as highly developed as in a mental and a physical sense.

We are apt to think, alas, mistakenly, that all the early Christians were ready to die for their faith. This was unfortunately—though very naturally—not invariably the case, and the persecutions of Diocletian had appalled many of them; he was bent on the destruction of Christendom and made this all too plain. "The Christians, who were already very numerous, responded in various ways. The zealous ones faced death undaunted; the weak ones, the spiritless Christians, betrayed their corruption by apostasy or by offering sacrifices to idols, which entitled them to a certificate, though they were sometimes obliged to resort to bribery in order to obtain this. Such persons were known as the bearers of a Libelous Certificate and were the ones to whom St. Ambrose referred in his hymn, *Agnes Beatae Virginus,* when he said, 'Faith wavered among men and even old men yielded.' This was the hymn which, for many years, was always sung on her birthday, 'the second feast of St. Agnes.' The faithful, gathering around her tomb, chanted, 'When fear of torture and death terrorized the young and led the old men to buy a few days of life through apostasy, you, Agnes, have been the great witness of Christ with your youth, with your chastity, with your blood.' " [13]

A great witness indeed—one of the greatest. This is not legend, it is fact, as indisputable as it is glorious. This tells us why the name of Agnes is "still praised by people, whatever their tongue," why her story has survived the centuries and has had a universal appeal through the ages. She was steadfast and courageous to the end, and her courage made her death as splendid as it was sublime. "With a single stroke she was beheaded, death was faster than pain and her resplendent soul, made free, flew to heaven where the angels met her as she proceeded along the white path that leads to Paradise." [14]

Many have striven to follow her along that path. I know of none who has done so more faithfully than another Roman of gentle birth and blameless character who has come down to us in history as Santa Francesca Romana.

SANTA FRANCESCA ROMANA

1384-1440

1

HUNDREDS OF tourists, who would not think of missing the most picturesque sights, the most haunting sounds and the most savory scents on the Left Bank in Paris, never seek out their counterparts on the West Bank in Rome. They go, as a matter of course, to St. Peter's and, very probably, to the Castel Sant' Angelo and up the Janiculum Hill. But their acquaintance with the district known as Trastevere is likely to be limited to one or two noisy restaurants and one or two lovely churches if they stray into that region at all. Such an oversight can be laid partly to the fact that most tourists who tell you they have "seen" Rome have spent only a few days there; and no city in the world—at least within the range of my experience—takes so long a time to "see," even superficially, and so much longer to really know. The oversight can also be laid to another sad fact: namely that, even with time to spare, the average tourist does not seem to feel Trastevere can offer much to interest him.

I believe this is a mistake and I will try to explain why I feel that way.

In the Middle Ages and during the Renaissance, Trastevere was the most aristocratic section of Rome, the quarter where many of the great patrician families had their *palazzi* (palaces) and led lives of such pageantry that it is hard for us to visualize them in all their magnificence. One of the most perceptive among modern travel writers, H. V. Morton, declares that "If Trastevere were to dress in mediaeval costume once a year, as Siena does, it would provide one of the most remarkable spectacles in Europe." [1] I heartily agree. But, alas, Trastevere does no such thing and I doubt if it could be persuaded to. It does not live largely rapt in the past, like Siena, but very vigorously in the present and is equally proud of both. It claims to be the only part of the Eternal City whose denizens have never once been successfully dislodged, much less annihilated; and, to show their superiority, the Trasteverini speak with condescension of "going into Rome" when they cross the Tiber. It is now the chosen habitat of lowly but skilled artisans, who have inherited their knowledge and aptitude from their forefathers and who will pass their industries on to their sons. They ply their trade not in the stately buildings which surround the spacious piazzas, where fountains sparkle in the sunshine, but half in tiny cave-like shops in the basements of vast decrepit houses located on slit-like streets; and half on the sidewalks to which these shops lead through wide open doors. They are open at all times to customers and cronies. They are also easily observed by the casual passer-by, especially at night, when their interiors glow with a radiance which seems all the brighter because the narrow streets are so dark.

If there is a certain eeriness in the sight, this only adds to its fascination, even though the stranger may have been warned that Trastevere is the chosen locale not only of diligent cobblers, potters, ironmongers and mechanics, but of many who follow less honorable trades. There is a saying that the streets in Trastevere "are honeycombed with passages into which everything of value stolen in Rome finds its way" and another to the effect that more murders are committed there than anywhere else.[2] It cannot be denied that, occasionally, there is something sinister and something electric in the atmosphere, as well as something eerie. But, except for the timid soul, the disadvantages of this are offset by the feeling of clannishness, of bravura and zestful living which are also in the air. The Trasteverini have a dialect of their own which they prefer to speak and often to shout and scream, rather than the language which is used on the other side of the river. But even if you cannot follow what they are saying, you cannot fail to recognize the comradeship and gaiety, not only in the mirthful weddings and frequent *festas,* but among the habitués at the *cantinas* and *trattorias,* which, like the workshops, spill over onto the sidewalk, and in the congenial groups that gather round the doorsteps to gossip at the end of a day's work.

Squalor is there in patches, but so is the obvious well-being that goes with plenty of *pasta* and red wine and great hunks of cheese. Glimpses of family kitchens, devoid of gleaming white porcelain, but well supplied with huge black kettles whose contents are bubbling and steaming, set you sniffing enviously as you try to hurry along to the place where you yourself plan to eat. For suddenly you are ravenous, and you become more and more so, as you continuously pass stands laden with crisp green vegetables and brilliant fruit. Despite your efforts, your progress will not be rapid. For you will be dodging baby carriages and pushcarts and Vespas, and failing to wedge your way past loving couples walking with arms interlaced and larger groups which have no idea of interrupting their excited conversation for the benefit of some impatient outsider. But eventually you will arrive in the Piazza di Santa Maria in Trastevere, if that is your destination, and there you will feast your eyes on the mosaic façade of the magnificent church which gives the square its name, and the no less magnificent fountain which forms the piazza's central ornament, while you dine at Galeassi's or Alfredo's; or, if your destination is the Piazza di Mercan, you will be caught up in the medley of music that comes from a flute and small tinkling bells and all the paraphernalia of Roman *stornelli* and Sicilian *cantastorie* while you dine at Da Meo Patacca.

The buildings which surround such piazzas retain their stateliness, as I have said, and many of the palazzi still survive, for the medievalists were not given to building flimsy structures. But usually they are tenements now, with washing strung over their balconies and from their windows, and gaunt, unshaven old men, leaning on canes as they totter down the steps, or slovenly old women, with their hands folded over their enormous stomachs, sitting in the carved doorways. However, there are still exceptions. I would not dare to guess how many because—to repeat myself again—it takes a long, long time to know Rome and this is doubly true in the case of Trastevere. But of one palazzo, at least, I can speak from the vantage point of pleasant and illuminating acquaintance.

This is located on the Via dei Vascellari, near the Tiber, in what is now the very heart of the slums. In the Middle Ages, it belonged to the Ponziani family, then among the greatest in Rome, but now, unfortunately, extinct. It is presently known as the Pia Casa di Ponterotto and also as the Casa dei SS. Spirituali Esercizi.[3] Here, from September through June every year, sixty men and boys at a time are welcomed for a weekly retreat. They are provided with comfortable quarters for sleeping and recreation and hearty abundant meals. Their program is supervised by the twelve priests who act as their hosts and some of the younger ones share the boys' dormitory. Brief religious services, in one or both of the two small chapels, are always the order of the day; but much of the time during the first part of the week is devoted to conferences and informative talks, with ample question and answer periods for both groups and individuals and adequate opportunities for leisure and companionship. On Saturday confessions are heard and on Sunday comes the culminating celebration of Holy Communion. In addition to this regular weekly schedule, there are frequent festivities of variegated character, occasional weddings and christenings and, on March 9, one very special celebration.

There is a cogent reason why this date should have been chosen for a special celebration. March 9 is the feast day of a very great Roman lady, whom we know—though not as well as we should—as Santa Francesca Romana, and whose name in the world was Francesca di Bussi di Broffedeschi. The present Casa di Ponterotto was for many years her home. It was here that she came as the child bride of Lorenzo Ponziano, the proud heir to a great name. It was here that she dwelt in harmony with her husband's family and succeeded to the management of their large estate when his parents died. It was here that she bore her three children, made the headquarters of her private charities and laid her plans for the foundation of the Oblates of the Congregation of Mount Olivet, governed by the Benedictine Rule, which she later established in the magnificent Tor di Specchi (Tower of the Mirrors). It was here that she died, in an enormous room with a splendid beamed ceiling, which has been reverently preserved and identified with a suitable plaque. The cellar where she stored her supplies is still used as she used it. The great banqueting hall of the Ponziani is the dining room where the transient but honored guests of the Pia Casa are served their substantial meals. And—as seems eminently fitting—it is the Oblates from Francesca's foundation at the Tor di Specchi who minister to the needs of the men and boys who have been gathered in from the gutters and alleys that represent the saddest and most sordid side of life in Trastevere.

"Men who have neglected their Catholic duties for years come here to resume them," you are told by the Oblate who greets you as you enter the Pia Casa and then shows you every part of the building. "One regular communicant at our chapel is ninety years old. He made his First Communion here when he was ten and did not come back again until he was forty. But since then he has come every week. Many of the others who have lapsed themselves scrupulously bring their sons and grandsons at the proper age and take pains to set them a good example by mending their own ways. There are constant causes of encouragement. . . . Not once has any member of our Order been subjected to indignity by these visitors," she added proudly.

That such a record should have been unbroken for over one hundred and fifty years is in itself evidence of the Pia Casa's tremendous prestige and influence; and we share the regret expressed by Mariano Armellini in his great work, *Churches of Rome,* that its name, history and purpose are so little known.

It was at the very beginning of the nineteenth century, during the Napoleonic Invasion, that Dom Gioacchino Michelini, the parish priest of San Salvatore a Ponterotto (Holy Savior of the Broken Bridge), recognized the need for such a center in such a locality, and obtained permission to use the once proud palace of the Ponziani, which was in a state of semidereliction, for his work of salvage. In 1807, the project was officially approved by ecclesiastical authorities and, little by little, the palace, which became the property of the Vicar General of Rome, was suitably restored. Since the time of Michelini, many illustrious monsignori and cardinals have sponsored the undertaking; the Venerable Vincenzo Palotti and the Blessed Gaspare del Bufalo and Pope Pius IX, in the early days of his priesthood, frequently worked there and the latter remained greatly attached to the institution all his life. At one time, it was customary that all those serving the communicants at table on the last day of the exercises should be of cardinalate rank; and John XXIII followed the honored papal tradition of serving as celebrant at Mass.

On the day we were at the Pia Casa, the pleasant Oblate who was our guide took us through a long succession of rooms to the one set aside for His Holiness and showed us the mementos of his visit. By that time, the afternoon was almost gone—there had been so much for us to hear and see and admire; and, before we started home, we wanted to visit the nearby Church of St. Cecilia, not only because it has always been one of our favorite churches in Rome, but because, now that we had seen the home of the Ponziani, we wanted to see their family chapel.

Like many of the medieval dynasties, the Ponziani had a chapel in the parish church they attended, which was called by their name, where they were privileged to bury their dead; in their case the church was St. Cecilia's. Such chapels were not private in the sense that the public could not see them or worship in them; but no one could be buried in them without their express permission, and the altarpieces and frescoes were nearly always indicative of family history and devotion. Unfortunately, as these became obscured or hidden by the passage of time, some of the chapels were put to other uses; and, five or six years ago, necessary repairs to the sacristy at St. Cecilia's—where the crumbling remnants of tombs had been rather haphazardly scattered about—revealed the existence of superb frescoes beneath the plain plaster on the walls and escutcheons and inscriptions in the original pavement, which plainly indicated that this sacristy had once been a family chapel and that the family in question was the Ponziani. It was this that we had come to see.

We were richly rewarded. Above the altar is the figure of the Madonna della Misericordia, to whom the Ponziani had special devotion. She stands with her hands holding wide her ample cloak, beneath which a reverent group has taken refuge; and on either side of her are figures of San Lorenzo and Santa Francesca Romana. (Santa Francesca's husband was never canonized or even declared a Blessed or a Venerable; but San Lorenzo was, of course, his patron saint.) The side walls of the chapel present various scenes connected with Francesca's life, and all her children, her husband and various other members of the Ponziani family are entombed beneath the pavement.

She herself is not buried there, but far from Trastevere, in the church which now bears her name, coupled with its original designation of Santa Maria Nuova; or, rather, she is not buried at all. Her skeletal remains, clad in the habit of the Order she founded, lie exposed in a glass casket for all to see and, once every hundred years, this repository is opened to permit Oblates from the same Order to reclothe them in a fresh habit. The casket, encased in a tomb under the apse, was erected at the expense of Agatha Pamphili, an Oblate of the Tor di Specchi and a sister of Innocent X, who, as we have already learned, was responsible for the unique status of Agnes in Agone. It is one of several that command attention, for Gregory XI and Cardinal Vulcani are also buried here. The church is a splendid one, superbly located on a crest of the Palatine with the Colosseum behind it and the Forum below it, and it is approached through a rising avenue, bright with flowers and ennobled by columns, which are majestic even in their truncated condition. It was built early in the eighth century, partially destroyed by fire and restored and embellished by several successive popes and further enriched by funds from the Frangipani family, who owned a nearby palazzo. Urban II resided there in 1093, dating his Bulls from it; and Innocent II was ordained and consecrated there in 1136. As it was the favorite church of Francesca's father, Paolo di Bussi, and the one he most frequently attended, it seems likely that his daughter was familiar with it from an early age, that he was the one who first taught her its history and showed her the glories to which she herself was to add the most significant chapter and the greatest luster. It is now the scene, on March 9, not only of a religious celebration, in which the statues of Francesca and her guardian angel are both garlanded with flowers and which, in a general way, resembles those at the Tor di Specchi and the Pia Casa, but also one wholly modern in character. Francesca never left Rome but once—and even that short journey to Assisi is open to doubt—and when she went about it was often on foot, for her little donkey was generally laden with fagots; but she is revered in Rome not only as the special patron of wives and mothers, which is easily understandable, but—rather inexplicably to me—as *La Padrona degli Automobilisti* —the Drivers' Saint! So, outside the church are parked tiny Fiats, larger Lancias and more impressive Mercedes, their proud owners standing possessively beside them; and, as soon as Mass is over, the priests leave the garlanded statues and come out to bless the cars.

The splendid site of the church, its wealth of history and its architectural and artistic importance have always impressed me deeply; but the glass coffin with its tenderly clothed skeleton is not the feature of it which means the most to me. Rather, this is its proud position, the harmony of its several parts and of those with its surroundings. As far as Francesca herself is concerned, she seems much more real to me in the Tor di Specchi than she does in the church. For in the church she is dead; but in the Tor di Specchi she still seems alive.

This great palazzo which became a convent is dramatically situated on the Via Teatro di Marcello, not far from the Palazzo Orsini, which that family built in the tenth century on top of the Teatro di Marcello, and which they have occupied ever since. The Tor di Specchi, like so many of its kind, presents a blank façade to the street; and the entrance which was originally the main one is now blocked by the cheerful little tables of a sidewalk café. Only an unusually observant passer-by, without any special interest in the building, is likely to notice the stone medallion, representing Francesca with her guardian angel, which surmounts the doorway now in use at the convent; but once inside, the visitor is struck by another characteristic of Roman palaces—the almost innumerable apartments, all spacious and splendid, the long succession of patios and galleries. It seems impossible that so much could have been concealed by that blank façade, that there is room for such expansion in the heart of a great city. You feel as if you must have been walking for miles before you have left the gorgeous reception rooms behind you and reached the medieval kitchen where the great stone cistern is still in use, though no cooking is done there any more; and you feel that you have scaled a thousand steps before you reach the original refectory and the tiny room off it where Francesca was accustomed to retire for prayer and meditation. She did not live there herself until after her husband's death; but several years before that she bought this palazzo and installed her Oblates in it; and she spent as much time as she could with her spiritual daughters, riding back and forth from Trastevere, across the Tiber, on a donkey, which she stabled in the vestibule of the now disused entrance, where a stone manger, comparable in size and style to the cistern in the kitchen, was kept filled with provender for him.[4]

The Superior of the Oblates and her nuns are friendly and cooperative in their manner of receiving; though they live as a community and wear a habit, they are not cloistered, and there is no grille between them and their visitors, no warning bell to tell all but the one who is acting as guide that they must retreat and keep out of sight. Except during the octave of Santa Francesca's feast day, when they, like the Pia Casa, keep open house, the Oblates must limit the number of persons they can receive and the hours of reception; otherwise, their good works, both in and out of the convent, would be too frequently interrupted, their devotions subject to distraction; but once a welcome among them has been assured, it is a very warm one. After you have seen the reception rooms, the old kitchen and Francesca's cabinet, you are also asked if you would like to see the original chapel. To do this, you will have to go down another flight of steps, rather steep ones; it is in a different part of the building from that where you have just been; but perhaps you would find it worth the effort. For there, as in the family chapel of the Ponziani, a series of frescoes has been disclosed with the removal of plaster. They are in perfect condition, really rather remarkable. . . .

Of course, there can be only one answer to such a question, and if double the effort to reach the chapel had been involved, it still would have been more than worth while. The other frescoes were illuminating and interesting; these are extraordinary. There are twenty of them, besides the altarpiece, all in a state of perfect preservation; and nearly every one depicts, in a most unusual and effective way, some miracle performed by Santa Francesca Romana: at the left of the picture we see the difficult or tragic situation that has called for a miracle; at the right we see its happy solution. I do not know of any other representations of the supernatural aspects of a saint's life that are so original, so charming and so convincing.

After leading to the chapel, the steep staircase descends further and finally reaches the entry with the stone manger. This will be the quickest and easiest exit for a lame lady, the thoughtful Oblate says kindly; it will take only a moment to unbar the disused door to the street. It takes a little longer than that, but the wait is worth while, just as everything else has been. And when the door opens and you look out into the street, it is easy to visualize just how Francesca must have looked as she came riding up on her donkey and tethered it beside the manger, before she went quietly and gracefully up those steep stairs.

For here, even more than in the Pia Casa di Ponterotto, where you were conscious of her enduring influence; even more than in the family chapel of the Ponziani, where you were conscious of her bereaved maternity; even more than in the church that bears her name and enshrines her holy remains—you feel her presence. Here, truly, her heart was the foundation stone. Here she provided the way of life and of obedience for her spiritual daughters along the same pathway to heaven that she chose herself. Here, in spirit, she still presides—wise, serene, dignified, generous and gracious, the embodiment of loving-kindness: the great lady who, without condescension or criticism ministered to the needs of those less privileged than herself; the holy woman so inseparably a part of the Eternal City where she was born and bred and spent her entire life that she is always designated as Santa Francesca *Romana*—St. Frances *the Roman*. No other saint, so far as I know, has a prouder heritage; no saint, whatever her heritage, could have been more worthy of it than this one.

Verses with which we have long been vaguely familiar, but have almost forgotten, have a way of suddenly regaining the forefront of our consciousness. I thought of some such verses as I went home through the golden light of a late Roman afternoon after my visit to the Tor di Specchi. I had always liked them; but now they had a new meaning for me. They ran like this:

That you can be a saint,
In quite a rich home,
Is shown by the case
Of St. Frances of Rome.

She had plenty of children,
A husband, a cook,
A household to manage,
A housekeeping book—

And they kept her so busy
Both up and downstairs,
She couldn't think when
To get on with her prayers.

She no sooner was kneeling
Than someone would call—
She thought she would never
Get finished at all.

First her husband must see her,
Then up came the cook,
Then a little boy shouting
To please come and look—

Then a friend with a very
Long story to tell,
And a dozen poor people
With troubles as well.

And she never lost patience,
Or said "Not at home,"
And that's why we call her
Saint Frances of Rome.[5]

Well, of course, those are some of the reasons. But, apparently, there were a great many others. It seemed to me that it might be a good plan to explore these and share the knowledge thus gained with others.

2

As the fourteenth century drew to a close, Rome, far from glowing with the radiant light which illumined Tuscany with ever increasing brilliance, was still the scene of violence, outlawry and degradation.

Gregory XI, the amiable but ineffectual Pope, whose return to the Eternal City was instigated by Catherine of Siena, had died before the dimming flame—once so strong and bright—of her own light had flickered to its untimely end. Gregory's successor, Urban VI, himself a choleric and headstrong man, contributed to the prevailing chaos, instead of controlling it. His quarrel with his cardinals resulted in their revolt and in their choice of Robert of Geneva to supplant him. Though they could not dislodge Urban from the throne to which he stubbornly and angrily clung, the rebels, headed by Robert, who took the name of Clement VII, returned, rejoicing, to Avignon. Denunciations of Clement as an antipope rent the air in Rome, but such denunciations did not mend matters, especially in view of the fact that Urban quarreled with the ruler of Naples and executed six cardinals. The Roman nobles, a proud and self-willed group, who brooked no interference from any superior power, least of all one they neither feared nor respected, could hardly be expected to enforce order, if the head of the Church did not do so; the people followed the temper of their riotous leaders. The families which continued to lead quiet and orderly domestic lives and to cling to the Church for spiritual support were the exception to the general rule.

But, as always, there were such families and, since two of them are to figure importantly in our story, I believe it is well to begin by learning something about them. A distinguished Peruvian historian reminds us, "Accustomed as we are to see saints in the sky, we forget that their origin was the earth. Saints have never been wholly of legend. They were born in a certain country, they belonged to a certain city, they developed a certain social medium, they represented a certain epoch and, because of all this, it is of historical interest to become acquainted with their families. These can tell us many things which would otherwise be obscure in hagiography." [6]

The story of Santa Francesca Romana would indeed be obscure if we could not establish both her own parental background—the di Bussi—and that of her husband—the Ponziani. Her father, Paolo di Bussi, was connected with several other great families and, through his marriage with Giacobella di Broffedeschi, became connected with several others—the Savelli, the Mellini and the Montelluci among them. Wealth, stability and strong Christian principles all served to fortify them in their proud positions,[7] and their union was harmonious. But it was not until they were well along in years that they were blessed with a child.

This was a beautiful little girl who was given the name of Francesca. She was baptized on the very day of her birth, at the Church of St. Agnes in the Piazza Navona—the same sanctuary that surmounts the erstwhile brothel, famous as the site of the young martyr's miraculous escape from ravishment. Six years later, Francesca was confirmed in the same church. Therefore, the saying that Francesca di Bussi's devotion to St. Agnes was lifelong is not a figure of speech, for it began with her christening and continued with her First Holy Communion and Confirmation.

Giacobella insisted on feeding the baby herself. This in itself was a rare mark of devotion; most women of her station and standing handed their children over to wet nurses. The physical closeness of the tie, which bound mother and daughter together from the beginning, soon had its parallel in spiritual and mental ties. Just as she had declined to entrust the bodily nourishment of Francesca to others, Giacobella declined to risk, through her own negligence, any lack of teaching. It can truthfully be said that Francesca drank in the fear of the Lord, which is the beginning of wisdom, with her mother's milk and that she was an apt pupil.

She was a gentle and thoughtful child, naturally devout, happy in a quiet way, but grave rather than gay, undemonstrative, silent under circumstances when most little girls are prone to chatter, and given to self-denial from a very early age. Far from craving caresses, she shrank from them, and she was equally reluctant to sample the sweetmeats which most youngsters consume with avidity. The atmosphere of her home may well have had something to do with the development of these qualities and this attitude. She had no brothers and sisters with whom to frolic. Her mother was pious and purposeful; Francesca's education was of supreme importance to her and there were probably few holidays. Paolo di Bussi was a stern man, with a strong sense of his prerogatives as a Roman and as a father. Neither one cared for rich fare nor made any objections when Francesca stopped eating eggs and meat, as well as sweets, and limited herself to bread and vegetables. Both parents were past their first youth and its correlative enjoyment of conviviality; they entertained very little themselves and accepted few invitations. The prevalent corruption of the society in which they would logically have had a part was repugnant to their tastes and their principles and this increased their inclination to live in retirement, though they maintained a stately establishment.

Since Francesca had been baptized and confirmed at the Church of St. Agnes, we may safely assume that the di Bussi belonged to its parish, especially as it is located on the Piazza Navona in Parione, the same splendid *rione* (ward) of the city where they lived,[8] though it was not the church which the family attended most frequently. This was Santa Maria Nuova, close to the Forum, directed by the Benedictines. One of these, Dom Antonio di Monte Savello, was Giacobella's confessor and became Francesca's as well. The closeness between priest and penitent, so characteristic of those times, so difficult for the modern woman, especially the non-Latin woman, to understand, was very strong in this case. The confessor was not an unidentified, or scarcely identified, priest, concealed behind the curtains of a confessional and approached at infrequent intervals with a stereotyped patter of venial sins; he was an intimate of the family, a welcome habitué of the household, a guide, philosopher and friend, in temporal as well as in spiritual matters. He was never too hurried to listen to problems; these might be trivial, as far as he could see, but he knew they did not seem so to those who consulted him; and, if the questions were really complex, he gave them his carefully considered opinion. In the case of Francesca, he wisely restrained her childish impulse to rush headlong into acts of self-denial and self-sacrifice, an impulse which was also characteristic of the age, when a burning desire to emulate martyrs, even after persecutions were a thing of the past, animated many a zealous young Christian, especially those who had taken a lovely young martyr for their ideal, as Francesca had done. In like measure, when she first confided to Dom Antonio that she desired to become a nun, he reminded her that she was very young to make such a decision and, when nothing he said had the slightest effect on her resolution, he further reminded her that it would be several years before she could put such a plan into practice, because of the conventual rule placing age limits on the admission of postulants to an Order. In any case, he added, her father's permission would be an absolute requisite.

Thus cautioned, Francesca approached her father, not without misgivings, which proved to be only too well founded. Dom Antonio's admonition had been gently worded; Paolo di Bussi's, on the contrary, was couched in the severest terms. He began, as most parents apparently have done under similar circumstances, by telling her that she could not possibly know her own mind at such a tender age; the vision of herself as a nun was nothing but a childish fancy; a little girl could have no conception of the real meaning of a vocation. It would be quite possible to feel some sympathy for this viewpoint, had it not been coupled with another which strikes the unprejudiced observer as being contradictory: she was not old enough to give intelligent and serious consideration to a cloister; however, in her father's opinion, she *was* old enough to give intelligent and serious consideration to marriage. He had, in fact, already promised her hand to Lorenzo di Ponziano, the son of his old friend, Andreazzo Ponziano, and their distant kinswoman, Cecilia Mellini, and the scion of one of the noblest families in Rome.

Di Bussi may well have been gratified that his daughter's beauty and bearing had attracted the favorable attention that led the Ponziani to seek such an alliance; but, since he himself was a proud patrician, it does not seem likely that his insistence on this marriage was due to a desire for personal advancement of any kind; and the fact that the boy in question was personable and pleasant and that his character was above reproach immediately gives the lie to any fantastic story that Paolo was forcing his daughter to marry some hideous degenerate. On the other hand, it is hard to escape the impression that he enjoyed exercising the authority which Roman law not only permitted a father, but encouraged him to practice: he had absolute power over his children, even to the point of selling them into bondage or putting them to death; and if he carried his prerogative no further than to dictate their way of life, he was regarded as a considerate and even merciful man. But however his contemporaries felt about this, the fact that di Bussi had told neither his wife nor his daughter about his matchmaking schemes, until Francesca approached him with her pathetic little plea, and then broke the news bluntly as well as brutally, adds to the unfavorable reaction toward him which prevails at the present day.

Perhaps there was something about her helpless misery in the face of his declaration of power that made him add other arguments in favor of his decision—if it is true that he actually did so. Some historians believe that he tried to move his daughter by reminding her that she was an only child and if she did not marry and give him grandchildren, there would be no one left to carry on an honorable name; furthermore, if she entered a cloister, his last years and those of her mother would, necessarily, be very lonely. Unfortunately, there seems to be a flaw in this (alleged) argument. That Francesca was the di Bussis' first child and that she was born when they were already middle-aged seems a well-authenticated fact; but, apparently, she had a younger sister, Perna, who lived with her after the death of their parents and whose two sons, Giovanni Antonio Lorenzi and Giacomo Ceccolelli, were later befriended by their aunt when they were in sore need of both moral and physical support.

This being the case, the impression made by di Bussi upon the modern mind inevitably remains unchanged. So does the impression that Francesca went to her wedding in a sacrificial spirit. She had submitted to her father's will because she had no choice; but from her viewpoint he would have been more merciful if he had killed her than he was in forcing her to accept a mortal husband when she considered herself pledged to a Celestial Bridegroom. Even if there had been no such pledge, she was pitifully unprepared, both physically and mentally, for the round of banquets, balls and other forms of revelry that characterized the medieval marriage and became less and less restrained as they approached their climax.

The Ponziani, though they were righteous people, and extremely proud to number among their ancestors St. Polianus, a third-century pope and martyr, were much more wordly minded than the di Bussi and lived in an atmosphere of much greater sophistication and festivity. This was partly from natural inclination and partly because there were several pleasure-loving young people in the family. Lorenzo had an elder brother Paolo, generally called by his nickname of Paluzzo, who had married Giovanna (familiarly known as Vannozza) di San Croce and there were, besides, gay young cousins galore. To Francesca their very lightheartedness was baffling, their candid relish of fleshly delights a staggering shock.

We may take what comfort we can from the knowledge that a girl of twelve was not then generally considered too young for marriage; that Francesca was warmly welcomed and lapped in luxury by the family of which she became a part; and that the young man who claimed her as his own really loved her and would not consciously, much less wilfully, have failed to treat her with tenderness. The fact still remains that she had been brought up alone by a woman who laid great stress on piety, but little on conjugality, and by a man who believed that mastery over a maiden should be absolute, whether the relationship were one of father and daughter or groom and bride, and that her strength was sapped by fasting and her endurance by discipline, even though neither had impaired her beauty. From the portrait of a contemporary, who moved in the same social circles, we can form a fairly accurate idea of her appearance as a bride: her tall headdress consists of a gauze veil surmounted by a pearl crown and confined at the back with a small string of pearls, to which are added light pendant ornaments. Her black velvet robe is cut low to reveal a bodice of gold brocade, with sleeves slashed at the elbow to permit the passage of the chemisette. A golden cord is placed crosswise over the shoulder and afterward forms a belt which falls to the side of the hip.[9]

So adorned, the little bride must, indeed, have been a vision of loveliness. What is more remarkable, she must have had extraordinary self-control, for she moved through all the riotous celebrations, not only with docility, but with grace and dignity, to the immense satisfaction of her parents and the admiration of all who met her. However, almost immediately afterward, she collapsed completely and, despite devoted nursing and the best available medical attention, for months lay so gravely ill that it appeared only a miracle could save her life and restore her to health.

She was wholly unable to eat and, presently, lost the power to move or even to speak. We are told that to everyone around her, including her physicians, her malady seemed "mysterious"; but we are also told that, rather tardily, her father repented his course of action, which would seem to indicate he realized he was at least partially responsible for her breakdown; and, in the light of modern psychology, this seems the almost inevitable consequence of shock precipitated by violence. The miracle which finally effected a cure, when the end for which Francesca prayed seemed very near, was attributed to St. Alexis, who in life had himself been a Roman of noble family and whose feast day was being celebrated in the church which bore his name, near the Ponziani palace. He appeared to her in a glorious vision, saying he had been sent to ask whether or not she wished to recover. She did not answer at once, though the power of speech was now restored to her. The temptation to ask for release from human bondage was very great; but, eventually, she found the strength to murmur, "God's will is mine." The saint replied, "Then you will live to glorify His name." The vision vanished. The recovery was immediate and complete.

"Francesca was looked upon as one risen from the dead. The affection she inspired was mingled with awe; every one considered her as the special object of the Divine mercy, and venerated her accordingly. Not so joyfully had Lorenzo received her on their bridal-day, as when she came to him now, restored to his arms by the miraculous interposition of a merciful God." [10]

3

THROUGHOUT FRANCESCA'S long illness, her sister-in-law had nursed her with untiring devotion, and they had become deeply attached to each other. She had at first mistaken Vannozza's natural joyousness for frivolity; now she recognized it not as an impediment to spirituality, but as a quality that gave luster to good deeds and great faith. During the invalid's disability, she was continually discovering that she and Vannozza had many mutual tastes and ideals and, presently, they mapped out a program of devout practices that they would share. First and foremost, of course, must come their obligations to their husbands and their parents; these they would never shirk; and they recognized that, to fulfill these obligations, they must dress as became their rank, they must receive visitors graciously and make certain visits in return, they must do their part in helping to keep a large household harmonious and upholding a proud tradition; and they must do this not only willingly, but gladly, with happy hearts and smiling faces; there must be nothing reluctant, nothing somber about their attitude. But in the periods that they were free to spend as they chose, they would attend Mass together, they would pray together in a secluded garden oratory, they would visit the prisons and serve in the hospitals.

Soon the Roman world became accustomed to the sight of these two lovely girls, accompanied only by each other, going to the churches they most frequented and to and fro on errands of mercy which took them along the riverbank to the poorer sections of the city. They were the embodiment of gentleness and kindness and the so-called "common people" came to regard them as saints and wove legends around them. In their own social circle they quickly acquired imitators, some inspired by a true desire to lead similar lives of Christian charity and others by merely following what seemed to be the latest mode.

To the modern mind, with a leaning toward history, as well as philanthropy, their volunteer nursing is one of their most interesting and appealing activities. The Hospital of Santo Spirito, where most of this nursing was done, and which is still one of the most imposing monuments of Rome, was already a venerable building when Francesca and Vannozza ministered to its patients. It was the outgrowth of an eighth-century hospice, built by Anglo-Saxon kings and first used to house Saxon pilgrims, who gave their name, Sassia or Saxia, to the quarter which "sprawled haphazardly over this part of Rome to the very doorstep of St. Peter's." [2] About the year 1200 the hospice was turned into a foundling hospital by Innocent III, in response to an appeal from some fishermen, who graphically convinced His Holiness of the need for such an institution by bringing him the dead babies they had caught in their nets. The number of Roman infants who were abandoned was appalling, and the banks of the Tiber were the popular places for such heartless desertion. As a result of the fishermen's ghastly exhibition, a turntable in the hospital wall proved a merciful substitute for these death-dealing shores; it was provided with a basket in which a baby could be placed by a woman standing in the street, close to the outer wall; then she would ring a bell, wait until the revolving turntable convinced her that it had been heard, and then go away. The baby was in good hands.

There have, of course, been hundreds of other hospitals through the ages which have received foundlings in much the same way, but none, as far as I know, which owes its origin to such a dramatic and forceful approach and none in which the rescued infants have been treated with musical therapy. For "An army of foster mothers was organized and disciplined by an official known as the Master of Wet Nurses . . . and at feeding time a flautist played to them." [11]

Innocent III, a nephew of Clement III, was notable in many ways besides for the founding of a hospital. He was only thirty-six when he became Pope, but he had already been a cardinal for some years, and he had written a book, *On the Contempt of the World.* He is described as "vigorous and able, good and clever, a right man at a most critical period. . . . He demanded and received universal allegiance, the papal dignity grew and no monarch could escape, if the occasion demanded, from the sting of his ire or the lash of his chastisement. The scandals of princes were no longer protected by the complacency of private chaplains, for few courts were exempt from the scrutiny of this strong Pope. . . . In 1215, one year before he died, Innocent assembled the Fourth Ecumenical Council of the Lateran. For eighteen months he had prepared the event and an immense gathering of prelates justified his hopes. Seventy-one patriarchs and archbishops, four hundred and twelve bishops, and nine hundred abbots and priors came to Rome and from their discussions seventy canons were promulgated. Here was pronounced that famous law which imposed upon all Catholics the obligation of annual confession and communion and here was given the doctrinal definition of transubstantiation." [12]

Having provided an asylum for the babies who, without it, would have been doomed, the hospital was enlarged so that it might admit "every sick individual for love, without making any distinction about nationality." [13] It was entrusted by the Pope to the care of Guido of Montepellier's Hospital Brethren and achieved tremendous international renown as an apostolic foundation. Nearly two hundred years had elapsed since the fishermen's fateful visit to Innocent when Francesca and Vannozza began to plan their program of good works. In the meantime, it had become increasingly the custom for Roman ladies of their station and standing to set aside a certain amount of time for service there. Accordingly, no objection was voiced, even by Cecilia Ponziano, who was inclined to regard their austere way of life less leniently than their husbands, because her daughters-in-law went almost every day to the hospital "and nursed the sick with the kindest attention; consoling them by their gentle words and tender care, bestowing alms upon the most needy, and above all, tending affectionately the most disgusting cases of disease and infirmity. To serve Christ in His afflicted brethren was a privilege they never consented to forego." [10]

Francesca did not permit her labors at the hospital, intensive as these were, to interfere with the devotional habits she had formed before she began her nursing career. She continued to go every Wednesday for confession and communion at the Church of Santa Maria Nuova, where Dom Antonio still acted as her spiritual adviser; and to these weekly visits she now added another, going every Saturday to the Church of San Clemente, for a conference with Fra Michele, a Dominican monk who, besides being "a learned theologian, as well as a man of great piety and virtue," [10] was an intimate friend of her father-in-law, a fact which, no doubt, helped to relieve the feeling, in the Ponziani family and its immediate circle, that Francesca was overzealous when it came to religion and, consequently, somewhat remiss in fulfilling her social obligations.

But though this feeling was relieved, it was not entirely overcome. Cecilia Ponziano loved to entertain, and she had every facility for doing this in the grand manner—wealth, savoir-faire, a large and competent household staff, and an incomparable setting. Architecturally, the Ponziani palace was ideally suited to every sort of festivity, and both its exterior and interior proclaimed this suitability. The previous century had seen the beginning of a change from the Greek and Roman houses of bygone days, as severely plain outside as an Oriental house; a portico supported by columns, balconies surrounded by balustrades of carved marble or wrought-ironwork, terraces adorned with potted plants and pergolas, and loggias of every description had become attached to their facades, entirely changing their atmosphere, as well as their appearance. The guest was conscious of a sense of welcome as soon as he stepped inside the portico, before he even entered the house; the balcony permitted members of the household and their intimates to view the passing scene and, in a new way, to share this; the loggia, open to the sun and air, provided not only an ideal mise en scène for al fresco family gatherings, but also for receptions of every kind and even for banquets. No longer was the great interior *cortile,* surrounded by colonnades and embellished by sparkling fountains, the secluded meeting place for members of the immediate family and the carefully selected guests who were privileged to penetrate to it; a more ostentatious and expansive way of life was now the fashion and one in which privacy, far from being a paramount attraction, was lightheartedly dismissed from serious consideration.[14]

Cecilia, always abreast of the times, had welcomed the new order of things and had fully expected that her two charming daughters-in-law would cooperate with her in making her dinners and dances, her routs and receptions outstanding for their elegance and gaiety. She may, perhaps, be forgiven for feeling thwarted because neither one consented to dance or play cards and both were very reluctant to keep late hours. Very possibly she thought that if Vannozza had taken a firm stand, supporting her pursuit of pleasure and love of luxury, Francesca, who, as she must have known, had married in unwilling obedience to parental orders, might have been equally tractable when it came to matters which, though important to Cecilia personally, were admittedly minor in the general scheme of things; and, instead, Vannozza had supported Francesca's unwelcome schedule of austerity!

However Cecilia may have felt about this, she was careful not to let her natural disappointment blind her to the great qualities of her younger daughter-in-law. Not all of her acquaintances were equally perceptive or equally tactful. "So austere and devout a life in a young person of twelve years old could not fail to attract the attention and draw down the censures of the worldly. Many such began to laugh at Francesca, and to turn her piety into ridicule. They intruded their advice on Lorenzo Ponziano, and urged him to put a stop to what they termed his wife's eccentricities. But happily for Francesca, he was not one of those men who are easily influenced by the opinion of others. He formed his own judgment, and pursued his own line of conduct undisturbed by the comments and animadversions of his would-be advisers. His young wife was much too precious to him, much too perfect in his sight, her whole life bore too visibly the stamp of God's dealings with her, for him to dream of interfering with the course she had taken. On the contrary, he looked upon her with that affectionate veneration which the presence of true sanctity always awakens in a noble and religious mind." [10]

All Francesca's biographies stress the cooperative attitude not only of her husband, but of her brother-in-law. But none, at least none that I have read, makes any mention of Francesca's or Vannozza's attendance at Mass and visits to their spiritual advisers *accompanied by their husbands.* And such an omission seems to me rather significant. In most cases, the men of a patrician family set the pattern for observances, religious as well as secular. In this case, the gentlemen seem to have been merely bystanders who did not interfere with their wives' frequent attendance and, presumably, the same is true regarding penitential habits, though Francesca and Vannozza both wore haircloth under their beautiful brocades and velvets, both starved and scourged themselves. These practices were an essential part of the pattern of the times, when martyrdom was still the ideal of true believers and self-inflicted physical suffering the nearest approach to it that most were able to realize. This ideal is so far removed from present-day standards, that it is hard for us to view it tolerantly, much less approvingly. I can only say, as I have said many times before, that we must try to accept it because it *does* belong to a pattern and we have no right to blind ourselves to any part of this, when we are endeavoring to understand and interpret a way of life.

The Ponziani palace was located within a stone's throw of the beautiful Church of St. Cecilia, and Francesca formed the habit of slipping away to it, whenever occasion offered, for prayer and meditation. Silence, habitual to her since childhood, became a more and more distinctive trait; she was courteous in conversation, gracious in manner to all she met, but, in so far as she properly could, she avoided chatter with associates which seemed to her purposeless and associates who might engage her in it. It is quite possible, considering her normal bent, that this might have happened in the natural course of events. But, as a matter of fact, there was a supernatural reason for it.

Francesca had been vouchsafed an extraordinary favor: she had been given a guardian angel, not in the sense that we all have one, as an invisible and intangible guide, but, by a rare privilege of grace, as a being who revealed himself gradually, first to her spiritual and, eventually, to her physical sight. In the early years of her marriage, she did not yet see him, as she was later to do, so clearly that she could describe his build, coloring, and garments in the greatest detail and account for almost every word he said to her; but she was already conscious not only of his presence by her side, but of his touch, at times gentle, at times forceful, according to the nature of his admonition. "At the least imperfection in her conduct . . . she felt the blow of a mysterious hand . . . and every day her virtues and piety increased." [10]

Her awareness of a guardian angel has all the more significance since she seems, even much earlier and with almost equal frequency, to have been aware of the nearness of temptation and danger, in demoniac form. The devil was very real to her, and she never took an impersonal view of him. He was embodied in a physician, who suggested that she might be cured by magic; in a pseudo-hermit who managed to penetrate to the Ponziani palace and "by some artful words, to inspire Francesca with aversion and disgust for the solitary life"; [10] by an unseen assailant who hurled her into the Tiber, when she stopped on the river brink to refresh herself with a drink of water on a very hot day; and in numerous others. Her viewpoint concerning a personal devil, rather than general spiritual forces of evil, was shared with many other great saints, Teresa of Avila among them; so it is noteworthy in her case largely because, to a greater degree than any other of whose life we have a detailed record, she had an antidote for temptation and danger as real as these perils themselves: how was a fallen angel, however powerful, to prevail against one clothed in celestial majesty and might?

4

THE YEAR 1400, which marked the celebration of a Pontifical Jubilee,[15] was one of great personal rejoicing at the Ponziani palace. For over four years Lorenzo and Francesca had been childless and, before this, Paluzzo and Vannozza had lost their only son; [16] the great house had been without an heir. Now, at last, there were prospects of one and, in due time, Francesca was safely delivered of a son, who was baptized on the day of his birth, at the nearby Church of St. Cecilia, to which his mother had become so attached, and given the name of Giovanni Battista.

Like her mother before her, Francesca took the duties of maternity seriously and, contrary to current custom, insisted on nursing the baby herself, thus necessarily curtailing the charitable activities which she and Vannozza had so long shared and—it is to be hoped —the self-inflicted penances which she practiced in secret. Shortly after the birth of Battista, Paolo di Bussi died, and it has been intimated that, once his hope for a grandson, so long deferred, had been realized and Francesca had fulfilled her destiny, in his viewpoint, he felt he had nothing left to live for. This seems a rather unnatural attitude, since his wife and a younger daughter, Perna, were still members of his immediate household. However, considering his harshness, amounting almost to cruelty, in the case of Francesca, it is hard for us to think of him as having altogether natural feelings. Since we are told in the course of justice none of us would see salvation and that we must all pray for mercy, it is to be hoped he did this; he needed it more than many who thus pray.[17]

The prescribed period of mourning for her father had not ended when Francesca's mother-in-law, Cecilia Ponziano, died, and this second death marked not only an occasion for sincere grief, but the beginning of new responsibilities. Normally, Vannozza, as the elder of the two daughters-in-law, would have been the one to take over the direction of the household. But she and her husband, no less than the bereft widower, felt that Francesca was better qualified to do this, and joined their entreaties to his. In the face of such strong feeling, and the sincere expression of it, she could not refuse, especially as Lorenzo was much gratified by their choice; and, young and inexperienced as she was, Francesca quickly revealed great ability as an administrator. Since ostentation of any kind was distasteful to her, and she was quite without self-importance, she preferred to minimize, rather than exaggerate, her position as head of what was designated as "the most opulent house in Rome"; but she ran it competently and with befitting dignity. Moreover, the firmness with which she managed her huge heterogeneous household was tempered with a loving-kindness revealed in her pleasant voice, her quiet manner and her impartial ruling; she was a gentlewoman in every sense of that much abused word. She was watchful and her numerous employees were given no chance to shirk their duties; but she neither overworked them nor accused them unjustly of negligence, and she was rewarded by their affection and their willingness to serve her as well as by their respect. Possibly they were not all as enthusiastic as she would have liked to have had them over her careful provision that their labors should be arranged in such a way that they need never miss either Mass or family prayers and that they should be free to attend parochial instruction on Sundays and holidays; but they admired the motives which led her to make all this possible and complied with her wishes. Indeed—to present the other side of the case—it is not unlikely that many were moved to real devotion and renewed faith by her example.

Since the second period of Francesca's mourning was one that affected the entire Ponziani family, there was, of course, no question of asking her to preside immediately at functions such as Donna Cecilia had so greatly enjoyed and which, on the contrary, were so distasteful to Francesca; and, before another year had passed,

Rome fell under the double scourge of famine and pestilence, which automatically put a tragic end to any type of social festivity. Instead of opening her doors to personal friends, Francesca opened them to the poor and the needy. She gave strict orders that no one who came to the house asking for alms was to be turned away; and, fearful that even after taking this precaution, she might have left some suffering, which she could have alleviated, still unremedied, she went out among the nearby poor, offering them corn, wine, oil and clothing. Andreazzo, alarmed by such wholesale prodigality, took the keys of the granary and the wine cellar away from his daughter-in-law, to whom he had hitherto entrusted them without reserve. Then, fearful that he might yield to her entreaties and unlock these strongholds after all, he sold the corn that was not needed for the immediate consumption of his household and all the wine except that contained in one huge cask.

By this time, the famine had reached such proportions that Francesca was ready to go to any lengths to relieve it even a little. Since the birth of her child and the subsequent responsibilities she had undertaken, she had abandoned most of her excursions, on which she had been accompanied by Vannozza, into remote parts of the city; now she resumed them. Again the two young gentlewomen went to and fro, not only to pray in churches or to visit prisons and hospitals, but to beg for the largesse which they were no longer able to dispense themselves. Sometimes they met with a generous response; at other times, they met with none at all, because they had sought it in places which seemed favorable, but where there was nothing available; at still others, they were greeted only with sneers and insults for futilely debasing themselves. At last, in desperation, Francesca suggested to Vannozza that they should go to the denuded corn loft; perhaps among the straw, they might still find a few grains of corn. Accordingly, they summoned their faithful old servant Clara to help them and mounted to the loft, which was no longer locked, since, presumably, all its treasure was gone.

For several hours, working on their knees, the three women sifted the straw and, at the end of that time, had succeeded in collecting about a measure of corn. Then, Francesca's earliest biographer tells us, a miracle occurred:

"The God who caused the widow's oil not to fail, and made her barrel of meal last through a scarcely more grievous famine, was preparing their reward. Lorenzo had entered the granary just as they were carrying off their hard-earned treasure, and, looking about him, beheld in place of the straw which was lying there a moment before, 40 measures of bright yellow corn, so shining and so full . . . that it seemed as though it had been raised in Paradise, and reaped there by angels. . . . But corn was not enough; the sick wanted wine. They came, poor pallid ghosts, just risen from their beds of suffering, to beg it of Francesca; aged men and delicate children, mothers with infants at their breasts, poor worn-out priests sinking with exhaustion, and yet willing to assist others, they had recourse to her for a little wine to strengthen them in their works of mercy, and she had no wine to give, save out of the single cask in the cellar. She gave it, nevertheless; and day after day drew from it, till not a drop was left. Andreazzo, provoked, waxed very wroth; he had never before been angry with Francesca, but now he stormed and raved at her; he had been to the cellar to see the wine drawn for that day's use, and not a drop was in the cask. 'Charity indeed!' he exclaimed, 'charity begins at home; a pretty sort of virtue this, which, under the pretext of assisting strangers, introduces penury and privation into the midst of a person's own family.'

"He vented his anger in bitter reproaches; Lorenzo and Paluzzo were also inclined to take his part, and joined in severely blaming Francesca. She the while, with a gentle voice and quiet manner, breathing most probably a secret prayer to her who at the marriage-feast of Cana turned to her Son and said, 'They have no wine,' doubtless with an inward assurance that God would befriend her in an extraordinary, but not to her an unprecedented manner, thus addressed to them: 'Do not be angry; let us go to the cellar; may be through God's mercy, that the cask may be full by this time.' They followed her with an involuntary submission; and on reaching the spot, saw her turn the cock of the barrel, out of which there instantly flowed the most exquisite wine, which Andreazzo acknowledge to be superior to any he had ever tasted. The venerable old man turned to his daughter-in-law, and, with tears in his eyes, exclaimed,

" 'Oh, my dear child, dispose henceforward of every thing I possess, and multiply without end those alms that have gained you such favour in God's sight.'

"The report of this miracle spread far and wide; and, in spite of her humility, Francesca did not object to its being divulged, as it testified to the Divine virtue of almsgiving, and encouraged the rich to increase their liberality, and minister more abundantly to the suffering members of Christ." [10]

Other miracles of a minor nature had already been reported: once when the two girls were in their oratory, engaged in discussing their mutual heartfelt desire to leave the world altogether and live in the desert like the earliest hermits, "absorbed in the subject, Vannozza exclaimed, with childlike simplicity, 'But what should we have to eat, sister?' and Francesca replied, 'We should search for fruits in the desert, dearest; and God would surely not let us seek in vain.' As she said these words they rose to return home, and from a tree which grew out of a ruined wall on one side of the garden there fell at her feet a quince of the largest size and the most shining colour, and another similar to it was lying in Vannozza's path. The sisters looked at each other in silent astonishment; for the time of the year was April, and nothing but a miracle could have brought these apples to maturity at this unwonted season. The taste of the fruit was as excellent as its colour was beautiful. They were divided amongst the members of the family, who wondered at the marvels which seemed continually to attend the steps of Francesca." [10]

On another occasion, when Vannozza was dangerously ill and had been for some days unable to retain any food, Francesca inquired anxiously if her sister-in-law could not think of something that might taste good to her. "She named a certain fish, which was not in season at that time. The markets were scoured by the servants, but naturally in vain, and they returned empty-handed to the dejected Francesca, who, kneeling by the bedside of her friend, betook herself, with arduous faith and childlike simplicity, to prayer. When she raised her head, the much-wished-for article of food was lying before her; and the first morsel of it that Vannozza ate restored her to health." [10]

It is noteworthy that both these supernatural occurrences, like the miracles of the corn and the wine, were connected with bodily nourishment; to the modern mind, it seems as if they should have suggested to Francesca that a human being's welfare, if not his actual existence, is often dependent on food and encouraged her to mitigate her voluntary abstinence. However, they do not appear to have had any great bearing on her mental and spiritual attitude and the miracles of the golden corn and the replenished cask, though they marked a turning point in Francesca's life did so because of their effect on her husband rather than because of their effect on her. "A kind of religious awe seems to have taken possession of Lorenzo's mind, at the sight of so many wonders wrought in his house. The great esteem in which he had always held his wife, now took the form of a profound veneration. He recommended her to follow in every respect the divine inspirations she received, and left her entirely free to order her life and dispose of her time in any way she thought fit." [10]

Francesca acted promptly. She first consulted her spiritual director and then she sold not only her jewels, but all her beautiful clothes and distributed the money among the most needy of the many in want; from that time on her habitual dress was one made of coarse green cloth. She resumed her regular ministrations at the Hospital of Santo Spirito and similar activities and doubled and redoubled the amount of time she spent in churches and in private devotions. In the latter, she was joined not only by Vannozza, but by a certain Rita Celli, a devout young friend whom the sisters had admitted to their intimacy, and by their faithful servant Clara. Her mortifications became more severe, her fasts more rigid than ever; even the biographers who are unstinted in their admiration for this phase of her devotional life admit that "it is difficult to understand how she could have sustained such rigors without endangering her health, or how she could have found time to supervise her household, care for her child and perform an incredible number of good works." [10] But, apparently, her health remained sound and, unquestionably, she never wearied in well-doing. And when Battista was four years old—that is, when Francesca herself had just turned twenty—she gave birth to her second son, who was christened Giovanni Evangelista and who was to prove himself "a child of grace and an inheritor of the Kingdom of Heaven."

5

"Evangelista was old in sense, small in body, great in soul, resplendent in beauty, angel-like in all his ways."

THIS CHARMING description of Francesca's second son, originating in the work of a contemporary biographer, is quoted with understandable admiration by Lady Georgiana Fullerton, one of the saint's ablest modern biographers, who then goes on to say, "Supernatural had been the mother's virtues, supernatural were the qualities of the child; at the age of three years old he was endowed with the gift of prophecy, and the faculty of reading the unuttered thoughts of men's hearts."

We are prone to associate the ability to prophesy with some of the sterner figures of the Old Testament—Jeremiah, Nehemiah and others—rather than with the merciful Savior and His chosen saints, who exemplify an entirely different aspect of this divine gift. The case of Evangelista suggests that we may be doing so mistakenly, for a gentler and more lovable child or one who gave more joy to his mother would be hard to imagine. The two examples of his powers that Lady Fullerton gives are also given by other biographers and seem worthy of quotation:

"He was in his mother's arms one day, when two mendicant friars approached the Ponziano Palace. Instantly stretching out his little hands, Evangelista took from Francesca the alms she was wont to bestow on such visitors, and held it out to them; but at the same time looking steadfastly at one of the monks, he said to him, 'Why will you put off this holy habit? You will wear a finer one; but woe to you who forget your vow of poverty.'

"The friar coloured and turned away; but it was soon evident that the words were prophetic, for within a short time, and after obtaining a bishopric through a simoniacal act, the unhappy man died a violent death. That same year, Evangelista was in his parents' room one day; and his father taking him up on his knees, was playing with him, and devouring him with kisses. In the midst of his sport, the child turned suddenly pale, and laying hold of a dagger which had been left on the table, he placed the point of it against Lorenzo's side, and said to him, as he looked up into his face with a strange melancholy smile, 'This will they do to you, my father.' And it so happened that at the time of the invasion of Rome by the troops of Ladislas Durazzo, the lord of Ponziano was dangerously wounded in the exact place and manner which his little son had pointed out."

Undoubtedly, despite the political storms that were gathering over Rome and already menacing the security of the family, and an occasional bout with the persistent "demon," the next few years were the happiest of her married life. She had not yet become forcibly aware of disturbing extraneous conditions, which she had not been called upon to meet and which were foreign to her understanding and experience; on the other hand, the conditions which she *was* called upon to meet and which she did understand were all improved. The scourge of famine and pestilence which had so wrung her heart and taxed her resources had abated, and the piteous demands made upon her strength and her purse had ceased to harass her. The management of "the most opulent house in Rome" was a task with which she had learned to cope efficiently, graciously and without undue effort. Her circle of intimates, which already embraced Rita Celli as well as Vannozza, had been further enlarged by Lucia degli Aspalli, a congenial young matron who was a kinswoman of the Ponziani; and this friendship was rewarding in many ways. Francesca's relations with her father-in-law were now unstrained and amicable, with her sister-in-law and brother-in-law consistently affectionate, and with her husband harmonious. She had learned to accept matrimony, which at first had appalled her, as a holy estate, since it had been crowned with maternity. With the birth of her third child, a daughter, whom she named Agnes after her favorite young martyr, her cup of joy was very full. She was no longer a frightened and thwarted girl, cowed to submission, or a zealot, substituting exaggerated piety and asceticism for normal human emotions; she was a Lady Bountiful, whose charity was without either ostentation or condescension; an accomplished chatelaine in the best Roman tradition; a respected and cherished wife and a beloved mother; and—though this was not yet apparent—an embryonic saint.

However, during the years which had been so rewarding to her, the political situation in Rome had gone from bad to worse. The death of Urban VI in 1389 had put an end to at least one element of violence; but his successor, the Neapolitan Cardinal Pietro Tomacelli, who took the name of Boniface IX and ruled for fifteen years, failed to restore harmony to the Church and, consequently, lacked the force to impose it elsewhere, though he succeeded in effecting some greatly needed reforms. The antipope, Clement VII, continued to preside over the splendid palace in Avignon; and when he died, five years after Urban—that is, when Francesca was ten years old and completely absorbed in her childish plans for a cloistered life—a successor had been quickly chosen for him in the person of the engaging Spaniard, Pedro de Luna, who "reigned" as Benedict XIII. Christendom was still divided; Rome was still a battlefield.

The celebration of the Holy Year in 1400 should have given thousands grounds for hope of an era marked by religious rebirth; Francesca and her family, happily absorbed in the birth of Battista, the eagerly awaited heir of the Ponziani, had hardly been aware that these hopes, as far as the papacy was concerned, were alas, unfounded.

The kingdom of Naples was rent in two by a War of Succession with ramifications which agitated all Italy and especially Rome. Louis of Anjou, a younger brother of the King of France, had been nominated by Queen Joanna I as her successor; but while Louis had been recognized by the antipope, Clement VII, Urban VI had declined to do this and had declared Charles of Durazzo, who had married Joanna's niece (who was also his own first cousin) to be the rightful heir to the throne.

Whatever his rights may or may not have been, Charles conquered the kingdom, took Joanna prisoner and brought about her murder.

When he himself died, leaving only a seven-year-old son, Ladislas, Louis was promptly crowned by the antipope, and Urban, though continuing to refuse Louis his support, took no action to back up the rebellious barons who were determined to advance the cause of little Ladislas—an undertaking in which his widowed mother, Margherita, a woman of considerable courage and many resources, aided and abetted them. As a result, the kingdom was thrown into a state of anarchy.

Boniface IX acted with more determination than his predecessor, but the form it took was not calculated to clarify confusion or restore harmony, for it was Ladislas, now twenty-one years of age, whom he crowned! The Colonna family, for centuries one of the most poweful and the most contentious in Rome, had long been hostile to Boniface, not merely because—as a Neapolitan—they regarded him in the light of a natural enemy, but because they had consistently taken the side of the antipopes and were especially favorable to Benedict XIII (Pedro de Luna) who had now succeeded Clement VII. They organized an insurrection and marched through the streets of Rome shouting to high heaven, "Death to the tyrant Boniface!" and leaving death and destruction in their wake.

Thanks to the loyalty of other great families, the Ponziani among them, Boniface managed to outride the storm and survive the century. For a time, the rival local factions ceased to harass each other and Rome, as a whole, stopped seething over what was happening in Naples, where Ladislas was now firmly entrenched—so firmly, indeed, that he began to form projects for expanding his realm of power if not his actual kingdom. He has been described as "a great warrior," but also as "proud, ambitious, cruel and lustful"; and, considering his character, it seems probable he was moved by ambition, rather than gratitude, in planning his strategy, and convinced that the best way to attain his own ends was to remain on good terms with the papacy, not only during the lifetime of his benefactor, Boniface, but during the lifetime of the latter's successor, Innocent VII. Whatever his motives, his methods had the desired results: by the time Innocent died, after a short and ineffectual reign (1404–1406), and Gregory XII was elected, Ladislas was virtually master of Rome—where he was represented by his brutal governor, Pietro Traja—as well as Naples, and the political situation was more complicated than ever.

The Colonnas, no longer enraged because the Supreme Pontiff was a Neapolitan, now shifted their allegiance from the antipope back to the Pope. But, meanwhile, other great families, among them the Ponziani and the Orsini, who were traditional enemies of the Colonnas, had shifted theirs to a compromise candidate, chosen at a council in Pisa by twenty-four cardinals who were determined to end the schism that divided Christendom. Both Gregory XII and Benedict XIII had promised to attend this conference and both had promised to abdicate in favor of a newly elected successor. All these promises were broken and the exasperated cardinals announced the selection of one of their number, a Greek by the name of Peter Philargos, to reign as Alexander V.

As John Farrow points out in his excellent work, *The Pageant of the Popes,* "Such an election was of course illegal and both Alexander and his successor were antipopes. . . . Today, with the clouds of contemporary confusion and distortion and clamour removed, Pope Gregory stands as the validly elected pontiff"—and continued so to stand until his voluntary abdication in 1415. Authoritative lists of popes do not include the name of Alexander V or his successor, any more than they include the names of other antipopes. But as two other reliable authors, Domenico Grandi and Antonio Galli, point out in *The Story of the Church,* "The Church now found itself faced with a worse scandal than before, for instead of a dual there was now a triple schism; neither the Roman nor Avignon popes would yield an inch, even though Alexander V was recognized by the majority of states." And there can be no possible doubt that the Ponziani and many other upright and loyal Romans were convinced that Alexander V was the rightful head of the Church.[18] And when Alexander "recognized" Louis and the latter decided to make Rome the battlefield, which would enable him to regain Naples, Lorenzo became one of his most valiant and active supporters and was selected as the logical *caporione* (ward captain) for Trastevere. From that moment on, it was only a matter of time before he was attacked in one of those street brawls which the Colonnas did not consider beneath their dignity to precipitate; and, after fighting desperately to ward off his assailants, he was wounded in exactly the way which his little son had foretold—by a dagger thrust into his side—and taken home for dead.

Fortunately, Francesca was able to surmount the shock of her grief and horror to the extent of kneeling by Lorenzo's side and listening for his heartbeat, at the same moment that she prayed for both resignation and courage; and quickly convinced that, though he might be dying, he was not yet actually dead, she swiftly summoned a physician as well as a priest and, while awaiting the arrival of both, calmly murmured words of loving-kindness to her husband, hoping against hope that he might be conscious, even if only vaguely, of her presence and her support. Though Extreme Unction was promptly administered, it proved to be a precautionary, rather than a necessary, measure; Lorenzo's condition was precarious, but it was not fatal; and the experience that Francesca had gained at Santo Spirito stood her in good stead now. She was able to nurse her husband not only untiringly but skillfully, and her watchful and intelligent care was rewarded by his slow but steady progress toward recovery.

He was, however, barely convalescent when Francesca's brother-in-law, Paluzzo, the husband of her beloved Vannozza, who had somehow managed to escape the sort of fray in which Lorenzo had been wounded, was arrested and thrown into prison; and the stricken family was next informed that, unless it surrendered its heir, the nine-year-old Battista, to Pietro Traja, the deputy governor of Ladislas, as a hostage, Paluzzo would be executed. For the first time, Francesca's fortitude wavered. She was devoted to her brother-in-law, but the depth of her feeling for him could not be compared with the intensity of her love for her first-born; and she was convinced that, once Ladislas or his cruel deputy had Battista in his power, the child's life would be forfeited. This conviction was not based on panic, but on natural maternal instinct; and though she yielded to panic in obeying this instinct, I believe that every mother of an endangered child will sympathize with her and not condemn her for seizing the bewildered boy by the hand and rushing blindly out into the street.

Though intent on escape, she had not the least idea where she could turn for safety; and it was providential that, in her headlong flight, which took her through obscure streets and half-deserted corners of the city, she should suddenly come face to face with Dom Antonio who, for more than twenty years, had been her spiritual adviser and her most trusted friend. The very sight of him was soothing to her distraught mind; and, when he had questioned her about her extraordinary conduct, so alien to her habitual self-control, he gave her wise counsel.

"You are choosing the wrong way to save Battista," he told her, placing a reassuring arm around the frightened child's shoulders. "Instead of trying to flee and hide, you should go to the Church of Aracoeli."

A protest, wrung from her anguished heart, almost reached her lips. The Church of Santa Maria d'Aracoeli, surmounting the site of the ancient Temple of Juno, is located on Capitoline Hill; and it was at the Capitol that Francesca had been sternly ordered to surrender the boy; the church in question was the last place where she would have voluntarily sought sanctuary. But her lifelong habit of obedience to spiritual direction and the implicit faith in her confessor's wisdom were even stronger than her fears. The protest was never uttered. She bowed her head, tightened her grasp on Battista's hand and then, looking straight ahead of her, started toward the Capitol.

By this time, the news of Paluzzo's imprisonment and the threat to his life had spread like wildfire through Rome. As she went along, crowds pressed around Francesca, trying to block her passage or to wrest Battista from her and take him home to his father. She was pursued by shouted warnings that she was mad, that she could not save Paluzzo's life and that she would never see her child alive again after that day. But she went steadily on, across the Tiber, past Pompey's Theater, to the foot of the great flight of steps, built with the proceeds from offerings made to the Virgin during the Black Death, leading to the Church of Aracoeli.

Some two centuries later, a second flight of steps was built, going directly to the piazza of the Capitol; but at that time, the steps to the church were the only ones leading to the summit of Capitoline Hill. There are one hundred twenty-four of them and, though they are very beautiful, they are also very steep; it requires a considerable effort to climb them. That Francesca managed to do so, encouraging her son, who must have been very tired, to keep up with her, is proof positive that she had recovered from her panic, that her physical strength was still strong and that her spiritual strength had been renewed.

The Count of Traja was waiting at the appointed place for his victim and Francesca led Battista to him. There is no record—at least I have found none—which tells just how she explained to the boy that she was obliged to leave him for the present, but that the gentleman to whom she was entrusting him would be his friend and protector until she could rejoin him. She must have made a great effort, as she spoke, to keep her lips from trembling and her eyes from overflowing—an effort all the harder because she could see the one her child was making to keep a stiff upper lip, while two great tears rolled slowly down his cheeks. Perhaps, as they stopped for breath on the seemingly endless flight of steps, she had managed to prepare him for what was going to happen. I do not know and I wish I did, for this seems to me one of the most poignant moments in Francesca's story. I only know that, at last, she turned away and, without looking back, walked into the vast columned church and, weeping bitterly, flung herself down before the altar of the Merciful Mother.

How long she stayed there she was never aware; but gradually, for the second time that dreadful day, she regained her self-control and her sense of calm returned. And, before she left the dimness of the great church and went out again into the bright Roman sunshine and down the steep shining marble steps, she had proof that she had not appealed to the Merciful Mother in vain, that her prayers for the safety of her child had been heard and heeded.

For she had no sooner left Battista than the Count of Traja had ordered one of his officers to lift the boy to the front of his saddle and take him to the place which had been designated. Lifting him up was easy enough; taking him away was another matter. The officer's well-trained horse, hitherto tractable and instantly alert at the sound of his master's voice, suddenly balked; neither spurs nor whip had the slightest effect on him. We are told that, after having given up this horse as hopeless for their purpose, four knights of Naples, using four successive steeds, attempted to remove Battista from Capitoline Hill, but always with the same result. At last, obviously annoyed and secretly frightened by such a phenomenon, Traja ordered the child taken back to his mother. She was still kneeling before the altar when she felt his warm little arms stealing around her neck.

6

FRANCESCA CAN hardly have hoped that her troubles were at an end when she returned unharmed to the Ponziani palace with her eldest son, providentially restored to her, at her side. Her husband was now convalescent, but he was still very weak; her brother-in-law was alive, but he was still in prison; her father-in-law, if he were still living—and we do not know whether he was or not—was now an elderly man; she had no stalwart male defenders, other than the faithful members of her household, who were without authority and therefore could not present a formidable front against abuse or attack. The march of events in Rome was to reveal, all too soon, how much she needed one.

For Alexander V had died in Bologna, after he had occupied his disputed and shaky throne for only a year; and sixteen assembled cardinals had chosen as his successor one of their number, Balthazar Cossa, who took the name of John XXIII. The kindest thing that can be said of him is that he "lacked spiritual qualities"; and we scarcely need to be reminded that, some five hundred years later, when Cardinal Roncalli of Venice was elected Pope, he took the same name, on the ground that it was available because its first holder had been only an antipope and, indeed, he is so classified on all official lists. But the confused Roman nobles, the Ponziani among them, who had supported Alexander V, now gave their support, as in duty bound, to his successor. So did Louis of Anjou, who had succeeded in getting a foothold in Rome. This was enough to send Ladislas, his triumphant rival for the throne of Naples, into fresh frenzies; and, on the pretext of restoring the rights of Gregory XII —who was, to be sure, still the lawfully elected Pope—Ladislas hurled himself on Rome at the head of a new army, conquered the city, and "gave it up to pillage."

The Ponziani were faced with the fact that their palace was unquestionably one that would be marked for demolition when the insurgents turned their attention from the churches, which they had despoiled and desecrated, to the homes of the nobles and, this time, Lorenzo would be not merely wounded, if he were found there, but killed. Therefore, Francesca persuaded him to make good his escape while there was still an opportunity. Evidently, her first idea was that he should take refuge on one of the remote estates which provided the family with a large part of its fortune, as it was on these their vineyards and their extensive stock farms were located; if Lorenzo could have watched over these, he could have safeguarded at least some of their possessions and assured his wife and children and his sister-in-law of some sort of a country house in which they could live, provided they were driven out of Rome. Unhappily, while the question of his flight was still under discussion, his terrified vintners, shepherds and cattlemen came pouring into the palace with dreadful tales of death and destruction. Instead of being able to provide safety for their lord and master in the country, they were seeking it from him in the city. Lorenzo yielded to Francesca's entreaties and fled to "a distant province," not otherwise identified.

Again it seems strange to this biographer, as it did when she found no mention of his leadership in the religious life of the household, that Lorenzo did not play a more valiant part in the defense of his family and his property; but this viewpoint seems to be unique. Other chroniclers all speak of the weakened condition in which his terrible wound had left him, of the futility of his presence in Rome and of the impossibility of taking his wife and children with him when he fled, because there would not have been time to assemble them. So, perhaps, this biographer's viewpoint is unduly severe. Be that as it may, he had hardly taken to his heels when the expected catastrophe occurred: drunken invaders broke into the house; tortured and killed the servants, who would not and, indeed, probably could not, disclose their master's whereabouts; and then proceeded to demolish the palace: the great canopied beds, mounted on platforms or trestles, were overturned and, in some cases, hacked to pieces. The ornate doors of the *armoires* were wrenched off their hinges, the shelves stripped, the drawers emptied, the contents stolen; credences and marriage chests, enriched with tooled and painted leather and elaborately wrought ironwork, were given similar rough treatment and so were the lamps gracefully shaped in the form of tripods. As to the ornaments made of Venetian glass, the Pompeian vases of terracotta, the Florentine vases of black clay, the Etruscan chalices, they were all smashed to atoms. Even the household utensils, whether made of brass or bronze, in a palace like that of the Ponziani "always took a form that was pure and exquisite." Pails, kitchenware, scales—all revealed the pride the artisans of the period took in molding the materials with which they worked; handles and hilts bore witness to their painstaking skill. All were ruthlessly destroyed. When the marauders finally decided to depart, having reduced the entire premises to a state of wrack and ruin, they tore Battista from his mother's arms and, unhampered this time by a balky horse, bore him away in triumph.

Gone were the glories of "the most opulent house in Rome." No more could its loggias and its terraces serve as the setting for magnificent fetes; no more could a proud old patrician, assisted by his wife and his sons and their wives, make his fellow patricians and their families welcome at his groaning board, or permit the doorway of his dwelling to serve as the portal for unstinted largesse to the poor and needy. Somehow Francesca, with the help of Vannozza and a few faithful retainers whose lives had been spared, cleared away the wreckage and created the semblance of a home among the ruins. She had no tidings of any kind from Lorenzo; for all she knew, he might dead. According to reliable reports, Paluzzo continued to languish in a Roman prison; it was something to know that, for the time being at least, the threat of execution had not been carried out. Indirectly, she learned that Battista had been taken to Naples, and to her fears for his safety was added her deep concern for his spiritual welfare. The depravity of the court at Naples was a byword, even during a period notoriously lax as far as moral standards were concerned; what effect would this gilded vice have on a thirteen-year-old boy, who had hitherto led a sheltered life, guarded, as far as it was humanly possible and with the help of prayer, from every sort of sin? Francesca had no delusions about the type of talk he would hear, the type of sights he would see, the type of temptations to which he would be subjected. What were they doing in Naples, she asked herself, to corrupt this innocence? What were they doing to this ardent faith? What were they doing to this adolescence which only a mother could protect in its wholesome and normal development? These were the questions she asked herself with anguish. But she still had Evangelista and Agnes; to them she could still be guardian and teacher as well as mother; to her they were all that remained to help her recall the happy years before the division of the papacy and the sack of Rome.

And then, once again, came famine and pestilence, scourging the city. Two of the faithful servants were the first victims in the Ponziani palace. The third was Evangelista.

There are many that say no death can be beautiful; but I have never felt that way and, quite evidently, this gifted and lovely child was happily convinced angels had come to keep him company on his way to heaven and that he would be very contented there, even if this meant separation for a time from his mother. She was strong enough to prevent her own grief from marring his confidence by anything she said or did; and her sorrow may well have been somewhat assuaged by the vision of a little girl who lived next door and who had been seriously ill for a long while. This small sufferer suddenly sat up in bed, exclaiming, "Oh, look! oh, look! Evangelista is going up to heaven and two angels are with him!" No one who heard her or who reported the story felt that she might have been the victim of a feverish imagination.

Evangelista was buried in the vault of the family chapel at St. Cecilia's Church, beside the little cousin who had died the same year that Battista was born; and Francesca began resolutely to devote the time which she would have spent in caring for her younger son to an expansion of her good works. The great inner banqueting hall of the palace,[19] though the two sisters had not tried to use it since the pillage of the property, was not as badly damaged as most of the building; and they now set to work to clear it of its debris and convert it into a makeshift hospital; at least it would provide shelter for those who, besides being desperately ill, were entirely homeless and there were many such. A few foodstuffs were still smuggled in from the damaged vineyards and stock farms, and these provisions were rationed and gladly shared with the poor who, except for such manna, would have starved to death. Moreover, Francesca and Vannozza were now experienced nurses; without leaving Agnes, they could care for as many victims of pestilence and famine as if they had kept on going regularly to Santo Spirito. And they had volunteers to help them in their work. Rita Celli and Lucia di Astalli had been standing steadily by for some time now; two more friends, Margherita di Montellucci and Giacobella di Biunemonti, were welcome additions to the little group and shared both its religious fervor and its view that it should illumine not only thoughts but works. As yet, there were no formal ties binding these congenial spirits together; but their association formed the nucleus of what was later to become a powerful congregation.

Occasionally, Francesca did leave Agnes in the watchful care of one of these consecrated women and went herself to the family vineyard near the Church of St. Paul's-Without-the-Walls. This property was less distant from her home than the other Ponziani estates, and she could combine her devotions at the church with work at the vineyard. There she not only gathered grapes for food and drink, but the dry branches of the vines, which could be used to supplement the meager supply of firewood in the ruined palace and, also, to distribute among the poor who had no fuel at all. These branches were neatly made into bundles and slung over the back of a patient donkey, just as similar fagots are today. Once, as Francesca was coming home with the donkey well laden, he stumbled and fell, scattering the loosened contents of his burden far and wide. While she was trying to assemble the stray branches, a certain Lelli Petrucci, who was a friend of her husband's, chanced to pass by and, after looking at her in unconcealed astonishment when he recognized her, turned to and helped her pick up the wood. It was, perhaps, his first experience with manual labor; but this was by no means unfamiliar to Francesca any more. She could gather up stray fagots, strewn about the streets, with as little embarrassment and with as much dignity as she had walked among her guests, supervising the servants who were passing jeweled goblets filled with rare vintage wine and great golden platters laden with sweetmeats.

It was during this same period that Francesca began to reveal not only the natural aptitude for nursing she had shown from girlhood, but powers that far surpassed mere skill and gentleness. Unquestionably, she had the healing hands of the chosen few whom the Savior has permitted to share one of His greatest gifts; and, besides making use of this supernatural favor without the aid of any special remedies, she prepared ointments which were remarkable for their efficacy in relieving the effects of horrible accidents and still more horrible wounds.[20] She came to be regarded with such confidence that nothing was considered beyond the scope of her power, even apparent death. Once, when she was passing through a very poor district, she heard sounds of bitter grief coming from a miserable hovel and, going in, found a distracted woman weeping over the body of a baby. It was dead, the woman wailed; that in itself was bad enough; but it had not been baptized and for that lack there could be no comfort on earth and no welcome in heaven. Perhaps Francesca told the distracted mother that she must not be afraid, she must only have faith; the baby was not dead, but sleeping. Such "large, divine and comfortable words" have been spoken before, under similar circumstances.[21] At all events, she took the baby and cradled it in her arms, reviving it; and, after a few minutes, she smiled and gave it back to its mother, telling her to give thanks that it could be baptized, after all, and charging her to see that this was done at once. Then, hurriedly, she left the house, not wishing to be recognized and connected with this seemingly supernatural occurrence. But though the dazed woman, whose child had been restored to her, at first believed she had been visited by a ministering angel, Francesca's shabby green wool dress, girdled with a cord, was now a familiar sight to many in the neighborhood, and the miracle was duly attributed to her.[22]

Though there are many recorded instances of Francesca's miracles during this period, there is only one, at least that I have found, of a vision; but this is so extraordinary, and marked such a turning point in her life, that it transcends almost every other experience. One morning when she was at prayer, she was suddenly conscious that her oratory was illumined by a mysterious light, so radiant that all her surroundings were transformed and she felt as if her very being were penetrated by its rays. As she lifted her eyes and ceased to be dazzled by the supernatural brilliance, she saw a celestial figure which so closely resembled Evangelista that, instinctively, she stretched out her arms to embrace her son, only to find that the glorified body eluded her. Desperately she cried out, asking if this apparition were indeed he and begging him, if she were not deceived in so believing, to tell her about himself.

Her appeal was granted, as Evangelista said to her, "My abode is with God; my companions are the angels; our sole occupation the contemplation of the Divine perfections,—the endless source of all happiness. Eternally united with God, we have no will but His; and our peace is as complete as His Being is infinite. He is Himself our joy, and that joy knows no limits. There are nine choirs of angels in heaven, and the higher orders of angelic spirits instruct in the Divine mysteries the less exalted intelligences. If you wish to know my place amongst them, my mother, learn that God, in His great goodness, has appointed it in the second choir of angels, and the first hierarchy of archangels." [10]

While he was speaking, Francesca saw that he was not alone; a second celestial figure stood beside him, very like him in build and height, but even more beautiful. Evangelista turned in his direction and said, "This my companion is higher than I am in rank, as he is more bright and fair in aspect. The Divine Majesty has assigned him to you as a guardian during the remainder of your earthly pilgrimage. Night and day by your side, he will assist you in every way. Never amidst the joys of Paradise have I for an instant forgotten you, or any of my loved ones on earth. I knew you were resigned; but I also knew that your heart would rejoice at beholding me once more, and God has permitted that I should thus gladden your eyes." [10]

Again he paused for a moment and then continued in tones of infinite compassion, "I have a message for you, Mother—a message from God. He is asking for Agnes. So, before long, she will leave you, too. But the archangel will remain. To the moment of your death he will be ever present in your sight."

The message ended with this final assurance and the glorified form of Evangelista disappeared. The brilliant light which had suffused the entire oratory gradually faded, except where it rested on the form of the celestial being who remained at Francesca's side, not only for the rest of the day, but, as her son had promised, for the rest of her life. Around him, the radiance continued to be so dazzling that she usually could not look at it with a fixed gaze, though at night, in the most profound darkness, she could read and write by its lambency; and there were times when she could see her guardian angel so distinctly that, when her confessor ordered her to do so, she was able to describe him in detail.

"His stature," she said, "is that of a child of about nine years old; his aspect full of sweetness and majesty; his eyes generally turned towards heaven; words cannot describe the divine purity of that gaze. His brow is always serene; his glances kindle in the soul the flame of ardent devotion. When I look upon him, I understand the glory of the angelic nature, and the degraded condition of our own. He wears a long shining robe, and over it a tunic, either as white as the lilies of the field, or of the colour of a red rose, or of the hue of the sky when it is most deeply blue. When he walks by my side, his feet are never soiled by the mud of the streets or the dust of the road."

I have used this description verbatim from Lady Georgiana Fullerton, because it so far surpasses in simplicity and grace any adaptation I can make of the descriptions contained in French and Italian biographies. She does not, however, describe one attribute that is stressed in these and which I think should also be mentioned—the guardian angel's beautiful golden hair, which fell in soft curls over his shoulders and had a luminescence all its own. "When demons came to attack Francesca," Dom J. Rabory tells us, "the archangel tossed back his curls and the sparkling rays that escaped from these put to flight those creatures of darkness, who could not endure the light." Berthem-Bontoux is equally ecstatic in her description: "A great part of the beauty and power of the celestial protector lay in his hair, which as to color resembled molten gold; it fell in ringlets long enough to cover his neck and wave over his shoulders. If demons molested the saint, he sometimes lowered his gaze so that it would rest on her and calm her; and sometimes to conjure the plots of their hatred against their innocent victim, he shook his flaming locks, an action which sufficed to put the monsters from hell to flight."

There is no question that this guardian angel had become as real to Francesca as any mortal member of her household, and that it was his support which enabled her to face, with fortitude, first the prospect and then the actuality of Agnes' death. But after the little girl, whose brief and lovely life had been like a benison to her mother, was buried beside her brother and her cousin in the vault of the family chapel at St. Cecilia's Church, the bereft woman collapsed. She had been such a tower of strength to so many suffering souls for so many years; now she found that, for the time being, she herself had no more reserves of strength on which she could draw. For months she lay gravely ill, and horrible visions of hell disturbed her rest. Though she had erred, as do all human beings, she had striven for the right, confessed her sins and been absolved. She was not troubled with forebodings that she herself was threatened with everlasting torment; her fears were all for those who had lived wilfully evil lives and died unrepentant. Far from dreading death, she longed for it. She cannot be blamed for hoping and praying that her children would be restored to her in a heavenly reunion. Besides, without doubt, she had reason to believe that her work in the world was done and she was justified in asking that she might be allowed to depart in peace. But though Francesca made very few mistakes, even for a saint, she was making one this time; her work on earth was well begun, but it was hardly more than half done. She was twenty-nine years old when she lost everything that seemed to make life worth while; nearly twenty-six years of usefulness to God and man still lay ahead of her. She was to find, as so many lesser mortals, both before and after her, have discovered, that for every door that closes, there is another one that opens.

7

THE NEW door did not open very wide at first, and such pleasing prospects as were disclosed seemed indistinct, as if they were still far away. But, little by little, Francesca became conscious of a fresh outlook, both figuratively and literally.

The first event that was responsible for this was the death of Ladislas. He had lived violently and evilly, and he was destined to have a violent and evil end. His current mistress was the daughter of a Florentine doctor [23] who was willing to go to any lengths if he could rid the world of this tyrant. When the girl complained that she felt her power over her royal lover was waning, her father gave her some poison with which to anoint herself, telling her it would act as an aphrodisiac, and Ladislas died in agony, raging against his enemies. The only stronghold which his sister Joanna, who was his heiress, managed to retain in Rome was the Castel Sant' Angelo, and she was too engrossed with a succession of scandalous love affairs to devote much time to young hostages, who were of no particular use to her. Battista was returned to his mother and, to her overwhelming joy and relief, she found that neither his physical nor his moral welfare had been undermined by his long sojourn in Naples. On the contrary, while losing none of the spiritual graces which had been his since childhood, he had now acquired the social and cultural graces of a court which, though admittedly corrupt, fostered and encouraged all the arts. While the brawling barons, profiting by the absence of the popes, were reducing Rome to rubble, the Angevin sovereigns had built and adorned superb palaces, monasteries and churches in Naples; they had welcomed such painters as the Tuscan Montano d'Arezzo, and such writers as Boccaccio and Petrarch; and their adroit cooperation with bankers and merchants had enabled them to carry on their program unharassed by financial cares. In the urbane atmosphere resulting from all this, Battista had become a gifted, personable and charming youth. He was in the best of health and spirits and his very presence in the desolate Ponziani palace lightened its gloom and gave it a new raison d'être.

Fortunately, Battista's vitality and buoyancy did much to offset the depressing effect which Lorenzo's long-awaited return from exile would inevitably have produced. He had not been able to surmount adversity with the same spirit as his son; he was a broken man, old before his time and, when he reentered his palace "deep sobs shook his breast, and he burst into an agony of tears." [10] He could not reconcile himself to the death of his two younger children and, instead of trying to comfort his bereaved wife, he seemed to blame her, tacitly at least, because they were not there to welcome him. Moreover, the inroads made by sorrow and privations on Francesca's bloom, instead of arousing sympathy for her and compassion for its tragic reasons, only increased his self-pity. When he had left her, she was strikingly beautiful; now she was so wan and wasted that the very sight of her made him more melancholy. We cannot escape the impression that he had become morose, irritable and fault finding. It required infinite tenderness, infinite tact and patience to restore him to normalcy of both body and soul. It is not the least of Francesca's achievements that she succeeded in doing this. And, with Lorenzo's improvement, despite the fallen fortunes and the bereavements of the Ponziani, family life again became a well-ordered unit, harmonious, contented and useful.

So the new door was opening wider all the time, and the vistas it disclosed became less and less obscured by distance. Improvements in the Church were keeping abreast with improvements in the State which had permitted the return of Battista and Lorenzo. Much of the credit for these improvements is due to the King of Hungary and Bohemia, Sigismund of Luxemburg, who also achieved the title of King of the Romans, first by the action of three electors and later through the death of his greatest rival, Jobst of Moravia. True, he had an ulterior motive. He greatly desired to be crowned as Emperor in Rome; and he was well aware that such a ceremony could not take place until western Christendom was united under one head; but there were still three claimants for the papal throne. On the basis of his authority, Sigismund called a Council at Constance, which functioned far more efficiently than the previous Council at Pisa—indeed, it has been called the greatest assemblage of its kind ever yet convened. Besides "numerous bishops, and many doctors of theology, the clergy were present to the number of some eighteen thousand. John XXIII . . . the Pisan pope, who thought that his title would be confirmed by the council, found himself instead accused of various crimes and deposed because of his unworthiness. Then the Roman Pope, the magnanimous Gregory XII . . . offered it his abdication, which was accepted. Only the obstinate Spaniard, Benedict XIII, bereft of almost all his supporters, refused to bow to the wishes of the council and offer his resignation. After long and fruitless negotiations, including a personal visit by Sigismund himself, the council decided that he was being unreasonable and ordered him deposed as a promoter of schism and heresy. Then the cardinals went into conclave, in association with thirty representatives from the council, and after three days of deliberation elected as Pope Cardinal Ottone Colonna (November 11, 1417), who took the name of Martin V. . . . Thus, to the joy of Christendom, the terrible plague afflicting the Church was eliminated. As the historian Gregorovius truly remarks: 'A kingdom would surely have perished in such a fierce storm. Yet so marvelous was the organization of the spiritual society and so indestructible the ideal of the papacy, that this division, the most profound of all, only succeeded in revealing its indivisibility.' "[24]

There had been no personal satisfaction to Lorenzo and Francesca in the election of a man belonging to the Colonna family, so bitterly inimicable to the Ponziani; but whatever their private disappointment, because the choice of the council had fallen on an adversary, they could and did share in the general rejoicing that the Great Western Schism was at last ended and that one Pope, whose authority was undisputed, would reign again in Rome. They were among the first to admit, freely and gladly, that Martin V was an able ruler who created order out of chaos and restored the ruins of Rome to their pristine splendor. Moreover, his personal life was free from all scandal, except that of nepotism and, in this case, the city actually benefited by the help of the powerful Colonna clan which rallied around him, as well as his attitude toward his hereditary enemies, the Orsini. These he was wise enough to conciliate by showing them favors, at the same time he was advancing his own kith and kin, even going so far as to promote a marriage between his niece, Anna, and Giovanni Antonio Orsini, Prince of Tarente, an even more adroit move than that of promoting the marriage of another niece, Caterina, with Guido da Montafeltre and that of his sister, Paola, with Gherardo Appiani, Lord of Piombino.

The Ponziani, like all the other great Roman families, profited by these measures. Now that they were unmolested, their vineyards and stock farms became productive again, and their ravaged houses were restored. The betterment in their fortunes brought new and welcome calm to Francesca's life, and it would appear that she now spent more time than previously, and willingly, with persons of her own social class, whose problems she had been somewhat inclined to overlook, because of her rightful and greater concern with those who were in more desperate physical and spiritual need. Perhaps her awful visions of hell, and the impression that many of its victims were not unknown to her, was responsible for this expansion of her sphere, which still included work in the vineyard nearest her home and ministry to the poor.

Among those with whom she was now associated was a young woman identified only as Gentilezza, who had lived an exceptionally frivolous life and had been outspoken in her criticism of Francesca's charities. A bad fall, that occurred when Gentilezza was pregnant, threatened her not only with the loss of her child, but with the loss of her beauty, which meant almost as much to her; and the physicians who were speedily summoned told her they could neither save her baby nor prevent her disfigurement. Through tender and devoted nursing, Francesca was able to do both; and, at the same time, she extracted from Gentilezza a promise to live in a manner more befitting a Christian wife and mother—a promise which was faithfully kept.

Two young noblemen, Giovanni Antonio Lorenzi and Angelo Savelli, were also the beneficiaries of her solicitude. She persuaded the former to abandon murderous designs on an erstwhile friend; the latter, who was dying with vengeance in his heart against an antagonist who had mortally wounded him in a duel, was induced to forgive his enemy and died in the state of grace. A mission of quite different character had as its object the Benedictine, Dom Ippolito. After ten years of useful service in his monastery, he was appointed sacristan; and this appointment, which at first filled him with pride, became so distasteful to him that he was on the point of abandoning not only his work but his habit. Before he took this rash step, however, he was inspired to "communicate to Francesca his discontent, his restlessness, and the resolution he had formed. She listened attentively to his statement, and then quietly addressed to him some questions which placed the subject in its true light. She asked him with what purpose he had entered the religious state; whom he had intended to serve in doing so; which he preferred, the God who descends and dwells on the altar, or the servants who wait upon Him elsewhere? Which was the highest post, that of watching over the sanctuary, in company with the angels, or of ministering to men, however holy and eminent they might be, as would be his lot in another office? The wisdom and simplicity of this answer went straight to Dom Ippolito's heart. He instantly acquiesced in its justice, and went directly to confession. With earnest benevolence he betook himself to the duties of his at once humble and exalted office, edified all his brethren by his unfeigned humility, and became in time the model of his order. He was afterwards successively named sub-prior, and then prior of the monastery of Santa Maria Nuova." [10]

Francesca had the faculty of crowding an almost unbelievable number of varied activities into a single day, and it is noteworthy that she considered her obligations to her family came first and these must never be slighted in order to permit her to devote more time to deeds of charity or even to prayer. Neither did interruptions, of whatever nature, seem to disturb the tranquillity with which she pursued the even tenor of her ways. Vannozza tells us that one morning when Francesca was in her room, reciting the Office to the Blessed Virgin, her husband summoned her, asking her to perform some trifling service for him, though he must have been well aware this was a time which she generally allotted to her devotions. Instantly, she rose from her knees, went to him and pleasantly did what he asked; then she returned to her room and continued reading the antiphon. She had gone only a little further down the page when she was summoned again, this time by a member of her household staff; and once more, without the slightest show of ill-humor, she responded to the call. This happened four times. The fourth time, when she went back to her book, it bore little resemblance to the one she had left, for the antiphon was now inscribed on its page in letters of gold which remained there until the day of her death.

Though there had been frequent miracles during the earlier part of Francesca's life, these had usually been associated, as we have seen, with the basic necessities of life like bread and wine or with physical healing; now they began to take on a more mystic character. Like most of the saints belonging to her era, she yearned for suffering, and self-inflicted pain was an integral part of her daily routine, both because it was the nearest approach to martyrdom for which she could hope and because it seemed to bring her closer to the Passion of the Savior. Therefore, she was convinced that the mysterious appearance of a deep wound in her side signified an "extraordinary token of union between the crucified Redeemer and His favoured servant." [10] Only Vannozza, who dressed "that touching and awful wound," [10] and Dom Antonio, to whom Francesca revealed its existence in confession, were aware of this "token" which caused her the intense suffering for which she so greatly longed "of a nature too sacred for common mention, for man's investigation, but not the less real and true." Eventually, "the relief was as miraculous as the infliction. In a vision she saw herself transported into the cave of Bethlehem, and into the presence of the Infant Jesus and of His Mother. With a sweet smile, the Blessed Virgin bade Francesca discover the wound which love had made, and then with water that flowed from the rock, she washed her side, and dismissed her. When her ecstasy was over, she found that the miraculous wound was perfectly healed." [10]

Such harrowing and soul-stirring experiences as these did not divert Francesca from the normal design of living for a great Roman lady; and she wholeheartedly shared Lorenzo's viewpoint that the time had come when the question of a suitable marriage for Battista should be given earnest consideration. This only surviving son, now grown to manhood, more than fulfilled the promise of his earlier youth. His formal education had been resumed after his return from Naples, and he had proved an eager and responsive student; his appearance was not only pleasing but distinguished; his manners were charming, his character above reproach; and now that the

Ponziani properties were productive again, he would eventually inherit a substantial fortune. His parents were certainly justified in feeling he should be considered highly eligible as the suitor of almost any young girl, however well dowered herself; and, quite obviously, the parents of his chosen bride, Mabilia Papazunni, were of the same opinion. They were residents of Trevi, which, like Parione and Trastevere, was then an aristocratic section of the city, and their social standing was comparable to that of the Ponziani. They readily consented to their daughter's marriage, and she was received at the Ponziani palace with all traditional ceremony. Lorenzo, now the head of the house, stood at the door to welcome the bridal pair as they came from the church, just as his father had done when he himself had brought Francesca there for the first time. Around and behind him stood not only the members of his immediate household, in handsome livery and his men-at-arms in gorgeous uniforms, but his shepherds and vintners in their picturesque peasant costumes, all eager to do homage to the newcomer. Then came the entertainment of their many guests, the feasting and dancing, the elaborate preparation of the nuptial chamber, the long continued revelry and, finally, the exuberant accompaniment of the newly wedded pair to their very bedside.

Many aspects of this riotous celebration must have been distasteful to Francesca, but she was bound to accept them as inevitable and with her usual grace under trying circumstances. It had been her idea that Mabilia would probably be only too glad to help with the management of the establishment, as soon as she became acquainted with its elaborate mechanism, so that she could run it as she pleased, and that the older woman would eventually be freed from many of her responsibilities and able to spend more time in prayer and good works. However, Mabilia had not the slightest idea of burdening herself with duties which, as she could readily see, consumed a great deal of her mother-in-law's time and strength. She was pretty and pleasure-loving and her main idea was to enjoy herself; and the Ponziani palace, though it had never regained all the splendors of Cecilia Mellini's days, was in its restored state more than adequate for almost any form of entertainment. Like Francesca, Mabilia had been strictly brought up, but the effect of such an upbringing was entirely different in the two cases; whereas Francesca had shrunk from any change in the pious routine of Giacobella, Mabilia regarded her marriage as a welcome means of escape from restriction. Like Francesca, she was only twelve years old at the time of her wedding; but she had made no vows of virginity; she was eager for initiation into the mysteries of marriage and ready for the full experience of love. Battista, who adored her, at first saw no reason why her slightest whim should not be law. After all, he probably was not above respectfully reminding his parents that Lorenzo had upheld Francesca when *her* mother-in-law had tried to persuade her to follow an established pattern. Why shouldn't he follow his father's example? To be sure, Cecilia had wanted to entertain and be entertained all the time, and Francesca had wanted social amenities reduced to a minimum. Now the situation was reversed; it was the mother-in-law who wanted seclusion and the daughter-in-law who wanted gaiety. But, as far as the young husband was concerned, wasn't the principle the same?

With her unfailing sense of justice, Francesca must have admitted it was; but surely it was harder for her to keep from reflecting that, whatever her own feelings, she had always felt that Cecilia was entitled to hers and that she had treated her mother-in-law with the greatest respect, consideration and affection. Mabilia, unfortunately, was doing nothing of the sort. She soon rode roughshod over Francesca's principles and even showed the extreme bad taste of criticizing and ridiculing her in public. For the wedding ceremonies, Francesca had, of course, consented to dress as befitted her rank and station and had devoted her time to presiding at the customary festivities. Now that these were over, she resumed her charitable work and her labors in the vineyard, once more clad in her shabby green dress.[25]

Such an occupation and such a costume were alike obnoxious to Mabilia. In Rome, elegant and costly feminine apparel had become even more elegant and costly than it was when Francesca was married. "The ladies wear long full robes of velvet, gold lame and scarlet or purple wool," we are told. "One pays as much as twenty-five florins or sixty golden ducats for a coat with sleeves. Moreover, the sleeves are so long that they cover half the hand, the skirt trails on the ground and on these garments are from three to five ounces of pearls, which are worth ten florins apiece. Then there are great golden ribbons floating freely, hoods trimmed with precious stones, and wide silver girdles ornamented with pearls. Many rings are worn on the fingers. Ladies also wear *cypriennes* [26] and dresses wide at the bottom and narrow on top, which outline their bosoms; on their heads they have crowns of pearls and other precious stones are plaited into their braids; on their necks strings of coral and amber and over their brows veils of light silk." [9]

If this is a sample of the way Mabilia liked to dress, as doubtless it is, no wonder her mother-in-law's voluntary shabbiness was irritating to her. But this does not excuse her discourtesy in the matter, and it was not excused at the Ponziani palace by anyone except Francesca herself. Battista, infatuated as he was with his bride, not only loved his mother dearly; he also recognized her great, if not her saintly qualities; and was distressed because Mabilia did not recognize them also; and Lorenzo, to whom Francesca still represented the acme of all perfection, as she had from the beginning, again became a most unhappy man. In promoting his son's marriage, he had visualized the contentment that would come to him as a grandfather, if he could dandle Battista's children on his knee and gather them around him; the sense of fulfillment in knowing that a great name would go on. Instead of this peaceful idyll, this promise of perpetuity, there was discord, defeat and disgrace.

Francesca, with more spiritual support at her command, was able to dismiss the bitter thoughts that tormented her husband, overcome her personal disappointment over Mabilia's lack of cooperation, and possess her soul in patience, confident that, sooner or later, something would happen to change the situation, though she could not foresee the form this change would take: namely, Mabilia's sudden collapse on a cold winter's day when the entire household was gathered around a fire in the great hall. She had been railing against her mother-in-law's habits, dress and standards with unusual vehemence, when she suddenly turned very pale, trembled uncontrollably and fell over in a dead faint. Francesca and Vannozza carried her, still unconscious, to her bed; and, when she regained her senses, it was to writhe with pain and to cry out between her moans, "Oh, my pride, my dreadful pride!" Francesca succeeded in soothing her and, gradually, the pain subsided, the moans gave way to healing tears and a rapprochement, with the happiest results, took place between the two.

Eventually, Lorenzo's long deferred hope of grandchildren was fulfilled, and the pattern of life—at one and the same time patrician and patriarchal—which was his ideal became a reality. So did a greater consciousness of the many sacrifices his wife had made for him and the disappointments she had so bravely and so cheerfully borne; he was obsessed with the fear that he might lose her, that she might not be with him to minister to the needs which increased in number with his growing physical weakness or to stand by him when he entered the valley of the shadow of death. "Taking her aside one day, he spoke to her with the greatest affection, and offered to release her from all the obligations imposed by the state of marriage, to allow her the fullest liberty of action and the most absolute control over her own person, her own time, and her own conduct, on only one condition,—that she would promise never to cease to inhabit his house, and to guide him in the way in which her example had hitherto led him. Francesca, profoundly touched by his kindness, did not hesitate to give this promise," [10] and thus the door opened a little wider.

8

LORENZO'S "LIBERATION" of his wife, together with Mabilia's growing sense of responsibility, left Francesca free to profit by two great events which took place in Rome on successive years. The first of these was the celebration, in 1423, of a Jubilee, which a decree of Urban VI had made it possible to observe, although only twenty-three years had passed since the last one.[27] The second was the visit to Rome of the great Franciscan of Siena, whom we know as St. Bernardine. He was one of the most forceful and popular preachers of his time, who went from one end of Italy to another, denouncing a great variety of prevalent vices, among them civil and political strife, usury, gambling and vanity in dress and behavior. Evidently, he did this in such an original and effective way that vast crowds were ready and eager to listen to him for hours on end; and Francesca was frequently represented in one of his enthralled audiences. His oft-quoted advice to mothers is one which she must have longed to put into practice, though I doubt if it were very popular among light-hearted young girls: "Do not let your daughters sing silly songs, but see to it that they learn to spin and to read; then, on feast days, you can make them read holy books and legends of virgins; you will not permit them to be idle all day and you will watch over all their outings." In this denunciation of vanity, we have still another vivid survey of current styles, in addition to the one already quoted. He pictures a lady of fashion as wearing *cheveux pastiches* (that is to say, wigs or false hair) surmounted with a golden crown; and, on top of the crown, a sort of mitre, which Bernardine unflatteringly calls "a swollen bladder," covered with silk and marvelous embroidery. Combs and valuable jewels complete the embellishment of the head, and precious stones come down as far as the forehead. Around the temples are circlets of gold and in the ears rich pendants. He does not, like another chronicler of the times, refer at length to the craze for blond hair and give directions for dyeing and bleaching it; but he does go on to speak of depilatories, dentures and cosmetics in far from alluring terms. All this strengthens the conviction that there is really nothing new under the sun, and it seems to me unfortunate that we are not better informed about the subjects of some of Bernardine's other sermons in Rome, which, personally, I feel might make more inspiring reading! [28]

After this zealot's return to Siena, where he declined a bishopric, Francesca continued to lead the consecrated life to which she was already pledged and, also, to lay firmer foundations for the establishment of the congregation which was to represent her greatest achievement. She had never abandoned or curtailed her attendance at the Church of Santa Maria Nuova, which belonged to the Congregation of Mount Olivet, a division of the Benedictine Order; and, as we have already seen, her closest friends had formed the habit of frequently going there with her. One evening, as several of them were leaving the church together, Francesca talked with them, as she had many times before, about the sanctity of St. Benedict and of the good works performed by the members of the Order to which he had given his name. Its Rule did not, as did the Rule of the Franciscans and the Dominicans, provide for a Third Order, but she felt that it might very possibly provide for an order of "Oblates," whose opportunities and obligations might be very similar, and to which most, if not all, of them could belong. Her suggestion was received with enthusiasm, and she and her friends relayed it at once to Francesca's old confessor, Dom Antonio, who looked upon it favorably and agreed to submit it to Dom Ippolito, now Vice-Prior, who happened to be in charge of the monastery at that time, during the absence of the Prior. He will be recalled as the same man whom Francesca had persuaded to remain faithful to his vows and contented in his work; and his sense of gratitude to her made him all the more ready to do anything he could for her. He approached the

General of the Order and secured the latter's approval for the establishment of a small religious organization to be known as the Oblates of Mary, which was to become a particular aggregation to the monastery of Santa Maria Nuova and to share in the suffrages and merits of the Order of St. Benedict.

Supremely happy at the result of their application, the friends prepared with prayer, fasting and penance for their consecration as a group to the Blessed Virgin. Authorities differ as to the names and the exact number of noble ladies who were, so to speak, charter members of this new organization. Of course, Francesca and Vannozza were its prime movers, and there is no question that Rita Celli and Agnes Selli were among them; so probably were Anastasia di Clarelli, Perna Colluzzi, Caterina Manetti, Francesca di Veroli, Giacobella di Brumemonti, Agostina di Viterbo and Lella Maioli. In any case, all those present dedicated themselves in a beautiful ceremony, on the Feast of the Assumption, led by Francesca, who solemnly declared:

> *In nomine Domini Nostri Jesu Christi. Ego soror Francisca filia domini Pauli Bussa, offero me Omnipotenti Deo, Gloriosae Virgini Mariae, Beato Patri Nostro Benedicto, huic venerabili monasterio sanctae Mariae Novae de Urbe Ordinis Montis Oliveti, coram omnibus sanctis quorum reliquiae in hoc loco habentur, in praesentia Reverendi Fratris Hippoliti de Roma, Prioris dicti monasterii: qui quidem nomine et auctoritate multum Reverendi Patris. Fratris Hieronimi de Perugia, Abbatis generalis praedicti Ordinis, me recepit pro oblata ejusdem monasterii, et* promitto perpetuam stabilitatem *de dicta mea oblatione, conversionem morum meorum et obedientiam. In quorum fidem has literas propria manu et nomini subscripsi, Anno Incarnationis Dominicae* 1425 *die* 15 *mensis Augusti, Romae, in praedicta ecclesia S. Mariae Novae. Amen.*
>
> *Ego soror Francisca Bussa de Pontianis.*[29]

This was the same formula as was used by the monks, except that the phrase *"me offero"* was substituted for *"profiteor"* and that, instead of taking solemn vows, they simply affiliated themselves with the Benedictine Order of Mt. Olivet. They were not assigned any special occupations by their director, Dom Antonio; he urged only that they should be scrupulously obedient to the commandments of God and of the Church, that they should hold the Mother of God in tender devotion and be diligent in receiving the Sacraments, in the exercise of Christian virtue and in various works of mercy. The link among these women consisted in their constant attendance at the Church of Santa Maria Nuova, where they received Communion on all the feasts of Our Lady, and the affectionate veneration in which all her fellow Oblates regarded Francesca, whom they regarded as their spiritual mother and whose advice they constantly sought, though she assumed no power and disclaimed all authority.

The new door was opening wider all the time.

9

THERE IS an old saying to the effect that the inhabitants of Isfahan claim it is "half the world" and, this being the case, it is not worth their while to make an effort to see the other half! In my experience and with such knowledge as I have of Romans, both past and present, their attitude is much the same; they are, and always have been, convinced that theirs is the greatest city in the world and, to all intents and purposes, the only really important city in the world. They leave it reluctantly, if at all; they know and love its every nook and corner and, from one generation to another, teach their chlidren to know and love it and to inhabit, in whole or in part, the same houses in which they themselves have grown up. They throng its churches and its piazzas, its restaurants and its theaters; they gather gaily around its sparkling fountains; they bask in its sunshine; they climb its hills in order to look down, with unabated admiration, on a scene they have beheld hundreds of times already; they are able to understand the viewpoint of the person who is not proud of his city, only if this is not Rome; then they are sorry for him.

High among the reasons why Francesca di Bussi di Ponziano has earned her designation as "The Roman" is because she thoroughly shared this feeling, so typical among her fellow citizens; to the best of our knowledge, she left Rome only once and that briefly and on a very special occasion. An observant historian has asked, rather caustically, why the Romans should have been so excited about the

Sienese Bernardine who, as our French friends would say, was simply *de passage* in their city (though he did come there several times and make long stays) when they had a saint who lived among them all the while: a holy woman whose life was consecrated to the service of Romans, who devoted herself to deeds of charity and did everything she could to overcome the corroding evils of the time. "I will name her—she is Santa Francesca Romana" this historian adds, rather superfluously; for, strangely enough, very few saints have been *natives* of Rome or have left their imprint on the city for that reason, though many have died there. The only others who come readily to mind are Agnes and Cecilia; and these belong to the early days of Christianity, when Rome was still a pagan city, and not to the period when Christ had triumphed over Caesar and Christ's Church over Caesar's Empire. Medieval Rome in its final stages; Renaissant Rome in its first stages; Christian Rome tragically divided by the Great Western Schism; Christian Rome triumphantly united again under Martin V—all these are gloriously embodied in one superb feminine figure—Santa Francesca Romana.

So it is in Rome that we always visualize her, and fittingly so. But, as we have said, she did leave Rome once, briefly and on a very special occasion. And, since that special occasion was a visit to Assisi, the city of the "seraphic saint," Francis, for the "Great Pardon" at the Church of Santa Maria degli Angeli, we should follow her footsteps as she makes this exceptional journey.[30]

The word "footsteps" is used advisedly and literally. Francesca insisted on walking all the way to Assisi and on the return journey to Rome; and she went like the humblest pilgrim, accompanied only by Vannozza and Rita. Lorenzo had, at first, objected to this mode of travel; and we learn that Paluzzo, concerning whom we have heard nothing for a long while, also considered it beneath the dignity of a Roman lady. Evidently he had survived to be released from his imprisonment, and the logical time for this liberation, from a political point of view, would have been during the same period that Battista returned from Naples and Lorenzo from the unidentified "distant province." Only one chronicler—at least only one that I have found [31]—tells us this. However, here he is at the Ponziani palace again, requiring persuasion to allow his wife to set out on foot with her sister-in-law and his cousin, but finally consenting and joining Lorenzo in telling them to do as they wish, to go in peace and to pray for those they have left behind.

So the three ladies departed, apparently following much the same route that travelers take nowadays, for we hear that the "Gothic towers of Cività Castellana looked down upon the humble pilgrims as they passed by in pious meditation"; that the "sound of their sweet voices . . . mingled with the murmurs of the stream that bathes the old walls of Nurni"; [10] that they were convinced no countryside could exceed in mystic charm and loveliness the environs of Spoleto. They found Foligno in a state of war, but passed through it without untoward incident and, on the whole, they seem to have enjoyed their journey. It was midsummer and the heat was very great; but Umbria's is a dry heat, much less debilitating than that of our own South and, undoubtedly, they were wise enough to do most of their walking early in the morning and late in the afternoon and to rest in the middle of the day. As Rome is about a hundred miles from Assisi, it seems equally probable that they took several days for their journey, stopping off at hospitable convents, which would have been honored to receive them, along the way. When they were nearing the end of their long road, they were joined by a courteous stranger, clad in the Franciscan habit, who hailed them cordially and then spoke to them, with increasing eloquence and gentleness, of many divine mysteries, which were clarified and beatified by his speech. As they went along, Francesca noticed that the light which surrounded him had a more radiant quality than that which fell on the rest of the road; and the conviction that they had been privileged to see a reincarnation of St. Francis himself was strengthened when the stranger raised his hands to bless them and then touched a wild pear tree which grew by the roadside before vanishing from their sight. The fruit which then fell from the tree was large and juicy; it quenched their thirst and allayed their hunger; they went on their way refreshed and uplifted.

We are not told where the pilgrims stayed while they were in Assisi, but very probably it was at the Convent of Santo Damiano, where Santa Chiara—"the spiritual sister" of St. Francis—lived with her nuns and where the low-roofed, severely plain refectory remains unchanged to this day. This convent, near the church of the same name, which was the scene of St. Francis' conversion, is located on a hillside, amid olive and cypress trees and overlooking a valley. It is graceful in its simplicity, and it is surmounted by a small terrace, where St. Francis is believed to have dictated his verses, entitled *Praises of the Creatures.* In such a haven as this, the weary travelers, like many before them and many since, would have found the peace that surpasses all understanding.

Their first objective, the morning after their arrival, was, of course, the Church of Santa Maria degli Angeli, which encloses the Porziuncola, that we call the "little portion"—the chapel which St. Francis found in a state of dilapidation and restored, and where he afterward consecrated St. Clare as a "bride of Christ." The magnificent basilica which we see today was not erected until the sixteenth century, but the earlier church served as an adequate shelter for the "little portion"; and its very location, on the plain where the saint and his companions had built their huts, enhanced the sanctity of its atmosphere.

Innumerable pilgrims came there, as our travelers had done, for the "Assisi Blessing," which carried with it a plenary indulgence, on the first and second of August—the latter date commemorating the restoration of the church—and also on the third and fourth of October—the latter St. Francis' feast day.

After receiving Communion, Francesca had a vision, in which she was encouraged to persevere with her labors and promised that these would be blessed. Later, she and her companions visited the erstwhile hospital, where St. Francis had died, now transformed into a chapel called El Transito; also its cloister, where the rosebush into which St. Francis threw himself, to escape temptation, still blooms brightly and, since his death, has borne no thorns.

Santa Maria degli Angeli is about six miles from Assisi itself; so Francesca, Vannozza and Rita would already have walked some distance to reach it; then they would have had the same distance to cover before visiting the churches dedicated to St. Francis and St. Clare, where these saints are, respectively, buried. The immortal frescoes of Cimabue and Giotto had long since adorned the walls of the upper and lower basilicas, glowing through their gloom; and the great flying buttresses had recently been added to the striking red and white Romanesque church. It is to be hoped that the pilgrims allowed themselves all the time they needed to see these wonderful sights, for even Rome itself had nothing that could surpass them in beauty and significance.

They took their homeward way still suffused with rapture and it is also to be hoped that this sustained them through the sorrows that lay ahead. While they were gone, Dom Antonio Savelli, who had been Francesca's lifelong friend, as well as her first and, for years, her only confessor, had suddenly died. The loss was a devastating one; she felt, and not without reason, that he was irreplaceable. When she finally selected a successor for him, her somewhat hesitant choice fell on Dom Giovanni Matteotti, who was not one of the Benedictine monks of Santa Maria Nuova, but the curate of Santa Maria in Trastevere, with which Francesca had no previous close ties, though its proximity to the Ponziani palace made it convenient for her to attend. This may well have been one of the reasons for her choice and, as far as posterity is concerned, it was a fortunate one. Dom Giovanni enjoined her, as a matter of obedience, to relate her visions to him in minutest detail and kept a daily record of all she told him. Though this meticulous reporting may at first have been due to the fact that he was only thirty-three years old and did not have much confidence, either in her or in himself, as far as stories told from memory were concerned, the resulting notes became a treasure-trove of information for subsequent biographers; and, as his respect for her and his trust in her increased, he wrote a more general account of her ecstasies and, also, a history of her life. After her death, all this material was gathered together in a full-length biography, which has formed the basis of all subsequent biographies —including this one—and is still carefully preserved in the Bollandist Collection at Venice.

While Francesca and Matteotti were slowly and somewhat painfully adapting themselves to each other, she was called upon to endure a new trial: Dom Ippolito, because of his now favored position, became an object of jealousy to some of his fellow monks at Santa Maria Nuova and, when a Father Inspector visited their monastery, they complained that their Vice-Prior had exceeded his powers and transgressed the statutes of the Congregation in admitting women to the name and privileges of the Order, especially as these women, several of them married, were living in the world. Fortunately, the visiting Father was perceptive and thorough, as well as pious; he investigated the question from every angle, and thereby not only convinced himself that the institution of the Oblates "tended to edification," but that it was pleasing to God and, therefore, he would not only approve it himself, but advocate its cause with the Father General.

This was reassuring, but it was not reassuring enough. Increasingly, Francesca felt that the group of friends she had assembled should have a recognized center of their own and a standing so definitive that no one could successfully challenge it; the only way to bring about the latter was to have formal recognition from the Pope. If Martin V (Ottone Colonna), who has often been called the Second Founder of the Papal Monarchy, had still been the head of the Church, he would, no doubt, have acted with his usual vigor and intelligence in this matter. But, after calling a council at Basle in 1431, he suddenly died before the prelates could be assembled; and the papacy had again fallen on troubled times. Soon after the election of Cardinal Gabriel Condolmieri, who took the name of Eugenius IV, an untoward accident occurred: the floor of the room where he was holding his first Consistory gave way, a bishop was killed and several other persons were badly injured; inevitably, the superstitious, already disturbed by an eclipse of the sun, regarded this as an evil omen. Moreover, the delayed council at Basle began in an atmosphere almost automatically inimicable to Eugenius, since its members were convinced that, as a unity, they were superior to the authority of a pope; and they were upheld in this defiant theory, not only by the Emperor Sigismund, but by almost every other ruling sovereign. Nor was it only in Basle that the authority of the new Pope was flouted; the rumor had spread that Martin V, simply as he lived, had died possessed of considerable private treasure, and the Colonna clan was determined to retrieve this. The further fact that Eugenius was trying to oust its members from the position of power they had enjoyed, while one of their own had been the Supreme Pontiff, roused them to ire, and they were glad of a pretext to make trouble for him. They made so much that Rome was soon the scene of internecine strife again, with the death toll mounting to hundreds as the Colonnas and the Orsini called out their cohorts. The Pope was obliged to flee, ignominiously disguised; but, thanks to a Tiber boatman, who gave him such meager shelter as a poor river craft could afford, he escaped with his life.

Eventually, there was a happy ending to his exile. For the city where he took refuge, and where he was warmly welcomed, was Florence, then at the zenith of its commercial prosperity and artistic glory, under the patronage of the Medici. With all this as a not wholly unsatisfactory substitute for the Vatican, Eugenius was able to function in absentia with considerable success; and, when he finally returned to Rome, he induced a host of painters, sculptors and architects, including Michelangelo, to come with him, and a new era of magnificence began in Rome.

This, however, was still far in the hereafter, as Francesca's troubled thoughts dwelt on the necessity of safeguarding both the present and the future of her little band and tried to surmount the anxieties of her private sorrows. Lorenzo was now so enfeebled that he seldom ventured out of the house and was, therefore, unlikely to be the victim of another street brawl. But there was always the possibility of a second attack on the palace itself, in which case neither he nor anyone else in it would be spared, not even the two grandchildren, Girolamo and Vannozza (the namesake of her aunt). Battista, too, as *marechal de camp* (brigadier general) and probably the successor to his father as *caporione* (ward captain), was in constant danger. For all her faith, Francesca could not completely still her fears; and her prophetic vision, which was growing stronger all the time and which had enabled her to recognize the fresh and imminent dangers to the papacy before they actually took place, now forewarned her of a terrible private grief: the mortal illness of her sister-in-law Vannozza.

Evidently the end was a peaceful one—at least there are no harrowing details of it and, since early chroniclers take the same delight in lurid deathbed scenes that they do in self-inflicted torture, we have reason to hope that, in this case, they were lacking. Francesca was with Vannozza constantly during the latter's final days, and the other members of their little group, and the priest who was not only her confessor, but her friend, came and went; she was surrounded with affection and solicitude, and the Last Rites were administered with gentleness as well as solemnity. Then, as she ceased to breathe, a soft white mist enveloped her and, through its gossamer, a shaft of light slanted toward heaven.

Strangely enough, there is no mention of Paluzzo as her chief mourner; we do not hear of him again after learning of his reluctant consent to the Assisi pilgrimage. It seems strange that, if he had died before his wife, we should not have been told of this; yet, in such a closely knit family unit as that of the Ponziani, it is even more unbelievable that he would have left the fold for any other reason. Be all this as it may, the funeral, whether with or without him, was one of grandeur. Vannozza was buried, not in the family chapel of the Ponziani—which provides us with another mystery for, from time immemorial, married women have been buried with their husbands' people—but in the family chapel of the Santa Croce, in the Church of Aracoeli. The great cortege, as it proceeded from Trastevere to the Capitoline Hill, was accompanied by an immense throng of both rich and poor. The coffin was not immediately lowered into the vault, and the people continued to press around it, eager not only for a last look at the lovely woman who lay in state, but at Francesca, who had fallen into a trancelike condition as soon as she had knelt beside the bier. From time to time, those who stood nearby heard her murmur, *"Quando? Quando?"* ("When? When?") as if she were asking for enlightenment as to the time of her own death, which she so greatly desired. But if there were a mystical answer to this, no one heard it and, presently, the officiating priest touched her compassionately and reminded her that those who still lived, but were suffering, had need of her. Instantly, she rose from her knees and, with no remaining traces of her trancelike state, left the church and resumed her ministrations.

However, ecstasies similar to these, like the prophetic visions, were of more and more frequent occurrence and—as in the case of the Great St. Teresa—it is hard to know how much of her course of action was due to the supernatural guidance which took these forms and how much to the sound common sense and the habit of calm and creative reflection which so characterized her. At all events, one day when Lorenzo was temporarily absent, she invited the group of Oblates, whom she held so dear, to join her for a simple supper at the palace, just as many other women have invited their friends under similar circumstances; and, when they had eaten and gathered around the fire, she reminded them that it was now seven years since they had consecrated themselves to the Virgin and bound themselves to live in charity and obedience and to observe the Rule prescribed for them. Then she said that she had long felt they should be as united in their outward mode of life as they were in spirit and intention; and now the Lord had revealed to her His will that she "should found a new spiritual edifice in this city, the ancient stronghold of religion and of faith." [10] She had besought Him to find some leader other than herself for this new undertaking; but He had remained unmoved and she was therefore prepared to do His bidding. Then she continued, " 'But without you, my sisters, what can I do? You are the foundations of the building, the first stones of the new spiritual house of His mother. You are the seed from which a plentiful harvest is to spring. Earthly cares, the temporal affairs of life, must no longer take up your time. He summons you to a retreat. . . . He bids us unite, and stand in the breach between Him and the daring sinners who each day defy Him.' " [10]

Francesca was already in a state of ecstasy as she spoke the last words. But, when she regained her normal senses, she realized she needed to say no more. Her companions were ready to adopt any mode of life which she would suggest and make any sacrifices that the Lord might require of them. The next step was to determine exactly what these should be.

10

First of all must come the selection of a house suitable for community living. In this selection, the Oblates, guided by the Blessed Virgin and under the protection of St. Paul, St. Benedict and St. Mary Magdalene, were aided by the three "procurators," that is to say, assistants and advisers, whom Francesca had been instructed to choose, also by supernatural means: her director, Dom Ippolito; her confessor, Dom Giovanni Matteotti; and Fra Bartolommeo Biondii, a Franciscan monk who was a brother-in-law of Agnes Selli and a theologian and orator of exceptional talent. Naturally, financial considerations entered into the picture; Francesca had spent most of her patrimony on charity, and she was unwilling to use Ponziani money for an undertaking uniquely hers and not her husband's or her son's, especially as their circumstances, though materially better than at one point, were still considerably reduced from their once high level. Besides, there were the future needs of the two beloved grandchildren to consider. (Eventually, she did accept, for the congregation, the deeds to the vineyard near St. Paul's-Without-the-Walls, so long the scene of her labors, and another vineyard known as Porta Portere.) Francesca's fellow Oblates, though all members of noble families, were no more independently wealthy than she was herself; it was natural for the prudent procurators to hesitate about pledging large sums which they might not be able to produce. But, again, Divine Providence showed the way: once the proper house was chosen, the means to support it would be forthcoming.

However, another natural objection remained to be overcome: the parents of the Oblates, in several cases, viewed with alarm the prospect of such definite separation from their daughters as community living would entail. (There was no question of separating husbands and wives, for Francesca was to make frequent visits to the community house and direct it, while continuing to reside at the Ponziani palace, and other women, who had been married and whose husbands were still living, would do the same; only those who were already widows would enter the community house.) It was one thing for them to go to church together, to visit hospitals together, to have an occasional meal together, while continuing to live with their families; it was quite another for them to leave home altogether. Patiently, Francesca pointed out that the widows had already achieved a certain amount of independence and had reached an age when they were entitled to more if they wanted it. As to the young girls, they would have left home if they had chosen, or if their parents had chosen, that they should be cloistered nuns; though no grilles were planned for the proposed community house and seclusion would be voluntary, there would be sufficient supervision to make sure that, once sought, it should be continued. With her usual tact and tolerance, she made all this clear and, gradually, the objecting relatives saw the wisdom of her ways.

The choice of the procurators and the Oblates finally fell on a building in the Campitelli district, the site of an old tower known as the Tor di Specchi (Tower of Mirrors). The usual reason given for this is because its caissons had been compared to mirrors by the people who lived in the vicinity, but this seems rather far-fetched; and in one biography—though only one—I have found a much more logical and appealing explanation:

The escutcheon of the nobles who owned the first tower to stand on this site was adorned with three silver mirrors in a golden frame; and this device formed the basis of a fantastic legend about a very high tower, made all of gold, from which a shining light served as a beacon for navigators. Within the tower a mirror was so arranged that it revealed everything happening in the outside world. Its purpose was to alert defenders against any treacherous attack on Rome. Persuading the Roman people that an immense treasure was hidden beneath the tower, the city's enemies induced them to seek permission from the tower's owners to dig under it. They dug so deeply that the tower fell and with its fall the magic mirror was shattered. By way of revenge, the Roman people compelled the instigators of the undertaking to drink molten gold; and the tower was rebuilt with less resplendency. But its title, the Tor di Specchi, remained unchanged. Whether or not the designation was apt, it was certainly arresting and, fortunately, it was officially recognized and has been preserved. When the papal bull, so ardently desired and so eagerly sought, was finally issued, the congregation was described as that of "the Oblates of Tor di Specchi" and they and their Foundation are thus known to this day.

Once provided with a place to live, a place not only suitable but beautiful, the next need of the Oblates was a set of Rules, more formal and more extended than the ones that had so far bound them together. A series of visions revealed to Francesca what they should be and, again, we may be permitted to believe that her sound common sense was closely allied to her mystic powers. At all events, the division of the Oblates' days into periods of work, rest and prayer was clearly set forth; so was the manner in which they should dress, the degree of their separation from the world and many other details. "Admit without distinction virgins and widows of every age; establish them firmly in obedience and let them open their consciences with simplicity. All must be at least old enough to discern the significance of their determination. Before you admit them [to your Congregation] you should examine them carefully, to make sure they are naturally joyous and will be content in such a design for living and whether or not they are sufficiently detached from the world. . . . You must be careful to have strong proofs of their willingness and ability to obey, since obedience is the armor which the tempter fears most of all. You should not allow the postulants to mingle with persons already established in the house until their dispositions and their habits are well known to you. You should observe, during the period of probation, whether or not they follow orders quietly and courageously and refuse to admit them if you discover otherwise. Reject those with presumptuous or devious traits; that sort is difficult to correct. Insist strictly that they must be faithful to the Rule.

"Since all their garments are symbolic, make sure that the postulants understand the nature of this significance. Their undergarment, which is white, signifies purity and faith, spirituality and single-heartedness, as well as innocence. It also signifies an intention, upright and founded on divine will. The second garment should be black, of rough material, in order to remind them [the Oblates] that they are dead to the world, that they will soon actually die, and that they must appear before the throne of God, where they will be judged without partiality.

"The veil which envelops their body should be of linen and they should remember, in putting it on, that linen is steeped, that it is beaten, that it is shaken over and over again; that next it is spun, that it is warped and woven, that it must undergo all these preparative measures before it can be bleached. Thus they should understand the meaning of the obedience by which they must permit themselves to be governed and disciplined. When they are white in the eyes of God, the Savior will welcome them and will share with them His great treasures. He will change lead into gold, he will share with them the possessions of His Kingdom." [9]

All these things having been decided, their new home in readiness and the papal bull in their possession, ten Oblates moved into the Tor di Specchi on the Feast of the Annunciation and chose Agnes Selli as their first Superior. I have found the list of necessary qualifications for these Oblates fascinating reading.

"Anyone wishing to follow the Oblates' way of life must incorporate in her person the following qualities:

"She must be free in body and soul.

"She must be firm in faith and sacred humility.

"She must deprive herself of every possession, both at home and abroad, in order to give herself to Christ without reserve.

"She must come to her consecration with clean hands and a pure heart.

"She must acquit herself with great gentleness in regard to everything which the Rule of Obedience requires.

"She must have great confidence in the goodness of the Creator.

"She must resolve to guard her chastity inviolate.

"She must recognize that she will have trials, but that they will be assuaged by the consolation of divine love.

"She must have the courage of a brave man and, withal, a peaceful disposition or, if her temperament is different, she must know how to control it. If she has these qualities, she will find tranquillity in obedience." [9]

I have found equally fascinating the details of their chosen way of life and of obedience.

"The Lady Oblates have a complete separation from the world, though they are not cloistered. If they go out, whether it be for the oblation that is made at the Church of Santa Francesca Romana, or to help those in need, or to be with their relatives in the latters' last moments, it is always in a closed carriage. The strict rule of poverty is scrupulously observed by them and gifts are made and received only by permission of the Lady President, who has to assist her a Lady Treasurer and two or three Lady Procurators.

"The dress is very modest and remains the same as that worn by the Oblates in the time of Santa Francesca Romana. Work is not done in a community, but the Oblate, after the hours devoted to the Office, and asking the benediction of the Lady President, returns to her cell and occupies herself with reading or work. The entire Office, from Matins to Compline, is said in the choir and, while it does not have the solemnity of an Office said by monks, the psalmody reveals these Oblates to be true daughters of St. Benedict, making the work of their God the basis of their lives.

"Abstinence and fasts are observed at the Tor di Specchi according to the Rule of St. Paul and the practice of incessant and rigorous obedience makes up for the lack of vows." [27]

A seventeenth-century author, Hélyot, called Père Hippolyte, gives us curious complementary glimpses of the Oblates of his time and, without doubt, of preceding periods, since his work is consecrated to the "History of Religious Orders." According to Hélyot's recital, the Oblates did not constitute a regular religious body, but an association of pious women, voluntarily submitting to a rule which, as a matter of fact, was necessary for the government of the community. "They have," he tells us, "a year of probation when they make their oblation in the Church of Santa Maria Nuova beside the tomb of their foundress, one of the most beautiful monuments in Rome. They may leave the Congregation to marry; they number about fifty girls and widows and thirty lay sisters.[32] Besides, each has a maid, whom she dresses like a lay sister, and a lackey to run errands, for only very great ladies are received into the society. These take their outings in coaches, and are allowed to spend a certain amount of time at their country seats. Although they follow the Rule of St. Benedict, they do not bind themselves to it in its entirety. They eat meat three times a week, though only at dinner. In addition to the fasts ordained by the Church, they also fast during Advent. Their house is as magnificent as their chapel, one of the most beautiful in the city; their sacristy is one of the richest in Rome, both in the amount of its silverware and in the beauty of its ornaments. They have, among other treasures, a monstrance which has immense value, because of the quantity of diamonds and pearls with which it is adorned. These diamonds are the presents of several princesses who, in retiring to this holy house, have divested themselves of such jewels, in order to clothe with greater glory Him whom they have taken as their celestial Spouse. They are very charitable and are especially concerned with alleviating the lot of unfortunate prisoners to whom they send food on the occasion of solemn feasts, as well as certain days of every week."

We are indebted to Berthem-Bontoux for quoting this picturesque description, but she herself wisely qualifies it by the reminder that many of the great customs therein mentioned have fallen into desuetude. The Oblates no longer have maids and lackeys attached to their service, nor do they ride in coaches or closed carriages any more. They go on foot to perform their deeds of charity in the same way as the humblest people. Berthem-Bontoux also reminds us that, despite its monastic way of life, this community is not, properly speaking, an official congregation. For this reason, it has been able to justify its economy and escape the Italian expropriation of 1870—a point of resemblance—of which there are several—between them and their predecessors, the French Sisters of Charity.

The Counsel of Perfection has been the ideal of many earnest human beings who have failed to achieve it. Indeed, perhaps its chief merit lies in the fact that, *if it is an ideal,* we come nearer to achieving it than if we had no such goal; and certainly Francesca and her Oblates came closer than most of us. From the beginning, she remained the guiding spirit; she visited the Tor di Specchi as frequently as her obligations at the Ponziani palace would permit, and that, apparently, was often. She came there riding or leading the donkey which had so long been her burden bearer when she went to the vineyard; and, while at the community house, she insisted on doing whatever was most necessary, whether this was in the drawing room or in the kitchen; and, on arriving and leaving, she kissed the hand of her old friend and kinswoman, Agnes Selli, now her Superior, as a token of obedience. And after she had followed this schedule and these customs industriously and contentedly for several years, at the same time ministering to the needs of her ailing husband, Lorenzo died and thus another door closed and still another opened.

11

DURING THE last months of her husband's life, Francesca had redoubled her efforts to secure his physical and spiritual well-being; she had been untiring in her care of him, both day and night; she had made all the necessary arrangements so that he might confess and communicate often and, also, receive such informal visits from priestly friends as might give him comfort. There were, apparently, a few bouts with the "demon," who never left the household undisturbed for long, but he was routed, and Lorenzo's end, like Vannozza's, was peaceful. He was buried with appropriate ceremonies in the family vault at St. Cecilia's, where his parents and two of his children were already interred; and Francesca, wearing suitable widow's weeds, provided first that Masses should be said for the repose of his soul and next that his estate should be properly settled.

The former office could safely be left in the hands of the clergy once the first arrangements were made; the latter required greater attention from her as executrix. The liquid assets presented no problem; Lorenzo had left a fortune of ten thousand ducats, immediately available for any necessary purpose; it took more time to make sure the real estate should be handled in a way that would assure its continued productiveness and hence its value as a source of income. Battista's position as *maréchal de camp* fitted him for military authority rather than agricultural activity; and he had been more than willing to leave the nominal administration of the vineyards and stock farms to his father and their actual administration, as well as that of the palace, to his mother. Now his father was dead and his mother determined to retire. But first, with her usual patience and efficiency, she did her best to fit her son for his role as head of the family; then, quietly but firmly, she told him and his wife that she was leaving the Ponziani palace to take up her permanent residence at the Tor di Specchi.

Of course, there were angry protests, tearful reproaches; but they left her unmoved. She would come to see her children and grandchildren from time to time, she told them—at *any* time if they really needed her; and they could come to see her, as often as they wished, as long as they did not infringe on the Rules of the Oblates. Next, without further futile argument, she took leave of them. Appropriately, the day she chose for her installation at the Tor di Specchi was the Feast of St. Benedict; and she entered it "not as the foundress but as a humble suppliant for admission."[10] Once inside the door, she removed her shoes, her widow's veil, her outer garments and the belt which confined them and placed a cord around her neck before kneeling to kiss the ground; then, having called the Oblates together in their main hall, she made her general confession in their presence and asked permission to dwell among them. Her spiritual daughters hastened to embrace her and, clothing her with their habit, led her to the chapel. While she knelt there in prayer, Agnes assembled the sisters in the chapter room and told them that, of course, it would be absurd for her to remain in her present office as Superior now that Francesca was among them to stay. She would instantly resign her authority. As might have been expected, Francesca objected but was overruled, first by the Oblates themselves and then by Dom Giovanni, who begged and then commanded her to take charge. Accordingly, on March 25, 1436, she was duly elected Superior of the Tor di Specchi.

That same night she was vouchsafed one of her most extraordinary visions: the archangel who had so long been her guide and companion took his leave of her, but not until he had presented to her his successor, whose rank in the angelic hierarchy was even higher than his own. In appearance, there was little difference between them; the newcomer also wore a dalmatic, but of more precious tissue than that worn by the previous protector; the light which surrounded him was even more dazzling; and his power was so great that he did not need to shake his locks in order that they might emit sparks and thus put demons to flight—his very glance was sufficient to do this! In his hand he held "three golden boughs, such as grow at the top of palm trees and from which hang the fruit; from these he continually drew golden threads which he wound about his neck or made into balls, to provide for a mysterious tissue that would be used later on." [9] St. Benedict himself explained the symbolism of all this to the saint: "The boughs signified love and charity; the palms vigor and force; while the angel's work represented the discretion and regularity necessary in his new office." [33]

The next few years were notable for a constant increase of Francesca's mystic powers; they were also distinguished for great executive ability and wise administration. Without doubt, this was the happiest period of her life. She had always been a nun at heart and a virgin in spirit; when she entered the bare little room in the Tor di Specchi, which was henceforth to be hers, she felt certain that she had come home at last.

She did not, however, forget her promise that, whenever she was needed by a member of her family, she would go instantly to the Ponziani palace. In March of 1440, Battista succumbed to a fever and sent her a message begging her to come to him. Although she was not feeling well, she instantly responded to his summons, taking with her the Oblate Augustina; and, when she reached his bedside, she found him so much better that he was already preparing to rise. However, she yielded to his entreaties that, since she was there, she would stay all day. By evening, it was evident she was really ill and he implored her to spend the night. This she refused to do, and she also refused to return to the Tor di Specchi in a litter. She set out on foot, stopping at the nearby Church of Santa Maria in Trastevere to ask for her spiritual father's blessing and, as he talked with her, he was struck by her extraordinary pallor and obvious exhaustion. Abruptly, he commanded her, as a matter of obedience, to return at once to the palace.

Very reluctantly, she did so. She had an instinctive feeling that the hour of her death was at hand, and she wanted, as most of us do, to die at home; and home to her was the Tor di Specchi, rather than the Ponziani palace. But it did not occur to her to disobey her confessor. The next morning she was so much worse that she asked him to inform her spiritual daughters of her illness and invite four of them—Agnes, Rita, Caterina and Anastasia—to visit her briefly. She would not, however, permit them to remain at her side, as they yearned to do. She dismissed them gently, keeping only Augustina with her to watch during the night; and it was in the dark watches of this that Our Lord, surrounded by angels and saints, appeared to her in a vision and announced to Francesca that, in seven days, she would die and receive the crown that was prepared for her in heaven. The next morning, when Dom Giovanni saw her, she appeared to be rallying; but when she told him about her vision and asked him to tell the Oblates, he did not disbelieve or deny her; and to all those who expressed the hope that she would recover she answered quietly, "God be praised, my pilgrimage will end from Wednesday to Thursday next." Every day she repeated, as if in perfect health, the rosary and all her usual prayers; she confessed, communicated and received Extreme Unction. The Oblates took turns in watching beside her and Mabilia was constantly with her. The "demons" no longer tormented her, for the archangel stood beside her and the light which surrounded him grew brighter and brighter until Francesca lay enwrapped in its radiance.

Only one untoward incident seems to have marked the serenity of the death chamber. Battista's attendance upon his mother had not been as faithful as that of the others and when, at last, he entered the room, she raised herself in bed and, looking at him anxiously, inquired if it could possibly be true that he was quarreling with poor shepherds and robbing "God of His glory by unlawful dealings with hell?" [10] The action and the question were both so astonishing that Francesca's attendants feared that she might have become suddenly delirious; but, after a moment of stunned silence, Battista confessed "that he had been guilty of striking, in his anger, some peasants who had injured his fields, and had gone to consult in secret one of the persons who dealt in occult sciences, as to the possibility of his mother's recovery. No one but himself knew of his twofold sin; and the rebuke of the dying Saint came upon him as a direct reproof from God, and an awful warning for the rest of his life." [10]

It is to be hoped that he heeded it, for it was the last his mother gave him. As the day wore on, "a sublime expression animated her face; a more ethereal beauty clothed her earthly form." [10] Her confessor, seeing that her lips were moving, but failing to hear her words, asked her what she was saying. "I am finishing my vespers," she said. And did not speak again.

The cause for the canonization of Francesca di Bussi di Ponziano was introduced almost immediately and had the great advantage of witnesses who had known her in the flesh; they and many others who had been recent beneficiaries of her miracles testified to the great holiness of her life and her supernatural powers. "The materials were ample, and the evidence complete; but a variety of circumstances interfered with the conclusion of the process; and though several Popes, namely Eugenius IV., Nicholas V., Pius II., Innocent VIII., and Julius II., promoted the question, it was not much advanced till the accession of Clement VIII., who had a great devotion to the Saint, and brought the matter nearly to a close; but his death occurring in the meantime, and his successor, Leo XI., only outliving him twenty-seven days, it was Paul V. (Borghese) who decreed the canonisation of Francesca, to the joy of the Oblates of Tor di Specchi, of the monks of Santa Maria Nuova, [which now bears her name] and of the whole people of Rome. Her festival was appointed to be kept on the 9th of March." [10]

We have already learned where and how it is kept, with mingled solemnity and rejoicing in the three places most closely associated with her—her church, her palace and her foundation; and to a lesser degree, but still a very great degree, in every section of the city of which she was so essentially a part. She has earned this tribute for, to the very end, she remained the faithful disciple of the ardent young martyr who was her ideal and, throughout her life, trod the "white path to Paradise" which Agnes had revealed through her death. Francesca's way of love not only complemented that of Agnes; it became closely interwoven with this. The more we learn about one saint, the more we learn about the other; thus the better we understand and the more we revere both.

We have still to learn about a different way of love as embodied in Catherine of Siena.

SAINT CATHERINE OF SIENA

1347-1380

1

IN TUSCANY, the fourteenth century was a period of dawning glory.

In England, the great Elizabethan Era was not so much as foreshadowed. Richard II, a weak and ineffective ruler, was deposed and imprisoned by his cousin, Henry Bolingbroke—a ruthless opportunist—and done to death, doubtless by Henry's orders, just as the century itself was dying. Chaos and crime were rampant throughout the land; no really great political or spiritual leader dominated the scene, no sculptors or painters arose to embellish it, and only one major literary figure, Geoffrey Chaucer, loomed above the illiteracy which surrounded him; for though Oxford and Cambridge were already long since founded, the rays from their lamps of learning were still faint and flickering.

In Spain, five warring kingdoms wrought havoc and laid waste, both within their own borders and in their conflicts with each other. It was not until the marriage of Ferdinand of Aragon and Isabel of Castile—thereafter known as the Catholic Kings—in 1479 that a semblance of political unity was achieved; more than twenty years later still that Granada was wrested from the Moors and the great days of exploration and conquest begun; and over fifty years were yet to pass before the birth of Miguel Cervantes, who was to set standards, unsurpassed to this day, in romantic and allegorical literature.

In France, the accession of the Valois had become the pretext for a dynastic quarrel between the King of France and the King of England. This quarrel, the Hundred Years' War, effectively obscured an economic crisis in which Flanders, so necessary to the wool trade of the Cotswolds, was the stake. The French were completely destroyed in battle, first at Crécy and then at Poitiers. In the latter conflict, John II—the Good, so-called—was made a prisoner by the Black Prince. The country, still further ravaged by the plague, seemed on the brink of annihilation. But the Dauphin Charles, having rid himself of Stephen Marcel, Provost of the Merchants of Paris, took the kingdom in hand and, with the help of Bertrand Du Guesclins, drove out the English. His reign was, unfortunately, of brief duration and a child of twelve became king under the regency of his uncles, dominated by Philip the Strong, to whom John, as a final aberration, had given the Duchy of Normandy and, thereby, dismembered France. The pure Gothic style of the cathedrals, begun in the thirteenth century, became increasingly flamboyant. Froissart wrote his endless chronicles of the war and manuscripts were magnificently illustrated by the monastic illuminators; but neither poets nor painters, who worked except in miniature, enlivened the scene. The agonies and ecstasies of Abélard and Héloïse had already been entombed for more than two centuries; the gorgeous daredeviltry of Villon was not to find expression for nearly another hundred years.

There was, of course, no Italian nation at that time, or for centuries still to come, in the sense that England was already a nation, Spain was groping toward national unity and France, despite its many calamities, was finding a way to liberate the commons and organize urban life. Naples was a kingdom, nominally independent, but actually insufficient to sustain itself and therefore the pawn of scheming popes and emperors, who placed first a French figurehead, then a Spanish figurehead, then a Hungarian on its unsteady throne, before again beginning the dismal merry-go-round. The rest of the peninsula formed part of the Holy Roman Empire, but the current emperors made their headquarters in Central Europe, whence they came; and Rome, deserted by the popes for Avignon in 1305, was in such a state of anarchy that it is hard to define its so-called government. However, going further north, we find the picture very different: allegiance to the emperor was largely a matter of lip service; what really counted was the republican form of government, as this was locally interpreted, and its strength was phenomenal. The two great maritime republics, Genoa and Venice, deadly enemies because they were bitter rivals, were already mighty sea powers; Pisa had also become an entity with which to reckon, and nearby Lucca, even with few resources, commanded and earned respect for its flourishing independence. As for Florence, this had become "the greatest and most triumphant republic of the Middle Ages" and had adopted "the constitution under which the most glorious culture and art of the modern world was to flourish." [1]

As far as military status was concerned, however, Florence had been obliged to acknowledge the supremacy of Siena ever since the Battle of Monteaperto in 1260, which had resulted in an overwhelming victory for the Sienese. If their city had not achieved quite such a supreme position politically and culturally as Florence, it had certainly approached *this*; it owed its democratic form of government to elected officers, who comprised what was known as the *Governo dei Nove* (Government of Nine); it possessed a well-established university, where the school of medicine was considered especially outstanding; it had amassed enormous wealth through its commercial dealings with France, England, Flanders and the East; it had completed construction on one of the most superb cathedrals in all Europe; and it had instituted the loftiest standards in art. "Siena had always been as eager for knowledge as she had been a lover of beauty and heroic virtues, even during her centuries of greatest splendour. This is exemplified in the 'Statute of the Sienese Artists' of the thirteenth century, which concludes with this declaration: *Neuna cosa, quanto sia minima può aver cominciamento o fine, senza queste tre cosa: senza potere et senza sapere, et senza con amore volere. . . .* (Nothing, be it ever so small, can have beginning or ending, unless possessing these three things: ability, knowledge, and earnest desire.) In no other Italian city during the thirteenth, fourteenth and fifteenth centuries was Art so closely bound to life as it was in Siena. Sienese artists were verily the most faithful interpreters of the sentiments and ideas of their great mystics. In this little Tuscan city Art never bent itself in order to magnify or satisfy the private ambitions of the cardinals or powerful nobles, but remained constantly at the service of a religious and civil ideal which was strongly felt by all the people." [2] And whereas Florence could—and did—claim Giotto for its own in the field of art at this period, just as it had previously claimed the Pisanos in the field of sculpture and Petrarch and Boccaccio as worthy successors to Dante in the field of literature, Siena could claim not only Guido di Siena, Duccio di Buoninsegna, Simoni di Martino and Jacopo della Querica as noteworthy, if not pre-eminent in these fields. It could also claim a citizen so outstanding, both politically and spiritually, that she was recognized and acknowledged in her own time as a power in Lucca, Pisa, Rome and Florence itself, as well as in her own city: namely, Catherine Benincasa, who has come down to us in history as St. Catherine of Siena.

Hers was a city of steep, winding streets, very narrow but well paved with brick, and lined with tall tower houses, whose plain stone facades were only sparingly relieved with ornamentation, but which, for the most part, were nevertheless stately rather than grim of aspect. Very often, their severity was relieved by the presence of a graceful, arched niche, which enshrined a holy image, and that, in turn, was kept banked with flowers and illumined, both day and night, with a flickering light which was never extinguished. Less prevalent, but still by no means infrequent or inconspicuous, were stone statues, mounted on high pedestals and representing a variety of figures. Outstanding among these was the familiar she-wolf, suckling Romulus and Remus, for Siena claimed the same right to this as Rome.

According to one cherished Sienese legend, only Romulus was responsible for the foundation of Rome; Siena owed its very existence to Remus. According to another version of the story, it was the sons of Remus, Ascius and Senius, who fled from Rome, one on a black horse and one on a white horse, to escape their uncle's wrath, and reached a haven which they called Castelsieno. There they built separate campfires. The smoke which rose from one was white, from the other black. Either for that reason or in compliment to their mounts, the brothers bisected the standards they raised, making one half black and the other half white, and thus created the flag which Castelsieno or Siena, as it soon came to be known, used from that day forward.[3] But even those citizens who clung to this version of the story and pointed to the flag to authenticate it, also insisted that they must have statues of the she-wolf with her nurslings to which they could point with justifiable pride, and their will became amply manifest in Siena.

The palaces of the patricians often faced piazzas, but otherwise were distinguishable rather by their size than by any other outward attribute which set them apart from the humbler dwellings of the populace; it was inside that their luxury became apparent: high, vaulted ceilings; stately stone staircases; frescoed walls; and, for furnishings, great beds, canopies above them and platforms beneath them; high-backed settees and sturdy trestle tables; painted marriage chests and other caskets and coffers; magnificent mirrors and hangings of linen, wool and silk, beautifully embroidered.

The exteriors of most churches were plain too; it was their glowing frescoes and their glittering altars which gave them their radiance. Only the Duomo, its black and white marble gleaming in the sunlight, its great central tower soaring above its dome toward the brilliant sky, was magnificent in all its aspects, both inside and out, as befitted a cathedral dedicated to the Virgin of the Assumption. And, just as this was the supreme shrine of the city, its bell, the Sovrana, was the voice of the city. When it rang, the bells of other churches—San Domenico, San Agostino, Santa Maria dei Servi—pealed, too, and Siena became a city of bells.

Whereas the Duomo was alone among churches in its magnificence, the great town hall, the Palazzo Pubblico, was magnificent, too. It dominated the enormous shell-shaped Piazza del Campo—generally called just the Campo—which sloped gently upward on one side of the palazzo and gently downward on the other. The palazzo, too, had a soaring bell tower and its battlement was crenellated; and the brick of which it was made looked warm even on the coldest and dreariest day, since its color, for the most part a tawny rose, defied the powers of gloom. In its great halls the Commune met to make the laws by which the city was governed—some wise and weighty, some seemingly trivial. On workdays, the huge open area in front of it became the market place, where not only foodstuffs of every description were sold in open stalls by hawkers, but rare silks and velvets and jewels were displayed in tents and shops by more pretentious merchants and great craftsmen. Here, too, the barbers and apothecaries, the cobblers and tailors plied their trades; there was no lack of buyers for all the wares or of patrons for all the services offered.

On holidays and holy days, the Campo became the accepted center for games, parades and every form of *festa.* Among these was the

Elmora, characterized as "a most cruel and dangerous pastime," but much favored by the Sienese. In 1291, the people of the ward of Cammolia with those of St. Martino had battled the people of the Cittá with stones as well as lances, and though this was in accordance with the rules of Elmora, so many fatalities resulted that the Commune prohibited combatants from using anything except their fists in the future. But, in its modified form, the game continued.[4]

The steep and narrow streets branched upward from the lower levels of the city, which were characterized by beautiful fountains. These were not the tall soaring fountains of Rome, which sent their sparkling spray high into the air. They were covered with flat roofs, which in some cases were surmounted with small houses, in which the guardian of the fountain lived and, in others, by the flowering terraces adjoining such a house. Beneath the roof rose a high, vaulted ceiling. On at least two, and sometimes on three, sides, the fountains were further protected by solid masonry, embellished by bas-reliefs and graven inscriptions; and on the remaining side, or sides, they were sheltered by graceful open archways. Thus shielded, the water flowed freely but gently into deep quiet pools or basins from openings that sometimes took simple and sometimes fantastic forms —they might be merely a round hole in the masonry, or they might be shaped like the mouth of a lion or a wolf or even of some legendary creature.

In the fourteenth century there were eleven of these fountains[5] and they served several useful purposes: they assured the entire city of an abundant water supply and from them pipes extended to the cisterns of the better private houses. They also served as giant watering troughs for livestock of all kinds, and stone benches were provided in front of them where the owners of horses, donkeys and cattle could sit and pass the time of day with each other, while their animals drank under their watchful gaze; in this way, the fountains developed into important communal centers. In other sections, the humbler housewives did their laundry work; and because these sheltered pools added such a distinctive note to the urban character, they became celebrated far and wide as "the covered fountains of Siena" and gave their names to the districts where they were located.[6]

In one of these, the Fontebranda, was a thoroughfare variously known as the Vicolo del Tiratoio (the Street of the Dyers) or as the

Via Benincasa—Giacomo Benincasa being the name of one such artisan who had achieved enough material success to be outstanding among his fellow craftsmen. Like most of these, he conducted his business in the same house where he and his family lived. His workshop, large enough to accommodate barrels, vats and mortars, was on the ground floor. Three of his sons—Bartolommeo, Orlando and Stefano—were his junior partners; and the business was sufficiently flourishing for them to employ two journeymen and two apprentices. Above the busy workshop were the small, scantily furnished bedrooms and the large cheerful kitchen, which served as the family living room. There was nothing scanty about the furnishings of this, nor the fare for which they were used. A flour chest, a meat safe and a sugar barrel were all well filled; so were great copper water jars and great earthen oil jars. In the huge fireplace at one end of the room, two simmering iron pots hung on the chain above the coals and meat was always turning on the spit: sometimes game, which was abundant around Siena; sometimes poultry, sometimes a whole pig or a whole lamb, for such provender was also abundant on the family farm. The walls of the room were hung with pots and pans in which the rest of the food was cooked. Most, but not all, of these utensils were made of copper; for certain purposes, terra cotta was considered preferable. Beans, for instance, never tasted as good as when they were baked in terra cotta. Plenty of beans, as well as plenty of other vegetables, were always available, for the sloping ground on which the house stood provided ample space for a kitchen garden, and the savory smells indoors mingled with the spicy scent of herbs and the fragrance of flowers drifting in through the open doors and windows.

Taken as a whole, the Benincasas' was a compact and complete establishment, well suited to the requirements of a family in moderate, but unstraitened, circumstances, even though this increased constantly in size. The prosperous and kindly dyer was already the father of twenty-two children when, on March 25, 1347—Annunciation Day—his shrewish, domineering wife, Lapa, gave birth to twin girls, who were christened Catherine and Giovanna. Giovanna lived only a few days. Catherine survived, to become not only one of the most powerful and extraordinary figures of the age, but of any age before or since. "Siena may well be called the 'City of St. Catherine' for every stone seems to have a heart which beats for the maiden who was able to take such a hold of her soul and lift it up to the highest heaven of love. She is the living poetry of the mystical mediaeval city. Everything there breathes of her, the legends and tales of the people, the art, the walks, the very sky, all seem fragrant with the memory of the sweet Saint. The greatest monuments of the city show forth the sovereign qualities of her indomitable spirit . . ." [2]

2

NOTHING POINTED to such a remarkable destiny. On the contrary, the baby was so small and frail that her chances of survival seemed almost as forlorn as those of her twin. But Lapa, who had been obliged to make the difficult decision as to which of the children she would nurse—for she did not have enough milk for two—proved to be a better provider than the foster mother to whom she had entrusted Giovanna. She "fed the child with great care and diligence"; and when the time came for Catherine to be weaned and she began to eat bread and to walk "everyone found her so pleasing and so sensible in the things she said that her mother had difficulty in keeping her at home, because all the friends and neighbors used to carry her off to their own homes, so that they could enjoy her wise little sayings and the comfort of her delightful childish gaiety." [7]

From this attractive picture, which we owe to Catherine's first biographer, Raymond of Capua, it would seem that her ability to charm began with her infancy, and there is nothing to indicate that it lessened to the very day of her death. True, there were a few years —a very few—when she lived in seclusion, managing somehow to do this in a house so small that it remains a mystery how it could have provided living space for an enormous family, let alone privacy for any member of it. A twenty-fifth child was born after the twins and named Giovanna for the one who died and, though she lived only a few years, thirteen of the brood did live to grow up and all remained at home, at least until they married—several of them afterward; and eventually eleven grandchildren were included in the household. Yet somehow space was found for a little foster son, Tommaso della Fonte, whose parents, intimate friends of the Benincasas, died in the plague of 1348; and he remained with his benefactors until the Dominicans, of whom he eventually became an outstanding member, undertook his education. As we have already seen, three of the sons, Bartolommeo, Orlando and Stefano, became their father's junior partners; and the dyeing, like all the rest of the work, was done on the premises. But apparently Catherine found quietude in the midst of this turmoil; and as long as she wished, she lived a life almost completely apart from all fellow creatures, even her nearest and dearest. Probably this interlude gave her the respite she needed to recover from the struggles of her earlier youth, when she was constantly pitting her will against her mother's, and to prepare her for the ceaseless activities of her adult life. Without it she might not have had the physical and spiritual strength to prevail against all the forces which threatened to overwhelm her. But it cannot be too strongly emphasized that, both as a girl and as a woman, her very being mingled with that of her fellow creatures and that she was always a source of comfort and delight to them.

Catherine did not spend all her time in the crowded house in the Vicolo del Tiratoio. The Benincasas owned a small farm on the outskirts of San Rocca a Pilli, a village some fourteen or fifteen kilometers from Siena, "and here among the vine and olive trees she enjoyed the sweetness of spring time, and the poetic melancholy of autumn. She saw the peaceful changes in the labour of the peasants; she felt the poetry of Mother Earth, the beauty of the trees and flowers, of the herbs and of all the minute creations of the great God. She had a passion for flowers, and, rambling through the garden, would gather tiny buds and weave them into little crosses, which she gave to her confessor, Padre Tommaso, as gifts for his friends. She often dreamed that angels descended from Heaven and crowned her with white lilies. These dreams, together with her poetic contemplation of the beauty of Nature, [later] became to her visions. Many of her words in the *Epistolario* and in the *Dialogo* were suggested by what she saw and felt in this little farm." [8]

It is easy to believe this. The site of the Benincasas' property permitted a beautiful view of the hills and valleys beyond. These were mantled with vineyards and olive trees, studded with prosperous farms and crowned with towering castles. Patient, long-suffering donkeys plodded along the winding paths, and snow-white oxen, hitched to scarlet carts, transported the heavier loads and plowed the fertile fields, where the color of the rich earth gave its name to the pigment known as raw sienna or burnt sienna, according to the amount of processing it had undergone. The unique tawny rose of most Sienese buildings owes its beauty to the fact that this earth forms the basis of the brick from which they are made. The pigment, sometimes used as ink in those days, became closely associated with Catherine; and, considering her sensitivity, so early developed, she could hardly have failed to be moved by such a scene as she beheld from the grounds and windows of her parents' house. Not only her lifelong love of flowers, which was very practically revealed in the fostering care she gave the plants in the garden that adjoined the kitchen of the house in Siena; but also the appreciation of the Tuscan countryside which made her travels a source of pleasure, as well as a means to a purposeful end, may be traced to these sojourns in the country.

Catherine was not a pretty child, in the generally accepted sense of the word. That is, when she had outgrown her infantile chubbiness, she was not plump and rosy, nor did she have big blue eyes and clustering curls. She was slight and pale, her features delicate, the texture of her skin exquisite, and her hair long, thick and lustrously golden. But without other actual beauty she was attractive, because she was animated and cheerful and friendly, and these qualities, like her sensitivity, were revealed in her expression and her manners. In a word, as we have said before, she was charming.

She developed early, physically, mentally and spiritually. All her movements were swift and graceful. She ascended the steep stairs of the house with such effortless speed that she seemed not to touch the steps—in fact, her mother asserted that sometimes the child did not actually do so, and the effect she gave was certainly one of upward flight. Yet at other times she paused on each tread to say the Ave Maria, which she had learned to recite, without difficulty, almost as soon as she could talk. Indeed, all forms of prayer came to her naturally; and when she was only seven, she returned from visiting one of her aunts with the report that, as she was walking down the steep hill by St. Dominic's Church, hand in hand with her brother Stefano, she had seen a celestial vision: the sky had suddenly opened to disclose the Son of God, seated on a throne and surrounded by saints, and the Savior had blessed her by making the sign of the cross.

The story of this vision, when she reported it at home, was greeted with scepticism. Stefano, admittedly, had seen nothing. Indeed, he had not understood why she had loosened her clasp on his hand and lagged behind him; he was disturbed when he found she was not following closely and puzzled when he learned the reason. But he did not attach much importance to it; it was not the first time he had thought that his little sister had a vivid imagination. Lapa, on the other hand, was distinctly annoyed. She did not talk about imagination, she talked about prevarication; and, anyway, she thought it would be much better for Catherine to watch where she was going, especially on a narrow crowded street like the Valle Piatta, than to stand gazing up at the sky.

Catherine certainly did not lie, either then or at any other time in the course of her life; neither did she nor anyone associated with her ever come to harm because her gaze was so often directed toward the sky. It is quite probable that she had a vivid imagination and it is, of course, hard to determine, even in the case of a saint, exactly where imagination ends and clairvoyance and clairaudience begin. But it has likewise always been hard, at least for me, to understand why so many persons who accept verbatim statements made by or about biblical characters find it impossible to believe that these special gifts were confined to the periods covered by the Old and New Testaments.[9] It seems safe to assume that clairvoyance and clairaudience are as old as time, and that persons who deny their existence in some cases are illogical if they accept them in others. Furthermore, the fact that such powers are not universal seems to me no more extraordinary than the fact that the ability to play the piano or paint pictures or write sonnets is not universal, either.

During my formative years, I not only learned, with delight, all the Bible stories referring to visions, but a bedtime hymn, which I confess I had not thought of for years, but which I suddenly remembered when I read of Catherine's first vision. It begins:

> Now the day is over,
> Night is drawing nigh,
> Shadows of the evening
> Drift across the sky.

After this opening, the hymn continues with a variety of petitions:

Jesus, give the weary
Sweet and calm repose,
With Thy tenderest blessing
Let our eyelids close.

Give to little children
Visions bright of Thee,
Keep the sailors tossing
On the deep blue sea.

Evidently, it seemed quite as logical to the writer of this hymn to pray that little children should have visions of the Savior as that the weary should be refreshed by sleep and the traveler saved from shipwreck; and this certainly implies belief not only in the existence of visions but in their value. Obviously, this belief has come down through the ages and is almost certain to endure, if for no other reason than because, over and over again, visions have had a tremendous influence on the lives of those who experienced them and have played an important part in the shaping of their destinies.

This was certainly so in the case of Catherine. From the day she saw the Savior surrounded by His saints, raising His hand in blessing as He looked down at her from the sky, her life was consecrated to His service. Raymond of Capua makes this situation vivid to us:

"From that moment it became clear from Catherine's virtues, the gravity of her behaviour, and her extraordinary wisdom, that under her girlish appearance there was hidden a fully formed woman. Her actions, indeed, had nothing childish, nothing girlish, about them, but showed all the signs of a most venerable maturity. From now onwards the fire of Divine love burned within her, enlightening her mind, kindling her will, strengthening her power of thought, and enabling her external acts to conform to the laws of God.

"To me, unworthy as I was, she revealed in all humility in confession that at this time, without the aid of teachers or books and taught entirely by the Holy Spirit, she had come to know and value the lives and way of life of the holy Fathers of Egypt and the great deeds of other saints, especially Blessed Dominic, and had felt such a strong desire to do what they did that she had been unable to think about anything else.

"This knowledge was the cause of certain innovations in the young girl's life which filled all who witnessed it with amazement. She would seek out hidden places and scourge her young body in secret with a special rope. She gave up all childish games and devoted her time to prayer and meditation instead; unlike most children, she became increasingly silent, and took less and less food to sustain her —a thing unheard-of in the case of growing children.

"Inspired by her example, a number of other little girls of her own age gathered round her, eager to hear her talk about salvation and to imitate her as best they could. They began to meet secretly in a corner of the house and scourge themselves with her, repeating the Our Father and the Hail Mary as often as she told them to. These things, as we shall see, were a sign of things to come." [7]

3

WE MAY feel, in this day and age, that Catherine's mind was not wholly "enlightened," as far as conforming to the laws of God was concerned. Increasingly, we have come to believe that the body is the temple of the soul and that it must be protected and even revered as such. But this was not the viewpoint of the age in which Catherine lived and we must consider her "external acts" from that angle, not from ours; and we will certainly agree that her will was kindled and her powers of thought strengthened. Had they not been, she never could have pursued, unswervingly, the way she had chosen, for the opposition she encountered was formidable.

There was, apparently, no objection to the hours spent in prayer and meditation, which she managed to keep from obtruding on the normal daily pattern of family life, just as she managed to obtain solitude when such an achievement would seem unobtainable to most of us. "Make yourself a cell in your own mind from which you need never to come out," she admonished Fra Raimondo not many years later; and it would seem as if she herself had always been adept at doing this, though, whenever possible, she chose an actual rather than an imaginary cell and, once at least, lingered in a cave which she had discovered by chance on her way to visit a married sister. The scourgings, in which several little girls took part, were also without doubt viewed tolerantly, as a sort of game, no more essentially morbid and cruel than many other games in which children seemed to take a grim satisfaction—and their elders, too, for that matter, as witness the popular Elmora. The fact that Catherine did not always pursue these practices alone, but encouraged her friends to join her in following them, was probably likewise considered a good sign; such periods of companionship, however spent, helped to offset the periods which she preferred to spend alone; and Raymond of Capua was entirely right in feeling that it was in such ways as these that coming events cast their shadow before them .

Just as the older neighbors had enjoyed her "wise little sayings" and her "delightful childish gaiety" when she was a prattler, so her youthful contemporaries now began to find her an example and a leader. Her power to charm and to influence was becoming increasingly stronger. Her parents could not have failed to be gratified by what they regarded as popularity, without taking it too seriously in any of its aspects.

It was, therefore, not until several years after the first momentous vision that the stress and strain began, which were to test Catherine's powers to pit her will against those of her parents. These conflicts were probably inevitable under the circumstances. It was natural for Giacomo and Lapa to hope that their youngest surviving daughter should marry and marry well; this seemed to them the manifest destiny for her, as it had been for her elder sisters, and as indeed it was for all the young girls of their acquaintance. She was encouraged to make the most of her looks, which were by no means negligible, even though she remained pale and slight, instead of becoming rosy and buxom, as her mother would have liked to see her. The cosmetics of that day provided artificial color for cheeks that lacked it, even as similar preparations do now; and these were applied to correct her pallor. Above all, much was made of her hair. There were masses of it, so it could be arranged in any way that was most effective, and its gorgeous color made it conspicuous in a city where brunettes were far more numerous than blondes; and the current fashions—long flowing skirts, close-fitting, low-necked bodices, tight full-length sleeves—were well suited to her slender figure. Becomingly rouged, becomingly coiffed, becomingly clothed, she was taken to all the proper places where her good looks could be seen to the best advantage; and the Benincasas' acquaintance with respectable well-to-do families, which numbered eligible young men among their members, was carefully fostered.

For a time Catherine submitted docilely, if reluctantly, to this program of propaganda. It was not until she realized that she was practically face to face with a definite courtship that she told her mother, calmly but unequivocally, that she could not marry. She had taken a vow of perpetual virginity when she was only seven years old.

Lapa's reaction to this was as natural as her desire to see her youngest daughter well married. She did not take the vow seriously, nor is there any really sound reason why she should have. Unless a little girl is very precocious, she hardly knows the meaning of the word virginity at the age of seven; and, granting that she does know it, vows taken at that age have no legal validity; it is not even necessary to be officially released from them. All Catherine had to do, her mother assured her, was to forget she had ever made such a promise and go happily forward with the preparations for her betrothal.

Catherine answered this admonition with action instead of words. She cut off her hair.

It was probably not the first time that a young girl took such a drastic step in the days when a woman's hair was still considered her crown of glory, and it was certainly not the last. (It will be recalled that Santa Rosa de Lima, who strove to be as much like Catherine of Siena as possible, in every way, did exactly the same thing, under much the same circumstances.) But, as far as Lapa was concerned, it was unprecedented—and disastrous. She rent the air with screams of rage and wept bitter tears over the ruin of her hopes. When she succeeded in collecting herself, her mood was grim: this thankless, insubordinate girl should be punished. Since she was unwilling to make a good appearance and mingle with pleasant people, she should dress like a servant and perform a servant's tasks, which would effectively keep her at home until she came to her senses. Meanwhile, the maid of all work would be discharged. She was not much good anyway. If she lost her job, it would serve her right. It would also serve Catherine right, to find herself cook and laundress and scrubwoman for so large a family. . . .

Catherine made no protest and, as far as anyone could find out, felt no inclination to do so. She accepted the drudgery that had been forced upon her with cheerfulness and performed all her tasks capably. Her father and brothers felt that she was being treated with undue harshness and taxed beyond her strength; but when they attempted to put their feelings into words, they were quickly silenced by Lapa, who, so far, had never failed to keep all the others subordinate to her will. It seemed inconceivable that she should fail now.

Yet, as the months went by, and Catherine continued to work uncomplainingly and efficiently, showing no signs of insubordination except when the subject of marriage was broached, Lapa began to feel that she was not making much progress. She resented the fact that her husband did not give her proper support. Although he did not insist that Catherine's labors should be lightened, it was all too evident he thought this should be done; and he gave her his word, in the presence of others, that she should not be forced into marriage and that, when her work was done, she should be free to spend as much time in prayer as she pleased. He went further than this: he said that, somehow, they must manage to let Catherine have a small room to herself, instead of sharing one with Stefano. When his wife, angrily reminding him how crowded they were anyway, asked him why he felt this was necessary, he answered that once, coming upon their daughter quietly, he had seen a white dove hovering over her head; he thought this was some sort of a symbol. Of course, it was nothing of the kind, Lapa retorted; weren't there hundreds of doves in Siena? And so wasn't it inevitable that, sooner or later, one would get into the house? Giacomo admitted that she was right on both these scores; but he still insisted the dove he had seen was significant and must be regarded as such. Catherine was given her little room, which she quickly cleared of all the furnishings she considered superfluous, that is to say, most of them. It bore no resemblance to the luxurious maiden's bower of song and story; on the contrary, it closely resembled a nun's cell.

Having made sure that she should be undisturbed in her prayers, Giacomo next listened, quietly and kindly, when Catherine told him about a dream she had had. In this she saw "Many holy fathers, and the founders of various Orders, including the most blessed Dominic. She recognized him at once because he was holding in his hands a most beautiful dazzling white lily, which, like Moses's bush, burned brightly without ever being consumed. All the people present advised her in turn to enter one of their Orders but she kept her eyes fixed on St. Dominic and gradually moved towards him. Suddenly he came forward to meet her, holding in his hand the habit

Saint Agnes of Rome

"Only seven female saints have found a place in the Canon, but she is one of them." From a painting of St. Agnes by Zurbaràn.

"The Church of St. Agnes . . . is one of the most beautiful in Rome and on her feast day it is invested with additional splendor."

A portion of the convent of the Benedictine nuns of St. Cecilia.

A painting from the museum in Pisa which shows St. Agnes with a flock of sheep and the Dominican watchdog.

Above. The Martyrdom of St. Agnes, *a painting by Tintoretto.*

"The one to whom I am betrothed is Christ whom the angels serve." From a painting of St. Agnes by Carlo Dolci.

Santa Francesca Romana

". . . it was Paul V. (Borghese) who decreed the canonisation of Francesca, to the joy of the Oblates of Tor di Specchi, of the monks of Santa Maria Nuova, and of the whole people of Rome."

Francesca pictured with a group of the Oblates of Tor di Specchi.

" 'I am finishing my vespers,' she said. And did not speak again."
A painting which depicts the veneration of the body of Francesca.

The Church of Santa Francesca Romana in Rome.

"Above the altar is the figure of the Madonna della Misericordia . . . beneath [her cloak] a reverent group has taken refuge; and on either side . . . are figures of San Lorenzo and Santa Francesca Romana."

"The Ponziani had a chapel in the parish church they attended . . . where they were privileged to bury their dead; in their case the church was St. Cecilia's." This scene is from a fresco by Cavallini located in the Church of St. Cecilia.

Several frescoes have been disclosed in the convent of the Oblates of Tor di Specchi. Above, we see Santa Francesca Romana performing one of the miracles that have been attributed to her. On the right is a detail taken from the fresco showing it to be in a remarkable state of preservation.

A painting of St. Catherine of Siena by Domenico Beccafumi from the Accademia di Belle Arti in Siena.

Pictured above is the altar in the Chapel of Veneration of St. Catherine, in Siena. Below are two details from the painting which surrounds the altar.

Above: an unusual painting by Matteo Balducci showing Catherine sheltering a prayerful group within her cloak.

Left: a representation of St. Catherine taken from The Marriage of St. Catherine *by Taddeo Gaddi.*

Below: This Balducci painting portrays the reception of the stigmata by Catherine.

The Church of St. Maria Novella where Catherine was tried by the Council.

The Baths of Vignone where Catherine was scalded and contracted smallpox.

A mural in St. Catherine's house depicting the miracle of St. Agnes of Montepulcian

The Torture of Tuldo *showing Catherine with the gift of the stigmata.*

St. Catherine of Siena *by Vanni, her contemporary.*

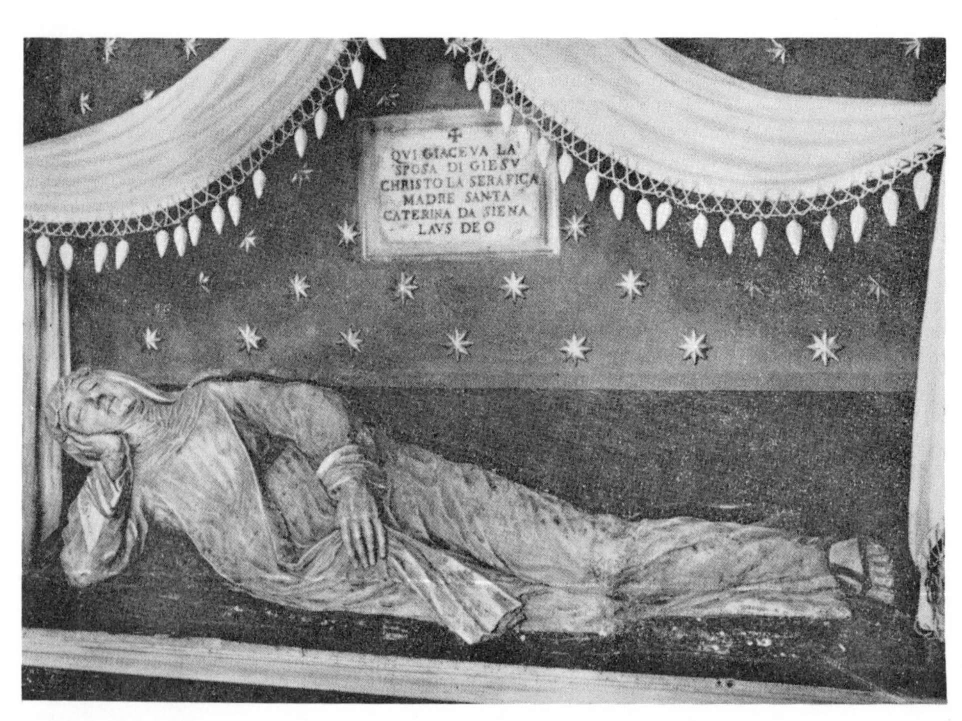

"The dyer's daughter . . . had transcended her womanhood." From a painting by Lorenzo di Pietro.

of the Sisters of Penance of St. Dominic. . . . When he came up to her he comforted her saying, 'Sweetest daughter, take courage and fear no obstacle, for you will undoubtedly put on this habit, as is your wish.' These words filled her with great joy, and with tears of happiness she gave thanks to God and to Dominic, the famous athlete of the Lord, for giving her such perfect consolation. Then she was awakened by her tears and came back to her senses." [7]

Having said this much and found her father a sympathetic listener, Catherine went on to say she felt sure this dream was an answer to prayer. She had long wished that she might give a more definite pattern to her religious life than she could do without direction and association and she had also long felt a special devotion to St. Dominic and yearned to join the Third Order which he had instituted. She was already well acquainted with it and so was Giacomo; for in Siena there were nearly a hundred devout women, among them several relatives and connections of the Benincasas, who belonged to this Order. Its members wore a habit and vowed obedience to a Prioress, elected by themselves; for spiritual direction they depended on the Dominican Brothers of St. Dominic's Church and often went to Mass in a body. Some, who had no settled homes of their own and no close kindred, joined forces and lived together in a house directed by the Prioress; but this had none of the attributes of an official community center. The rest of the members, more fortunately situated, continued to live with their families. Though they withdrew from the more frivolous pursuits, there was little or nothing in their proscribed routine which unfitted them for domesticity. They were pledged to extra periods of prayer, besides those regularly observed by all devout Catholics, but these took place during the night, when the rest of the household could sleep undisturbed. They were also pledged to more abstinence in their daily fare than was habitual, but this did not make their presence at table a source of embarrassment either to themselves or to others. They were in the world, though not of it and it was largely through the severity and simplicity of their lives that they succeeded in sublimating these. They were held in very high esteem by their fellow citizens and had become affectionately known as the Mantellate (wearers of cloaks) because of the black capes they wore over their white habits. Officially, they were called the Dominican Sisters of Penance. Catherine hoped she might have her parents' permission to join this Order, if the time came when she was not so greatly needed for household duties.

She had previously told her mother all this and had been answered with derision. The dream about St. Dominic was dismissed with the same scepticism as had greeted the story about the vision of the beneficent Savior. What was more practically to the point, the Mantellate were all elderly widows or spinsters; their Superior, Mother Neri di Gano, would never consent to introducing a girl of sixteen in their midst. Lapa had an idea, which she thought was a much better one: what Catherine needed was not more prayer and penance, but a complete change of scene, one that would afford pleasant diversion along with physical benefits. Admittedly, life had been dull for the girl while she was housebound and she had been losing weight, too, though she had none to spare. Lapa proposed to take her to Vignone, a resort some thirty miles from Siena. The hot springs were reputedly very strengthening and the best people frequented them.

Lapa's plan seemed to Giacomo very sound. He, too, had heard the springs well spoken of. They were supposed to contain iron and copper and possibly even gold and silver; they might well be strengthening and it would make him very happy to see Catherine looking stronger. At the same time, he ventured to remind his wife that, if Catherine became a Mantellata, she would not be a cloistered nun; she would continue to live at home, in much the same way she was already doing. Certainly, she would find it easy enough to obey the simple rules of the Order since she spent hours in prayer every day and, of her own choice, ate nothing but bread and fruit and vegetables.

Lapa, who had failed to observe this voluntary abstinence, was horrified; so it was lack of nourishment, not overwork, which made the girl so thin and pale! She must have a more substantial diet! Giacomo reminded his wife that she had called his attention to the fact that all the Mantellate were elderly women and, for the most part, they seemed to him very hale and hearty, as if their food agreed with them; surely, if Lapa were consistent, she would admit. . . .

Lapa admitted nothing. She cut short the argument and departed for Vignone, taking the unresisting Catherine with her. A week later they returned, Lapa again in a rage and Catherine swathed in bandages.

Whether by accident or design, the girl had slipped away from that part of the healing waters were these were tepid, and had approached the boiling springs from which they flowed. The attendants had shouted at her to stop, to turn back, but, instead, she had gone on and on. She had been terribly scalded and she had been ill ever since. It was now clear she was coming down with a fever.[10]

The next day the nature of the fever was apparent: Catherine had smallpox. Lapa, whose first fears were simply of disfigurement for her daughter, soon began to realize that she might lose Catherine altogether. Frantic with terror and grief, and possibly not unmoved by remorse, she was not only willing but eager to do anything that would bring relief to the sufferer, and Catherine was not slow to take advantage of this mood. She extracted a promise that, as soon as she showed signs of recovery, Lapa would go to the Superior of the Mantellate and ask her to accept the would-be Sister of Penance as a tertiary.

Lapa kept her promise and met with a rather frosty reception; it was quite unheard of to receive a girl of sixteen, Reverend Mother Neri di Gano assured Lapa curtly. Lapa returned to her daughter's bedside and made no attempt to conceal the satisfaction she felt in this reply. But Catherine did not react to it in the way her mother had expected.

"I am acquainted with the Rule of the Mantellate and there is nothing in it that says a girl of sixteen *cannot* be accepted," Catherine said calmly. "Please go back and remind the Superior of that."

On the occasion of her second visit, Lapa was received somewhat less frostily. The Superior admitted that there was no official rule which, in itself, would prevent Catherine's acceptance as a Dominican Sister of Penance. But the Reverend Mother had had one experience with an attractive widow, younger than most of those who joined the Order, which made her hesitate to consider an applicant who was too good looking; she would need to be assured that Catherine was not pretty; and, in any case, she felt a girl of sixteen was too young to know her own mind. . . .

At this point, Lapa was driven to saying that, alas, Catherine knew her own mind so well that she would go to any length to have her way. She had cut off her beautiful hair, so that she would not be presentable and she had walked into scalding water, probably with the same end in view. Now she had smallpox, which would doubtless result in further disfigurement. She might have been a very attractive girl; there was obviously little chance of that now. As Lapa said all this, she sounded aggrieved; for the first time in days, her sense of injury had triumphed over her anxiety.

The Superior, faintly amused, unexpectedly intrigued, said that as soon as the invalid was well enough to receive callers, she would come to the Benincasas' house, with two members of her Order, and interview the applicant herself. The results of this visit were satisfactory, both to her and to Catherine. A few weeks later, in the Cappella della Volte at St. Dominic's Church, Catherine was duly clothed in the white habit and black mantle of a Sister of Penance.

Thus clothed, she returned to her parents' house and retired to the bare little room which, thanks to her father's intercession, had already been set aside for her and where she had spent as much time as she could, after her household duties were fulfilled, in solitary prayer. Nothing in the vows she had taken necessitated any change in her routine—she had been careful, from the beginning, to point out that this would be the case. But some inner compulsion moved her to seek complete seclusion "for the purpose of purifying her way of thinking"; and she met with no objections, even from Lapa, when she made this known, or when she persisted in the new way of life which marked her period of preparation for still another way which she did not yet visualize. For three long years she left her cell-like room only to go to church and she broke her self-imposed rule of silence only to confess or to meet some emergency. She ate alone, and sparingly, of bread and vegetables and drank only water. She trained herself to do with very little sleep, in order that she might have more time for meditation and for her devotions; and, during the hours when she knew that the Dominican friars—her spiritual brothers—slept, she recited the Divine Office in their stead. And all the while she came closer and closer to the realization of her ideal—a life of union with Christ.

"Such was her novitiate: the novice master was our Lord Himself, who many times appeared to her and spoke to her heart." [11]

4

In *The Dialogue,* that remarkable document which Catherine dictated in five days, shortly before she left Siena forever, she gave, from memory, her own account of these appearances and these speeches. But a considerable period had elapsed between the time that they occurred and the time she herself caused them to be recorded, and many of her biographers have given their own versions of them, which I have found both moving and convincing. Left to myself, I should have vastly preferred to quote extensively and verbatim from those writers who, I feel, are much better qualified than I am to interpret the mystical aspects of this interval. Only the stern admonition that this is my book has driven me to attempt an interpretation, with a minimum of direct references.

Undoubtedly, Catherine was both clairaudient and clairvoyant during the interval in question. This was nothing new; it had been evident ever since she was six years old. She enjoyed the visible presence of Our Lord, Who sometimes visited her by Himself, at other times accompanied by His Mother and at still others by various saints. She listened to His voice, which He raised sometimes to speak words of praise and encouragement, sometimes words of reproof and sometimes words of explanation which clarified mysteries that were obscure to her. On other occasions, though conscious of His spiritual direction, she neither saw Him nor heard Him; but her awareness of communion with Him was such that she needed neither sight nor sound to satisfy her longing for Him. Like most saints, she also passed through periods of aridity—what John of the Cross called the dark night of the soul—when her Savior seemed completely withdrawn from her. These periods were very hard to bear until He told her something which gave her strength as well as consolation. "Lord, where were You when I sought You and could not find You?" she asked with anguish. "In your heart," came the reply. After that she never sought Him in vain.

For her, love of the Lord, rather than fear of the Lord, had been the beginning of wisdom. For a long time she had wished she could read her breviary, though this was not a requirement in the Third Order—indeed, it could not be, for many of the members were nearly, if not wholly, illiterate; but she found herself yearning increasingly for intellectual, as well as spiritual, growth. Now she realized this yearning. The accounts of how she did this vary with different biographers. According to some, her fellow Mantellata, Alessia Saracini, first tried to help her and found her an eager but unreceptive pupil. Alessia did, indeed, become her lifelong friend, who rendered her many services; but if Catherine's novitiate was actually as secluded as the best authorities maintain, she received no visitors in her cell, and her close companionship with Alessia did not begin until after she re-entered the world. On the other hand, she constantly saw her foster brother, Tommaso della Fonte, for he was now Fra Tommaso of the Dominican Order and her confessor; so he would have been the logical person to receive her confidences. It would have been both proper and natural for him to undertake her deliverance from illiteracy, when it was clearly indicated that this should be done; and it would also have been natural for him to pray that the Lord would help him to enlighten her, when the going seemed hard and slow. She herself may well have been discouraged, though this certainly was not in character—it was always her nature to persevere. And it may also well be that she is correctly quoted in saying, "If my Lord wishes me to praise Him through the daily office, then one day I shall be able to read. And if not I will content myself with saying 'Our Father' and 'Ave Maria' as other unschooled women do." Even so, it does not seem to me that this indicates a disposition to give up; rather, it indicates a disposition to be patient and resigned.

At all events, suddenly Catherine could read, and she and her friends were convinced that a miracle had occurred, that the Divine "Novice Master" was responsible for the teaching that had enabled her to overcome her previous difficulties with the written word. Doubtless He had—in the same sense that He helps all of us to overcome our difficulties, and as Fra Tommaso had hoped and prayed He might do in this case. But it does not seem to me that this sudden achievement should be placed in the same category as the mystical knowledge in which she had slowly progressed during the three years of her solitude. I believe it belongs in quite a different classification. Practically all human teachers and many human mothers in our time have watched children struggle with their primers until it seemed, as they went on and on without making any visible progress, that they would never advance as far as a first reader; and then, without any warning whatsoever, the youngsters have voluntarily opened their dogeared schoolbooks and proudly begun to read aloud from them, without hesitation, to the amazement of their hearers! [12] Somehow, in their subconscious minds, they have been absorbing more than their elders realized; and the results of their perseverance, instead of being revealed gradually, have been revealed abruptly, as some blossoms develop from tight little buds into larger and larger buds, while others burst into sudden bloom. I believe that much the same thing may have happened to Catherine; but this does not in the least detract from the principle of Divine Guidance, especially in view of her claim that, sometimes, when she was reading her breviary, Our Lord joined her and read the responses "as when two monks read the Office together."

Once she had mastered her missal, Catherine continued her quest for learning through the pages of other books which Father Tommaso made available to her: a short history of the Church, the lives of saints, the psalms of David and other portions of the Bible. Her understanding of these became perfect and complete because of that Divine Guidance which she never lacked. In due time, she was to astonish first her confessors and then many other learned ecclesiastics by her familiarity with such works and her grasp of their true lessons. But, after all, this was not astonishing, since Christ Himself had been her teacher.

Though Catherine had not been spared aridity, she had been singularly free from great temptations: on the eve of her clothing, she had, indeed, passed through a trying ordeal, when she envisioned a charming young man, whom she took to be the devil in disguise, and who urged her to accept his love. Suddenly, without warning, she had found herself a prey to violent earthbound emotion and this was one of the times when Our Lord Himself seemed withdrawn from her. Though she knelt and prayed for deliverance before the crucified Christ, her petition went unanswered; but when she felt she could endure no more, the Blessed Mother appeared to her and wrapped her in a miraculous cloak and thus she found strength to resist and to persevere. No similar temptation ever occurred—in fact, her sense of communion with Christ became so complete that she ceased to fear it might lessen and yet something still seemed lacking to make the unity complete.

She pondered this as she knelt in her cell on Shrove Tuesday in the Year of Our Lord 1367. She was now almost twenty and her life of seclusion had lasted more than three years. Probably some of her fellow Mantellate had resisted a natural impulse to join in the carnival madness, which had now reached its height; but it is doubtful whether any felt as much joy in their detachment from it as Catherine, for this wild carousal of singing and dancing and feasting, which marked the final day before the Lenten fast, was almost as essential to the average Sienese as breathing. But Catherine had no sense of loneliness, none of regret, because of her separation from it. She firmly believed that she and not the others had found true joy, that she had chosen the better part, and that such pandemonium as reigned outside her window had no place in her life any more. All she lacked was the mystical perfection for which she still yearned and which she had not yet achieved, despite all the divine favors with which she had been showered. "Grant me *fullness* of faith!" she prayed, over and over again.

And then the miracle happened.

Her Lord was with her, she could see Him standing close to her and hear His voice and He was saying, " 'Since for love of me you have forsaken vanities and despised the pleasure of the flesh and fastened all the delights of your heart on me, now, when the rest of the household are feasting and enjoying themselves, I have determined to celebrate the wedding feast of your soul and to espouse you to me in faith as I promised.'

"Before He had finished speaking His most glorious Virgin Mother appeared with the most blessed St. John the Evangelist, the glorious

Apostle Paul, St. Dominic (the founder of the Order) and the prophet David with his harp. While David played sweet strains on the harp the Mother of God took Catherine's hand in her own most holy hand and presenting her to her Son courteously asked Him to marry her to Himself in faith. The Son of God, graciously agreeing, held out a gold ring with four pearls set in a circle in it and a wonderful diamond in the middle and with His most holy right hand He slipped it on to the virgin's second finger, saying, 'There! I marry you to me in faith, to me, your Creator and Saviour. Keep this faith unspotted until you come to me in heaven and celebrate the marriage that has no end. From this time, forward, daughter, act firmly and decisively in everything that in my Providence I shall ask you to do. Armed as you are with the strength of faith, you will overcome all your enemies and be happy.'

"The vision disappeared, but the ring always remained on Catherine's finger and though no one else could see it it was always before her eyes. In fact she frequently confessed to me in all humility that she could always see it on her finger and that there was never a moment when it was out of her sight." [7]

5

THE MYSTICAL marriage marked both the climax and the conclusion of Catherine's novitiate. When Our Lord next spoke to her, He told her to join the members of her family at table, where they had foregathered for their midday meal, and begin her service in the world. For a few moments she demurred and hesitated; it seemed impossible for her to do this in a quiet and natural way. But she had learned to obey the first great Commandment: Thou shalt love the Lord thy God with all thy heart and all thy soul and all thy mind; it was now time for her to obey the second: Thou shalt love thy neighbor as thyself. And such love included the willingness to serve. She left her cell and went into the kitchen where the surprise with which she was received was tempered by joy and tenderness.

At first her "service" was limited to that which she gave at home; she had lived in solitude for so long that she could not readily mingle with people. But she loved to work in the kitchen garden, where she cultivated roses, lilies and violets among the thriving vegetables. Once, as she looked at a rose tree she was nurturing, she told herself—and afterward others—that "we must try to find in the midst of thorns the perfume of the rose which is just about to open." Very often she sang as she weeded. Her singing voice, like her speaking voice, was pleasing and she had a keen appreciation of all sorts of music. We are told that "she loved the organ and the sound of the evening bells, and in the twilight she would sit and lose herself in the contemplation of the firmament above." [2] It is easy to picture her, lingering in the garden after she had watered her flowers, listening to the canticles sung in the nearby Church of St. Dominic and the Angelus rung at the Cathedral and repeated by all the lesser bells of the city.

With such periods of respite as these and the still more precious hours given to retreat in her cell and attendance at Mass, she gradually adjusted herself to life in the world. She helped with the housework again, not under duress as she had done before, but easily and eagerly. She sat at table with her family, and though she ate more sparingly than the other members of the hearty brood, she made no parade of this. If she went to Mass more frequently than the others, she did not parade this habit either; and she showed herself glad of companionship when any or all of the rest wished to accompany her. She was passionately fond of children, and once confessed that "if it were not for the shame of it she would have liked to spend all her time playing with and petting her small nephews and nieces." [13] Several of these, still very young, were living in the Benincasas' home at the time; and, no doubt, the hours of mutually spontaneous companionship that Catherine spent with them helped her immensely in overcoming the first sense of strain which was natural under the circumstances. Her parents, her brothers and sisters were all delighted to have her with them again; and, as soon as she recovered from the first strangeness of her altered life, she shared their pleasure. She did not avoid their friends when visitors came to the house and soon she began to make friends of her own: first, among the Mantellate and the Dominican Brothers; then, among the priests and physicians at the Hospital of Santa Maria della Scala, where she began the nursing career for which, from the beginning, she showed remarkable aptitude; then among the intelligentsia who were intrigued by the reports of her cultural and mystical attainments and were eager to put these to the test.

Not everyone who sought her out did so from admiration. Many were prompted by curiosity, many by scepticism, many by downright malice. Rumors spread like wildfire in any small city and all sorts of interpretations can be given even the most reliable news. The gossip about Catherine inevitably led to a multitude of questions: how could the illiterate daughter of a dyer come to be regarded as such a font of wisdom? What sort of a girl would regard honorable marriage as a calamity, to be avoided at all costs, and then go so far as to incarcerate herself voluntarily for three years, claiming that during this time Jesus was her constant companion, but admitting no human being to her cell? Was it true that she had been forbidden to communicate as often as she desired, because she was apt to go off into trances on the very steps of the altar, to the great embarrassment of both priest and people? And what about these cures that she was alleged to be effecting at the hospital? Physicians could not account for many of them which did not belong in the realm of reason. And what about all the beggars she fed, because her father permitted her to draw on his resources, now that her vow of poverty prevented her from having any money of her own? Was it true that the number of these mendicants was increasing all the time, some of whom she claimed were saintly visitors in disguise? She had actually given her cloak to one of these charlatans, though this, as the Rector of the Misericordia Hospital had been obliged to point out to her, was part of her habit, without which she should not be seen in public, especially as no respectable Sienese woman, whether she were a religious or not, went abroad without a cape of some sort. Since Catherine was a Sienese, born and bred, she must be fully aware of this inviolable custom; and still she flouted it. And so on and so on. . . .

Sometimes those who wished her ill did not limit themselves to carping criticism. In one instance at least, she was so roughly handled by a powerful, disorderly lout, who tried to remove her bodily from her seat in church, that several of her fellow worshipers were obliged to come to her rescue and eject her assailant instead. And, more than once, groups of young men, who belonged to the gilded youth of the city, but who were more conspicuous for their lawless behavior than for their gentle birth, came roistering to her house in the dead of night and broke into her quiet cell, raging at her because some of their companions had deserted them at her instigation. They did not succeed in frightening her. She received them with the same serenity that she did those who came in tranquil friendliness. Then there were others among the gilded youth who, though far from being disorderly in the usual sense of the word, declined to take her seriously, flattered her and jested with her and tried to cajole her into merrier moods. One of these, Francesco di Vanni Malavolti, was a famous philanderer. Though married to a lovely and adoring girl, he spent much of his time in dalliance outside his own sumptuous home, and was very generally considered irresistible, which was not strange, since wealth, good looks, generosity and persuasiveness were also among his attributes. His peccadilloes were usually forgiven him; since his patient young wife was disposed to regard them leniently. His male friends did the same; and one of these brought him to see Catherine, so confident that he and she would please each other that he overruled Francesco's reluctance to making the visit, and declined to listen when the reprobate declared that if he heard a single word about reformation he would leave the premises immediately. As a matter of fact, he did not stay long, but this was not because of annoyance. It was because when he and Catherine looked into each other's eyes there came to both that instantaneous recognition of mutual understanding and sympathy which characterizes one of the rarest human relationships. She did not need to upbraid him or admonish him. He left her house to go to confession for the first time in many months, because he knew that unless he could free his soul from its burden of sin, she could not accept him as her friend, and he wanted to be her friend more than he wanted to be the lover of any other woman. It cannot be said that, from this moment on, he led a changed life; but it can be said that every time he fell from grace, he tried to recapture it and that, generally, he was successful.

Francesco's feeling for Catherine and hers for him was as lasting as it was immediate. It was a striking example of the fact that strong, abiding and unselfish friendships can and often do exist between sensual men and sanctified women to the benefit of both, because of mental harmony. Indeed, after the death of his wife—whom he had treated with increasing tenderness and consideration—he entered the Benedictine Monastery of Olivet and spent the remainder of his life there in prayer and contemplation.[14]

Francesco's story, though outstanding because of his engaging personality and the strong mutual attraction between him and Catherine, was not unusual in its broader aspects. In a surprising number of cases, "those who came to scoff remained to pray." Catherine managed to find the time, despite her discipline, her devotions and her household duties and the hours she gave to nursing and other works of charity, to welcome in her home everyone who wished to come there. She could do with very little sleep, as well as very little food, so most of these gatherings took place in the late evening and often went on far into the night—unfortunately, but not unnaturally, causing more adverse comment than if they had taken place in the daytime. In a different era, with less emphasis on the spiritual and more on the sophisticated, they might well have borne comparison with the assemblies of guests gathered together by the great ladies of France and their scene become celebrated as a salon. In this case, however, the scene became known as the *cenacolo Cateriniano.*

"She gathered together poets, artists, politicians, men of law and men of religion, all of whom deepened her culture and at the same time enlarged her field of action. She collected information from all her friends, information which she utilized in her public life. One of these friends, the artist Andrea Vanni, who has left to us, in the Church of San Domenico in Siena, the oldest picture of the Saint, was in 1368 one of the chiefs of the popular party, and took an active part in the revolution which led to the fall of the '*Governo dei Dodici*' (Government of the Twelve). He and Bartolo the brother of Catherine were nominated '*Difensore della Repubblica,*' and in 1373 Vanni went to Avignon as ambassador of the Sienese to beg the Pope, Gregory XI, to return to Rome. There is no doubt but that Catherine obtained from him a great deal of valuable information regarding those who formed the Avignon 'Curia,' the character of the Pope, and the real state of the politics of the time. From the English hermit, William Flete, a man of great political and religious power (who later, together with St. Catherine, must have inspired the government of Richard II in the famous *Rationes Anglicorum* in favour of Urban VI), Catherine received her information regarding the political condition of England. From her friends the Salimbeni, Saracini, Tolomei, Piccolomini and Malavolti, she learnt all about the Guelph and Ghibelline strifes among the Italian aristocracy. She discussed questions of art and poetry with Anastagio di Monte Altino and Giacomo del Pecora, who wrote poems in her honour; and with Raimondo da Capua and Tommaso della Fonte she discoursed of things Divine. Amongst these groups the one to whom she was most attached was the young poet, Neri di Landoccio dei Pagliaresi, who was also her first secretary. She knew him first in 1370, and he accompanied her in her travels, remaining with her until her death. He was a young man belonging to a noble Sienese family, of rather a melancholy poetic temperament, and extraordinarily sensitive. Some beautiful verses which he wrote gained great fame in Siena and captivated the sympathy of the Saint." [2]

The William Flete to whom this quotation refers belonged to a community of Augustinian monks whose monastery, San Salvatore di Lecceto, was situated on high ground above a grove of ilex trees which gave the place its name (Lecceto). The community had a notable history. According to tradition, the disciples of St. Ansanus fled to these woods to escape Roman persecution, and St. Augustine himself found hermits living there and gave them their Rule of life. St. Jerome and St. Monica were also said to have visited the place and St. Francis of Assisi unquestionably did so, plucking a branch from one of the ilexes which he afterward struck in the ground at Capraia, where it "grew into a goodly tree." The golden age of the convent began when Pope Alexander IV, a kinsman of his predecessor, Innocent IV, united all Augustine hermits into one order and Lecceto became the head house of Tuscany. Wonderful legends lingered around the place; angels were said to have descended from heaven in human form to eat with the hermits in their refectory or to help them when they were in need; and the flowers which grew in the forest allegedly healed the sick and worked other miracles. The priors were famous for the sanctity and severity of their lives; and one especially appealing story was told of a certain Frate Bandino di Balsetti "who was so strict in the rules that when he saw a thief taking away the convent donkey at the time of silence, rather than break the silence or cause the friars to break it, he let him lead it off, while he himself went into the church to pray for the redemption of the thief's soul. (Of course the thief was miraculously moved to repentance and the prior sent him away with a plenteous alms.)" [1]

The monastery itself was a spacious building of considerable distinction and dignity, its portico, cloisters and chapel adorned with frescoes of both allegorical and historical character, many of them noteworthy. Why William Flete, who was a man of great culture, a graduate of Cambridge University and a writer of remarkable talent, should have insisted on spending most of his time in a woodland cave, rather than in such a center, remains a mystery—but then it remains a mystery why he ever left England and came to Italy in the first place. Just how Catherine was persuaded to visit him is still another mystery. When she first did so, she had never left Siena, except for sojourns at the family farm at San Rocca a Pilli and the disastrous expedition to Vignone; but she finally consented to join some of her companions who were making the ten mile trip to Lecceto. Perhaps it was the fame of the convent, which she eventually visited many times,[15] and the much heralded beauty of its situation and frescoes, that first irresistibly attracted her. Be that as it may, almost from the first moment of their meeting, she and the eccentric but scholarly hermit became close friends.

She needed such friends, all the more because her family life at this time was shadowed with sorrow and corroded with anxiety. Her kind and loving father died, and two of her brothers became involved in a local uprising of revolutionary character and were obliged to flee for their lives to Florence. Their precipitate departure naturally had an adverse effect on the family business, already suffering from the loss of Giacomo's guiding hand; and when they decided that they would not return to Siena, but would establish themselves permanently in its rival city, the material prosperity of the establishment on the Vicolo del Tiratoio came to an end. After her husband's death, Lapa herself fell grievously ill; she and Catherine and all the other members of their immediate family were, for the first time, in really straitened circumstances.

Catherine was able to accept these, not only uncomplainingly, but cheerfully. Indeed, except for the fact that she now had no money to give the poor, they made little difference to her since, as far as she was personally concerned, she was vowed to poverty in any case. Instead of giving alms, she gave more and more time to nursing; and she had faith to believe that, somehow, the necessities of life would be provided for her mother and for the nephews and nieces who were still so young that they required more food and clothing than their elders. But she could not help being aware that the number of her detractors was increasing as rapidly as the number of her admirers and even her serene spirit was not proof against concern on this score. She had became conspicuous, for a variety of reasons, the more so because she was not as plain as the Superior of the Mantellate might have wished. Neither the burns from the boiling water at Vignone nor the smallpox which had attacked her soon afterward had left any scars; indeed, her appearance was already described as "beautiful" at the time of her clothing as a Mantellate. To be sure, she was still slight and pale, but neither her slenderness nor her pallor produced an effect of unhealthfulness; she was, as a matter of fact, strong as steel and her boundless energy, her almost incredible endurance, were evident to all. She gave an impression of physical, as well as spiritual and mental, force. Such attributes have always had great powers of attraction. And then, as we have pointed out several times already, she was almost irresistibly charming.

It may well have been this attribute which came closer than any other to getting Catherine into serious trouble. There can be no possible doubt that jealousy was responsible for many of the charges brought against her. If she had been elderly and plain and unpleasant, her activities and experiences might have been laid to the vagaries of a disagreeable, unbalanced old woman, whom nobody wished to imitate and whom almost everybody could dismiss with a shrug of the shoulders. Catherine's seemingly uncanny wisdom might also have been overlooked without envy—after all, what did a woman need of learning? Besides, when "two learned doctors attacked Catherine 'like raging lions' and bombarded her with the subtlest and most difficult theological questions they could invent, they were so abashed by her replies, given so clearly and wisely, that they wished they could withdraw from the whole affair when Catherine suddenly took the offensive." [13] Their humiliation was not the sort of feeling they wanted to have bruited about.

Her supernatural experiences presented more of a problem, when it came to comparative secrecy. She discussed these with Fra Tommaso, not only in his role as her confessor, as she was bound to do, but as her loved and trusted foster brother; and he, in turn, discussed them with his friend and fellow Dominican, Fra Bartolommeo, not sceptically or critically, but because he thought they needed more clarification than he could give them and because he believed, after receiving sage advice on the subject, he would be able to counsel Catherine more effectively on what course she should pursue as a result of her revelations. She said that Jesus had offered her a choice of two crowns, one made with gold and set with precious jewels, the other made of thorns, like His own. Which should she have chosen? The answer to that was fairly obvious: she had done right in deciding she should wear the crown of thorns in this world and then she would be entitled to wear the jeweled crown in the next. . . . She said that Jesus had taken away her heart and given her His own. Well, after all, was not that a figure of speech, an answer to the prayer which doubtless she had voiced like David when he said, "Create a clean heart in me, O God: and renew a right spirit within my bowels." [16] No, Catherine insisted, this had not been a figure of speech. It had been a physical experience, in which the pain had been almost unbearably great at first and the ecstasy equally great afterward. What should Fra Tommaso answer to that? He was by no means sure and neither was Fra Bartolommeo and the other Dominicans who were consulted. Some of them began to shake their heads and murmur among themselves. This was a more serious matter than going into trances at the Communion rail.

Perhaps the most serious of all was the situation precipitated by her statement, *"Vidi arcana Dei."* ("I have seen the hidden things of God.") She made this after she had lain for three days in a state of complete unconsciousness, during which bodily changes occurred, so similar to those of death, that all who surrounded her were sure she had died. A young friar who was apparently in the last stages of consumption was brought, at his urgent request, by Fra Tommaso and Fra Bartolommeo to the bier on which she had already been placed, and the blood pouring from his severe hemorrhage ceased to flow as soon as he touched her. Every one of the onlookers was convinced this was a miracle—just as they were convinced another miracle had occurred when, a few minutes later, Catherine opened her eyes and made her amazing declaration. But then they began to be troubled. Was this actually a resurrection? Was there at last a living human being who could, if so disposed, reveal what happened after death? These perplexing and disturbing questions remained unanswered.

Even so, Catherine's statement might somehow either have been explained away, to the satisfaction of the doubting clerics; or their thoughts might have been diverted by reminders of her invaluable services to the sick and suffering, and of the many conversions she had brought about, not only among the lax and the worldly, but even in cases of condemned criminals. At least that might have happened if she had not been slandered and attacked by members of her own Order, among them a certain Andrea, who had the most cause to be grateful to her, because Catherine had tended the vicious woman when she was stricken with a disease so loathsome that no one else would minister to her. "A host of witnesses appeared, eager to record what they knew of her wonderful life, of her charm, of her holy gaiety: everyone who knew anything about her burned to tell of the *'Beata Popolana'*—the Blessed Child of the People, as the Sienese loved to call the dyer's daughter." [13] But these did not suffice. As a result of Andrea's slanders and attacks from other quarters, Catherine was officially summoned by Reverend Mother Neri di Gano to answer the charges against her.

These ranged all the way from criticisms of her abstinence, which was regarded by many as a pose and by many others as a deception, to doubts as to the purity of her personal life. ("The scandalmongers did not limit themselves to the matter of eating and drinking; the more imaginative went on to deride the relations between the nun and so many persons living in the world, and between her and so many friars living in the cloister. The scandal mushroomed and soon became a pulpit theme.") [11]

There was, alas, one tragedy which gave the scandalmongers a foundation on which to base their malicious talk: a young friar, Pietro di Mastro Lando, committed suicide because of his hopeless passion for her. Of course, the very fact that it *was* hopeless, that Catherine had never by word or deed encouraged him or responded to him, was what led to his despair; but the fact that he was a religous was so especially damaging that one aspect of the case offset the other. The question was repeated again and again: was Catherine's relationship with men and women—especially with men—really on such a high spiritual plane?

It was these doubts and the manner in which they were expressed which came closer to breaking Catherine's spirit than anything else. ("All the holy doctors agree that a virgin's good name is a sensitive thing and maidenly modesty a very delicate matter, and that nothing is more unbearable for a virgin than the stigma of shame and nothing more upsetting than the charge of impurity.") [7] She managed to reply "modestly and patiently" to her accusers, who "attacked her with insults and reproaches and all manner of coarse vile words, asking her how she had deceived herself to the extent of losing her virginity: 'I assure you, ladies and sisters in the Faith, [she said] that by the grace of God I am a virgin.' That was all she would say, however much they went on lying and insulting her, 'Indeed, I am a virgin. Indeed, I am a virgin.' " [7]

But the iron entered into her soul as she said this, and she went on saying it, as if to reassure herself of its complete truth after she had been dismissed from the assembly which had so traduced her. Perhaps, unconsciously, she was also preparing herself to speak with assurance at a much larger and more formidable gathering. Pope Gregory XI (Pierre Roger de Beaufort), who was then residing in Avignon, had begun to hear some of the wild rumors circulating in and around Siena and had also received official reports from his legates, which had roused his suspicions regarding Catherine's integrity, though he had been favorably impressed with a letter she herself had written him. He finally decided that an investigation should take place, and this he entrusted to Fra Elia of Toulouse, Master General of the Dominican Order. Catherine was instructed to repair forthwith to Florence, where the Chapter, consisting of five hundred Dominicans, was to be convened in June of that year (1374) in the Chapel of Santa Maria Novella.

6

SHE DID not have to go alone. Her foster brother and confessor, Fra Tommaso, and his friend and hers, Fra Bartolommeo, had, of course been summoned also, not because they had to answer charges before the Council, but because they themselves were members of the Chapter and, hence, their presence in Florence was obligatory. And partly that Catherine might be shielded from the scandal which might arise if she went unaccompanied by any member of her own sex, and partly because they loved her and did not wish to be parted from her in her hour of trial, three of her fellow Mantellate went, too: Alessia Saracini, a beautiful young widow of noble birth, whose great family palazzo faced the Campo; Francesca Gori, an older widow, who came of plainer people and who had two or three sons in the Dominican Order; and Catherine's favorite sister-in-law, Lisa, who was very generally known by her maiden name of Colombini, instead of her married name of Benincasa, possibly because this emphasized her close relationship with the Blessed Giovanni Colombini, a wealthy merchant who had renounced the world, given all his goods to the poor and founded the Order of the Gesuati.[17]

Lisa had an additional reason for going: her husband, Bartolommeo Benincasa, who had once held a position of great importance in the Sienese government, was one of the two brothers who had fled for their lives to Florence after the revolutionary uprising of 1470; the moment had at last come when she could safely rejoin him.[18]

Dominican Brothers, unlike Franciscan Friars, were very generally provided with donkeys or mules for their journeys, and Alessia's comfortable circumstances would have assured her of a mount whenever she wished or needed one. But it is unlikely that the group of six would have had more than three among them and they probably took turns in riding. However, they were all good walkers, provided with stout staffs, who thought nothing of covering twenty miles or more in a day; so they may well have made the fifty-mile journey to Florence in three days, or even two; and there were no lack of convents and monasteries along the way where they would have been more than welcome to pause for a meal or spend the night. Aside from their natural anxiety—greater on the part of her friends than on Catherine's—as to how she would endure the ordeal she was facing, they enjoyed the trip, the longest that any of the young women had ever taken. Almost every time of year is beautiful in Tuscany; in late May there is something almost ethereally lovely about the landscape.

Bartolommeo and Stefano Benincasa were now safely, if unpretentiously, settled in Florence, and the family reunion, which permitted Catherine to see both her erring brothers for the first time in four years, and Lisa to join her husband, must have been a very happy one. The brothers' house formed a logical headquarters for all the travelers. Their arrival in Florence had been timed with a view toward permitting them to get settled and oriented before Catherine was called to the Chapter House. With her usual capacity for making friends, she quickly acquired three: Niccolo Soderini and Francesco and Agnese Pippino who were to remain steadfast in their admiration and affection for her as long as she lived. It was also characteristic that these newfound friends belonged to quite different walks of life, since she was equally at home with all sorts and conditions of men. Niccolo Soderini was an important member of the Signoria—the legislative body which governed Florence. He promptly invited Catherine and her companions to accept the lavish hospitality of his great palazzo facing the River Arno, where he habitually entertained large numbers of distinguished guests; he and they were eager to discuss matters of public interest with her. Francesco Pippino was a tailor, who lived with his wife Agnese in a small house near the corn market; with equal promptness, he assured Catherine that this would always be at her disposal for quiet family visiting or as an informal meeting place where their familiars, who had heard about her from them, could come to receive the benefit of her spiritual guidance.

The extreme cordiality of her reception by Soderini and his fellow legislators, and the respectful admiration of the Pippinos and their intimate friends, may well have come as a surprise to Catherine's brothers and fellow Mantellate and even to the two Sienese Dominicans. It was, of course, well known to them all that she had written the Holy Father, the papal legate, the Duke of Milan and other important personages. Copies of these letters were in the dossier which Fra Tommaso had brought with him for review by the Council, since the charge that Catherine had begun to take an actively unbecoming interest in political affairs was one of those which had been lodged against her and it had to be answered; the question as how best to do this must often have been discussed, gravely, in the little group. Catherine was still a prophet without honor in her own country; that she should have taken the initiative in writing such letters was adjudged presumptuous, even by her strongest supporters. That a Florentine as important as Soderini should have been in correspondence with her—as it was now obvious he had been —and that he considered this a privilege, was something else again. It is quite possible that, this, her companions did *not* know. At that stage, Catherine still dictated most of her letters to the friendly poet, Neri di Landoccio, who had acted as her secretary almost from the beginning of their acquaintance. It was only later, when her correspondence became so voluminous he could not handle it alone, that Alessia and Francesca and, eventually, a second male secretary, Stefano Maconi, were pressed into service. If Catherine had felt she should tell her confessor that she and Soderini were in touch with each other, she would certainly have done so; but, considering her conviction that she did nothing without Divine Guidance, and her extreme diffidence, when it came to presenting anything that might seem complimentary to herself, perhaps she did not feel that way. Such a confession might well have implied that, far from believing she had been presumptuous, she thought she had a flair for politics.

Whatever the degree of their surprise, her companions were certainly impressed by her reception. So were the members of the Council, who were now rapidly assembling. Many of them had felt annoyed at the prospect of having more important matters set aside while they used up valuable time in questioning an unbalanced, hysterical and self-willed woman; many others were so downright antagonistic that they felt it would be almost impossible to deal with her too harshly. But this young Mantellata who had arrived in Florence, chaperoned by outstanding members of her own Order—one of them a wealthy patrician—and by two Dominicans of unimpeachable character, did not in the least resemble the mental picture these inimical clerics had formed of her. She was quiet, she was modest, she was unassuming; and yet there was something so gracious and appealing in her manner, so dignified and distinguished in her bearing that she attracted a great deal of favorable attention wherever she went and, apparently, she went everywhere. Niccolo Soderini seemed to have a very high regard for the soundness and scope of her political views, and the wit and wisdom with which she expressed these; since she was his protégée, she was moving in the best social circles. As for the proletariat, as personified by the Pippinos and their ilk, it was simply feeding out of her hand. Perhaps her case was more important than it had seemed.

The Master General of the Dominican Order, Elia of Toulouse, spent hours going over the material Fra Tommaso had brought with him and studying the charges one by one: excess or pretension of excess in fasting; association with men and women of all kinds, both day and night, and acceptance of homage from many of these—consequently, neglect of prayer and devotion; in short, a way of life unbecoming a Sister of Penance; more vaguely, hints of witchcraft and unchastity; more seriously, the claim of performing miracles; many minor charges. . . .

After his thorough perusal of these and other complaints, the Master General sent for Fra Tommaso and Fra Bartolommeo and spent a long period in conference with them. Perhaps they could explain to him, he said rather drily, why Siena was so divided in its opinions about their fellow citizen; according to some, she seemed a most objectionable character; according to others, she was little short of a saint. The two Brothers did their best for their friend, but were obliged to leave the Master General without knowing what his convictions were. Possibly he had not formed any. In any event, at the end of this conference, he sent for one of the leading members of the Chapter, a certain Fra Raimondo da Capua, and talked with him at length.

Fra Raimondo, born Raimondo della Vigna, was an aristocrat,

a scholar, a theologian and a skilled administrator. He was now a handsome man of middle age, widely experienced, singularly refined, truly spiritual. At one time, he had been prior of the great Monastery of Santa Maria sopra Minerva in Rome; but the Master General had sent him from there to act as Chaplain of the Dominican Convent at Montepulciano, where he had dealt most effectively with several difficult situations and, meanwhile, had written a biography of the Blessed Agnes of Montepulciano, a Dominican nun for whom Catherine had great veneration and who was later canonized. Considering the variety of his attainments, it is not surprising that the Master General regarded his opinions as valuable; what is more surprising is the fact that Fra Elia had so quickly come to the conclusion that Catherine's case was sufficiently important to justify careful analysis and that he must not attempt to judge its merits alone, but must have expert advice on it. Fra Raimondo had never met Catherine Benincasa, he told the Master General, but he had heard a great deal about her and, though reports had been conflicting, he was inclined to think well of her; he would be glad of the opportunity to meet her. The opportunity, whether by accident or by design, very soon arose; their mutual understanding and sympathy were almost immediate.

Fra Raimondo was not the only cleric whom the Master General decided to consult regarding Catherine. Another was Don Giovanni delle Celle, a Vallombrosan monk, who had not wished to leave his lofty, mountainside retreat, at some distance from Florence. He had found peace there after storm; and sorcery, on which he had once been considered an authority, had ceased to be a welcome subject as far as he was concerned. He delayed coming to Florence as long as he could without actually flouting his superior's orders. But once he had met Catherine, it did not take him long to form his conclusions and make his report: she was anything but a witch; she was just the opposite. He begged to be allowed to return to the peaceful seclusion of the wooded hills where his monastery was located.

The Council, meanwhile, was nearing the end of its sessions. For several weeks it had been holding its meetings in the magnificent Chapter House of Santa Maria Novella, which adjoined the church by that name and was reached through a Romanesque cloister which later became celebrated as the Green Cloister, because of the *terra verde* (green earth) used for the beautiful biblical scenes painted in monochrome on its walls.[19] These were still unadorned in 1374; but the paintings, covering not only the walls but the ceiling, in the Chapter House itself had recently been completed and a splendid sight they were—superb in form and color, impressive in their historical delineation, inspiring in their allegorical aspects. Here in all their glory were St. Thomas Aquinas, St. Peter the Martyr, the Crucified Christ, the Church Militant and Triumphant. Here were Moses with the Tables, David with his zither, Solomon with the Book of Proverbs, the Evangelists with the Four Gospels, Peter with his barque. Here in solemn ranks were the figures representing the religious and liberal arts. Here was the Pope with a great group belonging to the religious state and the Emperor, with an equally great group, belonging to the lay state; and at the feet of these two supreme rulers, one spiritual and one temporal, were a flock of sheep, symbolical of humanity, guarded by black and white dogs, symbolical of the Dominicans, who were often called *Domini canes* (the hounds of God). And these trusty creatures not only guarded the lambs but, most realistically, devoured the ravening wolves that threatened them!

With these glowing walls for a mise en scène, the members of the Council, five hundred strong, were seated in tiers on either side of the Master General, who was enthroned, facing the entrance, before the recessed altar. As soon as Catherine came in through the massive gates of wrought iron, flanked on either side by tall grilled windows, she was confronted by him. She returned his gaze, conscious that this was the most crucial moment of her life, but undaunted by its implications. She knew the nature of the charges against her, and she was aware that, if she could not refute them, or if one of the judges did not refute them in her behalf, she could not keep her status as a Sister of Penance, and she might immediately be deprived of the habit which she had fought so long to wear and of which she had tried so hard to be worthy. She would have to face investigation of her alleged miracles, thus shorn. Just as the outrageous accusation that she had "deceived herself to the extent of losing her virginity" had seemed to her the supreme insult, when she had been questioned by the Superior of the Mantellate, so she now must have felt if she were divested of the robe which was the symbol of her "chastity, poverty and obedience," she would find her ordeal cruel beyond all human powers of endurance.

But she had never depended wholly on human powers of endurance. She was facing the Master General, but she was also facing the altar. She stood quite still and prayed—prayed so fervently that she hardly heard the man who had risen to accuse her, and who was describing her with vehemence in the way that would have given the greatest satisfaction possible to her enemies.

He finished his diatribe and sat down. Another man rose and quietly refuted the accusations, one by one. Catherine went on praying, her spiritual communication with God no longer taking the form of petition, but of thanksgiving. However, the examination was still to come, in which any member of the Chapter could ask the most sarcastic or the most searching questions. She knew that some of these would be deliberately phrased to trap her, that her kind and eloquent defender had by no means convinced everyone of her complete integrity; she knew that other remarks would not really be questions at all, but out and out accusations. She would have to be as adroit in evading the traps as her inquisitors were in laying them. She would have to suppress such a cry of outrage as had come instinctively to her lips, when she had repeated, over and over again, "I am a virgin. Indeed, I am a virgin." Reserve, not impulsiveness, imperturbability, not agitation, were what would count with these men; above all, dignity, combined with fearlessness, the outward and visible signs of inward and spiritual grace.

The association with improper companions—the acceptance of homage from these—the insistence on union with the Savior—the alleged miracles—one by one the dangerous subjects were introduced, discussed, dismissed. At length, the questioning was over. Then came a long silence. The Master General broke it by asking Catherine if there were anything she wished to say on her own initiative.

"No, Father General."

"Then you may retire while the Chapter considers what action it will take."

She inclined her head which, until then, she had held so erect. She bowed first to him and, afterward, to the groups on either side of him. Then she turned and went out through the iron gates as quietly as she had come in.

When the gates had closed behind her, the Master General asked Fra Livio Donelli to speak for the prosecution. He begged to be excused; everyone present had heard the accused; there was nothing he could add to what she had said. Another Brother, Francesco Adimari, was asked to speak for the defense; he, too, asked to be excused from comment for much the same reason as Fra Livio. Both were released from the obligation of speaking, but since they did not wish to exercise their right to do so, the Master General asked Fra Raimondo da Capua, who at the request of the former had been much in Catherine's company, to make a brief report. Fra Raimondo made it in a single sentence: it was his conviction that there was no truth in the accusations.

It was inevitable, after such a report, that the Master General would make a pronouncement to the effect that, unless there were dissent, the accused, Sister Catherine Benincasa, should be acquitted. One aged Brother, Master Ludovico of Verona, rose to remind the Chapter that Catherine had antagonized a great many people and that perhaps, even if she were guiltless of the specific charges brought against her, she should in some way be restrained, lest she antagonize still more. His objections were overruled. Nevertheless, the Master General, before declaring the session to be ended, announced that it was impossible to take Master Ludovico's opinion lightly. It was evident that Sister Catherine, even if she were not restrained, needed more expert guidance than had hitherto been available to her. With this in mind, he was appointing Fra Raimondo da Capua Lector of St. Dominic's in Siena and Catherine's spiritual adviser.

It proved to be a most momentous decision.

7

THE JOURNEY back to Siena must have been very pleasant. The weather was warmer now, for this was the end of June; but the travelers could rest during the heat of noon, and take advantage of the long twilight hours to walk and ride during the cool of the evening. With no interruptions except of their own choosing and no fear of being overheard, they were able to talk freely with each other concerning matters both temporal and spiritual. After having lived four years in Florence, Bartolommeo Benincasa was in a position to speak about the political situation there from his viewpoint, which would necessarily have differed from both Niccolo Soderini's and Francesco Pippino's. Catherine must have listened to him with avid attention, whether or not she agreed with this viewpoint; she would have asked many questions and, before the trip was over, she would have known more than before about many pertinent problems. Her friends, both Florentine and Sienese, had already been impressed by her acquaintance with the rivalry between the Guelphs and Ghibellines,[20] the development of the Commune, the rise of the Ciompi,[21] the increase in both Major and Minor Arts, the flourishing condition of manufacturies and banks in Florence. As she talked with her brother, the acquaintance deepened into better and better understanding.

With Fra Raimondo, on the other hand, she would not only have delved deeper and deeper into theology and mysticism; she would have discussed the chaotic condition of Rome, with which his position as Prior at Santa Maria sopra Minerva would have made him all too familiar. With him she could speak candidly about her concern over the so-called "Babylonian exile" or captivity of the popes in Avignon, which had begun with Clement V; continued, with more show of a desire for prolongation, under his immediate successors, John XXII and Benedict XII; and was accepted unquestioningly by Clement VI and Innocent VI, who followed next. Innocent's successor, Urban V, had indeed returned briefly to Rome and all Italy had rejoiced; but he had lacked the stamina to face the problems and endure the hardships there; he had followed the path of least resistance and gone back to Avignon, where he soon died. Now Gregory XI blandly regarded his sojourn there as permanent. The mission of Catherine's friend, the painter, Andrea Vanni, who had gone as Ambassador to the Papal Court the previous year, had proved fruitless; Gregory had turned a deaf ear to Vanni's entreaties for re-establishment in Rome. This was a constant source of grief to her. So was the friction between papal legates and the legislators and peoples of the Tuscan republics; of the ruthlessness of the Duke of Milan and the depravity of the Queen of Naples. While they were walking or riding along, these pregnant conversations must have been mostly dialogues between Catherine and her brother or Catherine and her new confessor; but, as the group stopped in some shady olive grove to rest or eat a frugal meal, Fra Tommaso and Fra Bartolommeo would have joined in both types of discussion and, sometimes, Alessia, Lisa and Francesca would have done so, too; at other times they would have contented themselves by being listeners, always interested and often fascinated.

They approached Siena joyously. To all but Fra Raimondo it was a homecoming; to him it was the beginning of a new and challenging career. But, as they drew close to the city, they were conscious of a change in the atmosphere: a strange, sickish smell suddenly pervaded the soft, fresh air of evening; and, as they sniffed this, in distasteful surprise, a heavy cart, laden with sacks, came rattling out of the Porta Cammolia. The next instant they realized that its burden was dead bodies. With horrible and devastating suddenness, the plague had struck again.

For Francesca and Fra Tommaso the moment of realization was even more appalling than for the others. Francesca, then a happy young wife, had lost her husband; Fra Tommaso, a cherished child, both his parents in the last epidemic. Catherine, mercifully, could not remember it; she had been only a year old at the time it decimated Siena before. Doubtless this oblivion was also a palliative; but even if there had been nothing to prevent her from visualizing the horrors ahead, she could not have acted otherwise than exactly as she did: that is, in going straight to the Misericordia Hospital and calling on the others to follow her.

From that moment, she worked unceasingly, going from the Misericordia to the Scala and then back again, as she found, or feared she found, that the need for her in the one was even greater than the need in the other. Sometimes she was needed even more at home. Her elder sister Lisa, whose mental or physical state had, apparently, never been quite normal, died almost before she could be made happily aware of Catherine's return; and that other Lisa, Catherine's beloved sister-in-law, was tragically bereft. Bartolommeo Benincasa survived his happy homecoming by only a few days. Then several of their children died too, and not only theirs, but, in all, eight of Lapa's grandchildren—the little boys and girls for whom Catherine's affection was so strong that she had confessed "if it were not for the shame of it, I would like to spend the whole day playing with them and petting them." Now she buried them with her own hands, saying with supreme resignation, "These children at least, I shall never lose."

But the children's deaths did not mark the end of the family's bereavement: from Rome came the news that Stefano had died, too, making, in all, eleven deaths among the Benincasas, besides that of a faithful maid. Lapa and Lisa were overwhelmed; Catherine was not. She brought what order and comfort she could to the desolate household; then she went back to the Scala, back to the Misericordia, dodging the plunging horses attached to the rattling carts whose drivers shouted hoarsely, "Bring out your dead!" and stopping along the way to rescue from the streets those who had been suddenly stricken and left there to die. Francesca went with her; she was not needed at home any more, for all her sons had died. Alessia went too; she was already alone in the world; there was no one left for her to lose.

In the basement of the Scala there was a tiny room, where Catherine went once every other night, to snatch a little sleep.[22]

Aside from this, she took no rest at all and, as far as anyone could see, she took no time to eat. Each night she was at work, carrying her little lantern, to light her way, and a pomander to serve the double purpose of providing a refreshing scent in the fetid wards and guarding against further infection. More and more, her endurance seemed like a miracle to those who worked with her. And not only her endurance in combating the plague; her achievements in curing its victims.

There are many accounts of these miracles and, unlike some aspects of her story, these agree in all their main points and all are arresting and convincing. But since "all of this he saw, part of this he was," the most vivid, as well as the most authentic, is the one written by Fra Raimondo. No one who was not Catherine's contemporary could possibly tell the story as well. So here it is, or rather part of it, just as he wrote it:

"While I was serving God to the best of my poor abilities, day and night I visited the sick, often retiring for rest and recuperation to the hospital of S. Maria delle Misericordia, which I was especially glad to do as its rector and head at that time was a certain Matteo.[23] He was a man of praiseworthy life, highly esteemed by all, and he was very fond of Catherine in the spirit of charity. I loved him dearly, and still do, for the virtues that heaven had granted him. . . .

"One morning after attending Mass in the monastery I went out on my visits to the sick and called in at the 'Misericordia.' As I went in I found Matteo being carried from the church to his own room by the brothers and clerks, like one dead. He had lost his usual colour and also all his strength and power of speech, for when I asked him how he felt he was unable to reply. I was very upset and I turned to the people who were carrying this very dear friend of mine and asked them what had happened to him. The reply I got was, 'Last night, at about seven, while he was tending one of the sick, the plague attacked him in the groin and in a short time reduced him to the state in which you now see him.' Upon hearing this I felt very sad, and I followed the company to Matteo's bed, where, as soon as he lay down, he recovered his spirits and called me over, and, as usual, confessed his sins.

"Having given him absolution, I asked him how he felt and he said, 'I have such a pain in my groin that it feels as though my thigh is breaking, and a dreadful pain in my head, which seems to have been split into four different pieces.' After these words I felt his pulse and found he was suffering from a very high fever, whereupon I suggested to the people present that they should take a sample of his urine to a very good, conscientious doctor called Master Senso; and a little later I went off to see him myself.

"The doctor, having tested the sample, decided at once that my friend had caught the plague. . . .

" 'Don't you think it possible for medical science to find some sort of remedy?' I asked. 'Tonight,' replied the doctor, 'you can try purging his blood with cassia juice, but I have not much faith in it because the illness is so far advanced.' . . .

"In the meantime the holy virgin had heard that Matteo had been struck down by the plague. As she was very fond of him because of his virtues, she hastened to see him, fired by charity and as though angry with the plague itself, and even before she reached him she started shouting from a distance, 'Get up, Messer Matteo, get up, this is no time for lying in a soft bed!' At the words of this command the fever and the swelling in the groin and all the pain immediately disappeared, and Matteo felt as well as if he had never been ill at all. Nature had obeyed God through the mouth of the virgin, and at the sound of her voice his body had been restored to perfect health. Matteo got up as cheerful as a cricket, convinced that the power of God dwelt in the virgin, and went away rejoicing. . . .

"And now, to the glory of God and Catherine, let us pass on to the [other] miracles that I myself saw and heard.

"During the plague mentioned above, a certain hermit called Santi, a saint in name and a saint in deed, who had for a long time been leading an exemplary life of poverty in the city of Siena, fell a victim to it. The virgin learned of this and at once had him moved from his hermitage outside the city to the Misericordia, where she went to see him with her companions and ordered him to be given all the attention he required. Then, going up to him, she whispered softly into his ear, 'Have no fear; however ill you may be you won't die this time.' To us, when we kept asking her to pray for his recovery, she would not say a word; so that it seemed to us that she nevertheless felt certain that he was bound to die. This made us sadder than ever, for we felt united with Santi in his sufferings because of the friendship that bound us to him. . . .

"Santi told us later what the virgin had whispered into his ear, and how he had felt the strength of her power holding back his spirit when it was about to issue from his body. He told everyone that it was no natural power that had cured him but the Divine Power alone, and added that he regarded the miracle as a real, genuine resuscitation. The sanctity of his life and his natural prudence guaranteed that he was to be believed in everything he said. For nearly thirty-six years he had been living an absolutely blameless life as an anchorite and he was held in the greatest esteem by all who knew him. . . .

"So far I have been speaking of others; now it is time for me to speak of the miracles that Catherine did for me.

"The plague, as I have said, having broken out in Siena, I made a firm decision, encouraged by the virgin, to visit as many of the sick as I could and comfort and instruct them. This I did, with God's help, and according to the grace granted me.

"But I was almost alone in the big city, and many were the calls I had from the sick, so that I hardly had time to eat and sleep or even breathe.

"One night, after I had had my usual brief rest, I was about to get up to say lauds, when I felt a great pain in my groin. I longed for the daylight to come, so that I could go and see the virgin before it got any worse. In the meantime the inevitable fever and headache came down upon me, but I forced myself to finish saying lauds.

"As soon as it was light I went as best I could to the virgin's home; but for the moment it was a fruitless journey as she was not there. I decided to wait for her, but was obliged to lie down on a bed, urging the people in the house to send for her as quickly as they could; which they did.

"When she arrived, and saw the state I was in, realizing what the matter was she knelt down by the bed and, putting her hand on my forehead, began to pray silently. I saw her go into ecstasy as on other occasions and waited for something unusual to happen. . . .

"As soon as the virgin of the Lord had obtained complete grace for me from her Heavenly Bridegroom, knowing that I was cured she returned to her senses and ordered a convalescent's meal to be prepared for me. This was done, I took the food from her own holy hands, and then she advised me to take a little rest, which obediently and gratefully I did.

"When I got up, I found myself as well as if I had never been ill. Seeing that I was better, Catherine said, 'Go and work for the good of souls, and give thanks to the Highest for freeing you from this danger.' And so I returned to my accustomed labours, giving praise to the Lord for granting Catherine such power." [7]

There was, indeed, great strength in Catherine's power. It was obviously supernatural power, but it was not omnipotence. That is the attribute of God alone. He gave her this power and, perhaps in His wisdom, He limited it to the cases where humanity would best be served by the recovery of the victim. Matteo di Cenni di Fazio, the Rector of Misericordia, was, as Fra Raimondo is at pains to point out, "a man of praiseworthy life, highly esteemed by all," and he was in a position to do incalculable good. Santi, the hermit, "was in truth well named for he was truly a saint." Fra Raimondo, though he refers to his own abilities as poor, was a great spiritual force. Each in his own way was indispensable to Siena at the time, and probably this was likewise so in the other cases where supernatural power seems to have played a part, but about which we know less. Catherine certainly effected many apparent miracles. But she did not cure everyone whom she attempted to heal. Neither Fra Raimondo nor any other chronicler of this tragic period, in which one-third of Siena's population perished, makes any such claim; and when the worst was over, she herself collapsed and lay dangerously ill for weeks. She had, indeed, reached the end of her endurance. There were limits to that, too.

8

THE TEDIUM of Catherine's convalescence was relieved and her recovery advanced by a sojourn with a community of Dominican nuns at Montepulciano, a hill city, distinguished for the classical severity of its buildings and its plazas, loftily situated above a valley of great productiveness and serene beauty, about forty miles from Siena. Almost certainly the idea of visiting there was first suggested by Fra Raimondo, who, it will be recalled, had spent three years as the chaplain of these nuns, meanwhile writing a biography of their founder, Agnes of Montepulciano, who had died only thirty years before Catherine was born and who was already venerated as a saint, though she was not formally canonized until nearly three hundred years later (1726). She had founded a second convent at Proceno, about thirty-five miles south of Montepulciano, and many miracles were ascribed to her, both during her lifetime and after her death. Fra Raimondo's description of these miracles and the place where they occurred was so vivid that Catherine longed to "venerate St. Agnes' corpse" and undertook the journey as soon as she was strong enough. Fra Raimondo and her "other confessor"—presumably Fra Tommaso—"followed her to see what would happen, and to see whether the Lord would perform any miracle at this meeting between two such privileged brides of His." When the priests arrived at Montepulciano, the day after Catherine, they "found everyone talking about the miracle that had been performed through the merits of these two virgins by their Bridegroom.

"Catherine at once entered the convent buildings," Fra Raimondo tells us, "and, in the presence of nearly all the nuns, and the Sisters of Penance of St. Dominic who had come with her, went devoutly up to Agnes' body, knelt down at its feet, and began to lower her head devoutly to kiss them; but in the sight of all the people present, without injuring Catherine as she bent down, the lifeless body, without a word of a lie, raised one of its feet up to her; whereupon Catherine, humbling herself more than ever, bent over still further, and gradually the virgin Agnes' foot returned to its original position." [7]

Obviously, Fra Raimondo was not an eyewitness to this miracle, since he arrived at Montepulciano the day after Catherine; but it is equally obvious, from the way he describes it in his biography of her that he did not doubt for a minute it had taken place.[24]

Such a supernatural episode and the excitement which followed must have been agitating, rather than calming, in its effects on Catherine. But gradually the even tenor of life was resumed and did its healing work. The convent was situated just outside the gates of the city and thus removed from its turmoil. The outlook over the valley was so lovely that this in itself was soothing to the spirit; the chanting of the nuns and the ringing of their bells were the only sounds that broke the beneficent silence. Little by little, the all-enveloping quietude relieved the tension of weeks spent without respite from physical and mental strain. The air was fresh and pure and the soft breezes blew away the remembrance of stench and miasma.

Catherine was certainly very happy in the monastic calm at Montepulciano and very loath to leave it—in fact, when the so-called Reform Government [25] sent her a peremptory message, recalling her to her native city, she calmly replied that she still had several things to do at the convent and that she would return when it was more convenient for her. Not until the very end of the year did she find it so. Meanwhile, she grew steadily stronger.

It was during this peaceful period of convalescence that Catherine received her first invitation to visit Pisa. Apparently, it was actually written by the Governor himself, Ser Piero Gambacorti; and though the letter stated that it was being sent at the request of certain Religious in the city, among them no less a personage than the Archbishop, and this was no doubt true, the governor would not have dispatched it if he had not also felt a lively curiosity about this Sienese Mantellata, who had made such an impression in Florence, and a keen desire to meet her. It required a certain amount of courage to do so since "relations between Siena and Pisa were, to put it mildly, strained; the Knights of St. John from Pisa had occupied Talamone, the port of Siena on the Tyrrhenian Sea. And while Pisa was still on the Pope's side, the government of Siena had not yet decided which side they would join. Catherine's presence in Pisa would also help to antagonize Bernabò Visconti, [the wicked and powerful Duke of Milan] who was intriguing to get the republic over to his side." [13] Nevertheless, Gambacorti sent the letter.

Catherine declined the invitation and, though she did so courteously, she did not lose the opportunity of making some cogent comments on the duties and responsibilities of Christian rulers, which were not always as scrupulously observed as they might be, and the sad results when they were not. Without actually saying that Gambacorti was among the backsliders, the inference that she thought so was plain. She added that she feared there might be some "murmuring" in Siena if she went to Pisa, which was true enough, for the hard feelings between the two republics were by no means all on one side. But this was merely an excuse. Catherine was never unduly disturbed by murmuring or even threats, as she had just shown by her independent reply to the so-called Defenders of Siena. She gave the state of her health as another reason for hesitating to undertake a hard trip. Hesitation was not in character, either, and she usually found the strength to do whatever she wanted or considered it expedient to do. She closed the letter by saying she hoped she might come to Pisa some future time—and this, being interpreted, meant at a time when she and her best advisers considered it propitious. That time had not yet come.

It was not, however, long in arriving. The following February (1375) she was on her way, again accompanied by Fra Raimondo, Fra Tommaso and Fra Bartolommeo—this time by all three officially, for Pope Gregory XI, who had begun to take due notice of Catherine's activities, had given orders that there should always be this number of priests in her company, to hear the confessions which would result from her teaching and example. The number of Mantellate who accompanied her had also been augmented, in a way especially pleasing to Catherine: Lapa, her solitude unendurable, her pride humbled, had joined the Order. She could not bear to stay alone in an empty house that had once been teeming with children and grandchildren, apprentices and journeymen; if Catherine would not stay there, she was determined that she would not stay there, either. She still did not understand why this strange daughter of hers had chosen an existence of austere celibacy instead of a lusty marriage, still less why anyone who could live comfortably in a civilized place like Siena should go traipsing off to distant unfriendly cities like Florence and Pisa. But if that was the way it had to be, she intended to have a share in it and to be worthy of it. She had always been virtuous; now she would also be valiant. Even if she were moved by no strong spiritual urge, which seems unlikely, in joining forces with her daughter, she intended to do Catherine credit. She had her pride, too.

The travelers were given a royal welcome in Pisa. The Archbishop, the Governor and other dignitaries of Church and State joined in their official reception and they were led through the cheering crowds which lined the streets to the palazzo of the Buonconti, where they were to be installed and entertained.[26] In this aristocratic family there were three brothers—Gherardo, Tommaso and Francesco, all extremely devout, who had long since been Catherine's followers in spirit, and who had been among those who were most insistent that she should visit their city. Through them, she was immediately put in touch with all the Religious who were waiting with bated breath for cures and conversions. She did, indeed, effect many of these, though at least one of the latter was far from welcome in many of its aspects: the Governor's daughter Tora Gambacorti decided to enter a Dominican Convent,[27] instead of making a brilliant marriage, which, besides being highly suitable from other viewpoints, would have had great political advantages for her father. It is hardly surprising that he was annoyed.

Inevitably, there were also other cases where her prayers met with no visible response and where her powers proved limited. These cases served to intensify the critical or incredulous attitude toward her that still prevailed in many quarters. Her abstention from almost all forms of food, as usual, furnished the basis for a great deal of petty gossip. Several self-important scholars, failing to learn a lesson from others elsewhere who had vainly tried a similar experiment, tried to trip her with theological questions. A minor poet took it upon himself to warn her, in verse, that she should be careful not to attach overmuch importance to the attentions which were being showered upon her, lest her vainglory should add to the downfall of others. Even Fra Raimondo rebuked her for allowing her disciples to kiss her hand and show her other marks of deference. As might be expected, she confounded the scholars, thanked the poet for his concern, which she said she was sure must be an indication of affection, and asked Fra Raimondo how homage could possibly influence her since she herself was all too fully aware of her unworthiness to receive it. In these and in every other instance of which we have a record, she disarmed her critics.

In a worldly sense, the Buonconti brothers were her sponsors in much the same way that Niccolo Soderini had been in Florence. As their house guest, she met the elite of the city on equal terms; and in her association with them, though the political questions were largely predominant, the religious aspects of these were also treated as being of the utmost importance. Bernabò Visconti was now openly seeking an alliance with the Tuscan Republics; if he were successful in obtaining this, the temporal power of the Pope would be seriously jeopardized. Yet it was by no means certain that the papal legates who were, of course, the official representatives of His Holiness and who were Frenchmen—as were all the Popes but one (Innocent VI) who had reigned since the beginning of the "Babylonian exile"—might not effect the compromise with the Duke. Catherine was convinced, as were many others, that only the departure from Avignon of Gregory XI and his return to Rome could save the situation. When she was not actually in conference with the leaders of the Pisan government, trying to find ways of strengthening its bonds with the Papacy, she was much of the time in correspondence with officials in other parts of Tuscany whom she thought might influence Gregory XI to end his "Babylonian exile." She knew that one of his pet projects had been a crusade against the infidel, yet, with characteristic inertia, he had done little or nothing to advance this. Catherine felt sure that if a number of independent rulers in northern Italy could convince him that they would unite in this common cause, it would have a great bearing on his willingness to return to Rome and direct them. That she herself was heart and soul in favor of such a crusade goes without saying; but the further fact she hoped it might be a two-edged sword strengthened the force of her appeal.

She lived most of the time in a crowd and had adjusted herself, with increasing aptitude, to this tumultuous form of existence. But her essential yearning for tranquillity had never been wholly suppressed and it was partly this which caused her to slip into the little church of Santa Cristina, which adjoined the Palazzo Buonconti, instead of going to the cathedral on Laetare Sunday. At Santa Cristina, the number of worshipers was automatically restricted by its lack of space; and because it also lacked architectural distinction, outstanding equipment and elaborate ornamentation, it failed to attract any except the truly devout, whereas the magnificent proportions of the cathedral, the tremendous volume of its organ and the splendor of its services made it the goal of many to whom the Mass itself had only limited spiritual appeal. Moreover, at Catherine's request, Fra Raimondo was to be the celebrant at Santa Cristina on this occasion which marks the fourth Sunday of Lent with a joyous note, instead of the somber ones that prevail through the rest of the penitential season. It meant more to her to receive Communion from his hands than to assist at a Pontifical High Mass.

When she approached the altar rail with her fellow Mantellate, there was nothing to indicate the imminence of anything exceptional, much less supernatural, nor did anyone suspect such an occurrence when Catherine did not leave with the others; it was not unusual for her to go into raptures at such times. "We were waiting for her to come back to herself," Fra Raimondo says, with his usual graphic simplicity, "so as to receive some kind of spiritual encouragement from her, as we often did on these occasions, when to our surprise we saw her little body, which had been lying prostrate, gradually rise up until it was upright on its knees, her arms and hands stretched themselves out, and light beamed from her face; she remained in this position for a long time, perfectly stiff, with her eyes closed, and then we saw her suddenly fall, as though mortally wounded. A little later, her soul recovered its senses." [7]

The accounts of what happened next, like the accounts of Catherine's miraculous ministrations during the plague, are moving in the extreme and must seem convincing to almost anyone except the most obdurate unbeliever. But again it is Fra Raimondo's chronicle which seems to me the most moving and convincing of all. "Then [after her soul had recovered its senses] the virgin sent for me and said quietly, 'You must know, Father, that by the mercy of the Lord Jesus I now bear in my body His stigmata.' I replied that while I had been watching the movements of her body when she was in ecstasy I had suspected something of the sort; I asked her how the Lord had done all this. She said, 'I saw the Lord fixed to the cross coming towards me in a great light, and such was the impulse of my soul to go and meet its Creator that it forced the body to rise up. Then from the scars of His most sacred wounds I saw five rays of blood coming down towards me, to my hands, my feet and my heart. Realizing what was to happen, I exclaimed, "O Lord God, I beg you—do not let these scars show on the outside of my body!" As I said this, before the rays reached me their colour changed from blood red to the colour of light, and in the form of pure light they arrived at the five points of my body, hands, feet and heart.' 'So then,' I said, 'no ray reached your right side?' 'No,' she replied, 'it came straight to my left side, over my heart; because that line of light from Jesus's right side struck me directly, not aslant.' 'Do you feel any pain at these points now?' I asked. She heaved a great sigh, and answered, 'I feel such pain at those five points, especially in my heart, that if the Lord does not perform another miracle I do not see how I can possibly go on, and within a few days I shall be dead.'

"While she was saying these things, and I was rather sadly pondering upon them, I was trying to see if I could discover any signs of this great pain. She finished telling me what she wanted me to know and then we came out of the chapel and went back to the house where we were being put up. When we got there, the virgin had no sooner stepped into the room she had been given when her heart gave out and she fell senseless. We were all called, and gathered round her, and as the occurrence seemed more serious than usual we all started weeping, afraid that we were going to lose her whom we loved in the Lord." [7]

Their fears were not without foundation; for nearly a week, Catherine was gravely ill. But Fra Raimondo summoned her spiritual sons and daughters and begged them "to unite with him in a joint prayer to the Lord that He would deign to leave us our mother and teacher for a little while longer, so that, weak and sickly as we were, not yet strengthened by heaven in the holy virtues, we might not be left orphaned amongst the dangers of the world. All, men and women, promised with one heart and one voice to do this." [7]

Their prayers were answered. On the following Sunday, Catherine again received Holy Communion from the hands of Fra Raimondo "and whereas on the preceding Sunday her body had been as though blighted while she was in ecstasy, on this day the ecstasy she fell into seemed to give it more life than ever." [28]

Though Catherine's prayer that the stigmata should not be visible during her lifetime was apparently granted, numerous witnesses testified that they saw it after her death and it is always shown in paintings of her that represent her later than 1374. While jealousy seems a strange characteristic to attribute to the feeling that members of one religious Order have for members of another, there was a widespread rumor that Franciscans claimed their Saint, Francis of Assisi, was the only one who had been honored by this outward and visible sign of the Crucified Christ's favor.

It is interesting to note that the supplementary figures in Sodoma's famous painting of the saint's reception of the stigmata are generally accepted as faithful portraits of her lifelong friends, Alessia Saracini and Francesca Gori, who were, of course, with her when the miracle took place.

9

"Her body seemed to have more life than ever."

DESPITE the intensity of her political and spiritual activities in Pisa, Catherine found the time and strength to visit its surroundings. In the picturesque village of Calci, six miles from the city—practically at its outskirts, from the viewpoint of such indefatigable walkers as Catherine and her companions—was a beautiful little church, a gem of eleventh-century architecture; and in the Valle Graziosa just beyond was a famous Carthusian Monastery; both made logical objectives for an afternoon's pilgrimage, and Catherine delighted in making it frequently. Less easy of access was the barren Island of Gorgona, inhabited largely by poor fishermen, some thirty miles out at sea; but the inconveniences connected with the trip left Catherine quite undaunted when the Prior, Bartolommeo di Ravenna, who was characterized by Fra Raimondo as "a devout and wonderfully wise Carthusian," invited her to visit his monastery there. After a courteous show of hesitation, she not only accepted the invitation, but persuaded quite a group of her followers to accompany her; and, as she had never been on the ocean before, and probably very seldom on a broad river leading to it, no doubt she greatly enjoyed the novel experience. Again, Fra Raimondo's account of the invitation and the visit, like his account of the miracles performed during the plague and the reception of the stigmata, seems to me of such vitality and importance that it should be quoted.

"This Bartolommeo had grown very fond of the holy virgin because of her marvellous knowledge and wonderful deeds, and he had implored her again and again to set foot on the island at least once to meet his monks. . . .

"One day the holy virgin decided to make the journey, and with her went almost a score of men and women. The night we arrived, the prior lodged Catherine and her women companions in a house about a mile from the monastery, and us men he entertained in the monastery itself.

"Early the following morning he took all the monks to see her, and entreated her to say a few words of instruction to them. At first she declined, saying that she was an ignorant and incapable woman, adding that it would be more fitting for her to hear the word of God from them instead. In the end, however, persuaded by their reiterated requests, she began to speak, saying what the Holy Spirit suggested to her . . . in such an orderly fashion that she filled me and all the others with amazement.

"When her speech ended, the Prior turned to me admiringly and said, 'Dearest Fra Raimondo, you know that it is one of our rules that I am the only person who hears these monks' confessions, so that I know whether they are advancing in virtue or not. Well, I tell you, if the holy virgin had been their confessor and not I, she could not have spoken better or more appropriately to every single one of them, for she left out nothing essential and yet wasted no time over irrelevancies. From this I can see, quite seriously, that she is full of the spirit of prophecy and that the Holy Spirit speaks in her.' " [7]

Strangely enough, considering the wealth of detail which accompanies most of his narratives, Fra Raimondo makes no mention of two episodes which occurred toward the close of this memorable visit. While it was apparently true that Catherine could not "have spoken better or more appropriately" in every case, when she was addressing the monks, there was one of these in particular whom her message touched so profoundly that he was saved from mortal sin. He had been going through a period of deep discouragement and depression and had been on the point not only of deserting the cloister, but of committing suicide. However, he "was so moved by Catherine's words that he returned to the complete ideal of Chartreuse and again found complete joy in the companionship of his brethren." [11]

Among Catherine's saddest memories must always have been that of Fra Pietro di Mastro Lando, the young friar, unrestrained by his priestly calling and by the veneration with which he should have regarded her, who had committed suicide because of his hopeless passion for her. Now that another man, vowed to the service of Christ, had been saved from breaking his vows and from self-destruction because of her, some of the shame and sting must have been taken from that memory.

That the Prior whole-heartedly meant every word he had said, regarding the blessing of her visit, became even more obvious than before when the moment of farewell arrived: he asked Catherine to take off her cape and leave it to be treasured at the monastery. If he did not actually use the words "as a relic," the inference was plain. Among her memories must have been another, less tragic than that of Fra Pietro's suicide, yet not without its own poignancy. When the great Rector of the Misericordia Hospital, Matteo di Cenni di Fazio, had rebuked her for giving her cloak to a beggar, he had called her attention to the fact that this was part of her habit, the insignia of her vows; and the local gossips had not hesitated to go further: they had reminded her that, in Siena, a woman who went abroad uncloaked was proclaiming herself a prostitute. Now she must have realized that the Prior considered she was no longer so dependent on the insignia of her calling that she could not safely be without it until another cloak could be found for her; her very life made her mission self evident; and as far as bringing the reproach of unchastity upon herself, such an idea was now so fantastic that it never would have occurred to anyone. When Catherine unfastened her cloak and handed it to the Prior, joy surely welled up in her heart.

During the periods when she did not leave Pisa at all, Catherine became more and more involved in correspondence. Alessia and Francesca had certainly been pressed into service by this time, and it is probable that the pleasant young poet, Neri di Landoccio, had now joined them in Pisa. As he had been Catherine's first secretary, this would have been entirely logical; and it may have been imperative as well, for Catherine thought nothing of dictating three or four letters at once, all on burning questions; the two Mantellate could hardly have kept up with her speed and her zeal. She wrote to

Pierre d'Estaing, Cardinal Bishop of Ostia and papal legate who, the year before (1374), "had descended on Italy at the head of mercenary troops." She wrote to Gerald DuPuy, Abbot of Marmantiers and the Pope's nephew, who had "roamed around the Peninsula setting the fire of discord among the powerful adversaries of the Holy See." She wrote to Guillaume de Noellet, Cardinal of St. Angelo, "a fitting successor to DuPuy who, descending again upon Italy, devoted himself anew to snares and traps, conspiracies and crimes, factions and internecine struggles, all intensified by simony and corruption of priests and monks. . . . On his part the ambitious and villainous Bernabò Visconti threw all his resources into the battle against the papal party. . . . Catherine, though a fragile creature, did not become discouraged and was not content with weeping; she reacted energetically. She would sue the forces of the Holy Spirit against the onslaught of evil spirits. An atmosphere of terror hung over Tuscany and, indeed, over all Italy; but Catherine feared neither the poison nor the dagger of Bernabò Visconti." [11] She wrote to him, too.

This violent man had actually forced the legates who arrived in Milan with a Bull of Excommunication to eat it—parchment, seal, silk cords and all—meanwhile shouting obscene insults at them. His terrible temper was such that, even without provocation, he often vented his wrath on innocent bystanders; and if anyone broke his hunting laws, which included provisions for five thousand hounds quartered among his down-trodden subjects and even in monasteries, the offender was tortured and often murdered. But there was no denying that, besides having incalculable strength as a warlord, Bernabò had amazing shrewdness as a politician and he schemed to capitalize on the antagonism of the Pope's Italian subjects against the French legates. If that antagonism could be fanned into open rebellion, he might well be the gainer; and he believed there were circuitous means of bringing this about. In short, he decided to play both ends against the middle; and he recognized the fact that Catherine's opinions were beginning to carry weight and that her influence with the people had great potential value. Far from threatening her with dagger and poison, he answered her letter promptly and respectfully. He even asked her prayers for Divine Guidance; and to his reply he attached a cordial message from his wife, inviting Catherine to visit them in Milan. Like Gambacorti, he was genuinely curious to see this phenomenon Siena had produced and, if possible, to profit by it.

In the light of subsequent events, it seems unfortunate that, though Catherine agreed to accept this invitation, she did not do so at once. It is, of course, true that there are no ifs in history. Nevertheless, it is interesting to speculate as to whether her powers of persuasion, which were later to save Florence from complete anarchy and impel an errant pope to resume his rightful throne, might not have prevailed to prevent a catastrophe which was already impending. In early June a courier arrived in Pisa from de Noellet, one of the papal legates who, only a short time before had been forced by Visconti to swallow the Bull of Excommunication which he himself had delivered. Now this treacherous Frenchman had debased himself by effecting a truce in Bologna with this same evil duke.

The news came like a bolt from the blue. Being interpreted, it meant that a new league threatened the freedom of the Tuscan Republics and that their small states might at any moment be overrun by the joint armies of the Pope and the Duke. It was now too late for Catherine to attempt a personal appeal to Visconti; and the fact that she had not done so sooner must be set down as one of her few recorded mistakes. But she did her best to make up for her error and though, like most compensations, this was something which did not quite compensate, it was certainly a step in the right direction. She decided to appeal to someone else in behalf of Pisa and, after due consideration, came to the conclusion that the person whom she could most effectively approach would be the notorious soldier of fortune, Sir John Hawkwood.

The choice was an amazing one, but Catherine was an amazing person. So, for that matter, was Sir John Hawkwood, whom the Italians called Giovanni Acuto. He headed a band of mercenaries, known as the White Company, who sold their services to the highest bidder and, very recently, this had been the Pope! Now that peace was declared between Gregory and Visconti, Hawkwood and his army were out of a job, for it was the Duke whom they had been hired to fight! The legate, with what seems like surprisingly little tact in an official supposedly skilled in diplomacy, at one and the same time forbade all export of corn from the Papal States and demanded sixty thousand guilders from Florence to free himself from his obligations to Hawkwood. The outraged Florentines decided, not unnaturally, that, rather than do this, they would hire Hawkwood themselves if they could meet his price. While awaiting an answer as to the value they put on his services, Hawkwood and his army encamped near Pisa, which was offering him thirty thousand guilders for its defense. It was here that Catherine approached him, on this occasion, without loss of time.

She wished to deliver her appeal in person, but apparently was forbidden by the Archbishop to venture into the camp; and when she attempted to argue with him, he invoked her vow of obedience, and she had no choice but to bow to his orders. So, instead of going herself, she sent Fra Raimondo, who probably undertook the mission with some misgivings. He could not be blamed if he thought there were some lengths to which even Catherine should not go in tempting Providence. However, neither he nor his alter ego, Fra Bartolommeo, was threatened or abused when they reached the camp of the White Company. They were led, with comparatively little delay, to Hawkwood's tent. It cannot be said that he received them with the courtesy due their cloth. He had been expecting a communication from the governor, bettering the offer of thirty thousand guilders for the defense of Pisa and Hawkwood thought that Gambacorti might have sent a more imposing delegation than two simple friars. However, his manner changed when he learned who *had* sent them; he, too, had heard a great deal about Sister Catherine Benincasa and what he had heard aroused his reluctant admiration. He accepted her letter and ordered it read to him.

It was certainly an extraordinary document. In the name of Christ Crucified and gentle Mary, she addressed Hawkwood and his fellow brigands as her beloved brothers in Christ and asked them to consider the terrible pain and trouble they had suffered in the service of the devil. She advised them to change their ways and serve the Cross; she expressed herself as surprised that Hawkwood was making war in Italy, since such a war was a poor preparation for a crusade against the infidel and she had heard of his promise to fight and, if necessary, to die in a crusade. Since this was the case, surely he and his companions should prepare themselves for such a mission by showing themselves true and noble knights. "Is it not a horrible thing," she asked, "that we who are Christians and are one, because we are the limbs of the body of Holy Church, should attack each other?" She closed by begging him, in the name of Jesus Christ, to fight no longer against Christians but against their common enemies and signed herself "Catherine, the useless servant."

The response to this letter was as extraordinary as the missive itself. The two friars, anxiously awaiting the terrible captain's reaction to it, must almost inevitably have expected and feared derision, if not actual ribaldry. Nothing of the sort happened. Hawkwood asked whether or not Pisa was about to join the rebels against the Pope and was told that the Governor and the Archbishop had both called on Catherine to help keep the city loyal; Fra Raimondo thought she would succeed. Hawkwood nodded reflectively and asked if there were any chance that the offer of thirty thousand guilders might be improved. Regretfully, Fra Raimondo was obliged to confess that there seemed to be little hope of that; the city was almost at the end of its resources. Hawkwood had already wrung a hundred more than that from Florence and expected the next bid to be higher. However . . . it was true that he had once promised to join the crusade and that he was still willing to do so, if and when definite plans for it were made. Meanwhile, he would accept the thirty thousand guilders as the price for which he would defend Pisa against its enemies, because the message had come to him from Catherine Benincasa. She was a woman of courage. He would seal both bargains by taking Holy Communion.

Hawkwood's defense offered nothing more than a breathing space, but it did offer that. Catherine had been away from Siena for a long while. She felt justified in telling her kind and grateful hosts that she felt the time had come when she should go home. They grieved at her departure, but they wished her Godspeed.

10

AGAIN, A journey offered a welcome opportunity for fruitful discussion and, again, the spring of the year proved a delightful time for traveling. The distance between Pisa and Siena was much greater than between Florence and Siena and a little over a week was required to cover so much ground; but it was time pleasantly and profitably spent, with home as its destination. Catherine was very glad to be back in Siena. She had enjoyed Pisa, as she had enjoyed Florence, but this was her own city, the one where she believed she belonged. It had not occurred to her that she was to spend a large part of her remaining years away from it. She had been summoned to Florence to answer a grave charge against her character; she had done so successfully, and she had no reason to believe that others of similar nature would be lodged, or that there would be any other reason why she should go there. The invitation to Pisa had been a compliment which she appreciated and of which she had tried to be worthy; but she had no reason to believe that this would be renewed, either. She settled down to her usually quiet and orderly routine: so much time for discipline and devotions; so much time for service in hospitals and other works of charity; so much time for her ever-increasing circle of friends and disciples.

There were, of course, interruptions to this schedule. One of these took a very pleasing form. A singularly successful financier by the name of Nanni di Vanni Savini was persuaded by the hermit

William Flete, with whom Catherine had hastened to renew her friendship as soon as it was practical for her to visit Lecceto, that he was making a great mistake in not cultivating the acquaintance of such a remarkable woman. Messer Nanni scoffed at the idea, but not for long; like many another man before and after, he was deeply impressed with her from the very first; and, as a token of his regard, he asked Fra Raimondo to present her, in his behalf, with the title deed to Belcaro, a valuable property not far from Lecceto, which comprised many hectares of fertile land and was dominated by a superbly located castello, somewhat run down, but essentially sound and well built. Catherine hesitated to accept so considerable a gift; but Fra Raimondo was not slow in pointing out that the castello could be readily adapted to serve as a much-needed convent for Dominican nuns; since this was the case, Catherine had no right to decline the offer. Happily, she began making plans for the creation of a Community which she proposed to call Santa Maria degli Angeli.

The next interruption to her routine took a very different and very tragic form; another friar, Tommaso Caffarini,[29] brought her terrible news: Niccolo di Tuldo, an attractive young man of good family, who had come to Siena from Perugia, had been arrested as a spy and all his efforts to establish his innocence had been unavailing. In his rage at his failure to do so, he had become so violent that anyone who approached him did so with peril. He not only refused the consolations of religion, he attacked any priest who tried to minister to him, shouting obscenities and blasphemies as he did so. He was condemned to die by decapitation the following morning and. . . .

"I will go to him at once," Catherine said firmly.

Fra Tommaso Caffarini was aghast. Probably Fra Raimondo could have argued with her more successfully than he could, he told himself desperately; but Fra Raimondo was in Pisa, where Catherine had persuaded him to go as her representative, because the people there were all clamoring for her return and she did not feel it wise to leave Siena again so soon. The Archbishop of Siena might well have ordered her, under obedience, not to pursue such a wild course, as the Archbishop of Pisa had done when she was determined to visit the tent of Sir John Hawkwood; but she did not risk such a prohibition. Keeping clear of the episcopal palace, she went straight to the Palazzo Pubblico, where she confronted Ser Alberto Varuzzi, one of the Defenders who had pronounced the death sentence; and though she did not succeed in changing the verdict or securing a stay of execution, she did persuade the magistrate that, if the accused died without being given another chance to confess, Varuzzi would be responsible for the sins on the soul of the condemned. Having got so far, she wrung from him an admission that Tuldo should have this chance; and, as far as she was concerned, permission to find out if there were anything she could do in the way of preparing the mutinous man to meet his death with more dignity, if not with more resignation. Varuzzi even accepted her stipulation that she should see the prisoner alone. Probably he believed that, once admitted to the prisoner's presence, she would be only too glad to retreat, but the magistrate was mistaken. She went calmly down the damp stone steps leading to the dungeons while the guard warned her against the prisoner: the man's hands and feet were chained and he was also chained to the wall; nevertheless, he could move about a little and he could, and did, strike out violently; she must stay well beyond his reach and shout for help if he tried to attack her. The guard continued to caution her as they went along a dim corridor, where the oppressive silence was broken only by his voice and by the rattle of keys as a keeper came lumbering forward to meet them. The guard rapped out an order which he was obliged to repeat before the incredulous keeper could believe his ears and grope for the right key in the bunch he was carrying. It grated as it turned in the massive lock. Then the door opened and Catherine stepped inside the cell.

This was even darker than the corridor. There, an oil lamp had at least given enough light to make the way passable without danger of falling; here, there was only a candle stub flickering in its socket. The shadows engulfed the huddled figure of the prisoner and he did not raise his head at the sound of the closing door. It was not until Catherine spoke to him that he looked up with a start to see what seemed to be an apparition. Catherine's face was almost as white as her robes, and her form was so fragile as to give an impression of ethereality. Only her voice suggested the presence of a human being and, even so, the words she spoke did not sound real. Why should a woman—if this actually were a woman and not a supernal being—come to solace and support him in his extremity? There must be cruel mockery of some sort at work. But as he shouted at her, ordering her to leave him, denouncing the treachery of his friends and railing against his undeserved fate at the hands of men and his abandonment by God, and she did not move or show any signs of taking offence or feeling fear because of his abusiveness and his blasphemy, his violence gradually subsided. In spite of himself, he began to find her presence welcome, her speech soothing and heartening. Catherine had never been afraid of anything in her life; but she had been able to understand that, though Tuldo's sense of injustice and desertion were partly responsible for his fury, the most powerful underlying reason for it was fear. He had none of the daring and dauntlessness of his times; he shuddered and cowered at the very thought of facing a terrible death and Catherine saw that she must try to give him courage to meet the ordeal before him as became a brave man. She chose her words carefully and Tuldo listened with increasing attention and increasing confidence. His sense of harmony with her did not come instantaneously, as it had with Francesco di Vanni, who had recognized their mutual understanding and sympathy the minute their eyes met; nevertheless, it came with surprising swiftness, considering the horrible circumstances under which she came to him. Falteringly, he consented to see the priest she wanted to summon and take Communion the following morning. But only—only—if she would go to Mass with him, if she would stay by him until the end. He could not persevere alone; it was from her that he must draw strength.

As always, she had it and to spare. She left him in the compassionate care of Fra Tommaso Caffarini to make his peace with God. But before daylight she was back again, to walk with him as he went, under heavy guard, to the prison chapel and to kneel beside him at the Communion rail. And when the cart came to take him to the place of execution, outside the city gates, she told him she would be there first, waiting for him.

This time, we do not have to turn even to so reliable a witness as Fra Raimondo for the rest of our story. We have it from Catherine herself in her own words:

"Niccolo arrived at the place of execution like a gentle lamb, and seeing me there awaiting him he began to smile. He asked me to make the sign of the Cross over him, and having done so I said to him, 'Hie thee upward to the marriage feast, sweet brother mine, soon thou wilt enter into life everlasting.' He knelt down with great meekness and being over him I spoke to him of the Blood of the Lamb. The only words he utttered were 'Jesus' and 'Catherine' and even as he said these words, I received his head in my hands, and fixing my mind on the goodness of God, I said 'I am willing.' " [2]

11

WHEN THE Governor of a sovereign state invited her to Pisa and the Prior of a Carthusian monastery besought her to visit Gorgona, Catherine could, to a certain degree, consult her own convenience and, meanwhile, show a proper amount of courteous hesitancy. When the Pope ordered her to Lucca, she had no choice but to go there immediately; and such an order, totally unexpected, was not long in forthcoming. Her stay at home, which she had expected would be indefinite, had lasted only a few months.

The mandate was, of course, a great compliment: it showed that Gregory XI had been duly impressed with her achievements at Pisa earlier the same year, and that he believed she might be equally successful in keeping Lucca from joining the anti-papal league, which was gathering force in Tuscany with alarming speed. She set out with her usual entourage and was "received with enthusiasm and honored as a saint." [13]

All things being equal, Catherine would have enjoyed her stay in Lucca very much. This little city, enclosed by walls so high that it cannot even be glimpsed from outside, is one of the most charming in Tuscany. The shimmering façades of its churches, the amplitude of its piazzas, the verdure of its gardens and its interlacing trees—all these must have been sources of delight to Catherine's beauty-loving nature. A distinguished lady, Monna Malina Balbani, welcomed her as a house guest and became so attached to her that

Catherine eventually reproved her gently for over-fondness, in the case of another human being, since such intensity of devotion was appropriate only toward God; and, as usual, Catherine made friends very quickly among all classes and moved many to lead better lives. For a time, it also seemed as if she were making headway in her mission. Florence, which had chosen a new government—called the Eight of War—was already flying a red flag, lettered in white with the word LIBERTAS, as a banner of rebellion, sent its most eloquent orator, Donato Barbardori, to counteract her teachings; and his diatribes apparently fell on deaf ears while her mild admonitions commanded attention. Moreover, the elders of the city outdid themselves in making her fair promises; but they probably had little or no intentions of keeping their pledges, which they regarded as part of a political game.

"Catherine did not hesitate to rebuke those heads of state who were willing to go through the motions of siding with the pope; however, with equal candor she declared to the pope himself that the rebellion against him was due principally to the actions of the evil pastors and rectors sent by him into Italy. She wished to eliminate the effects but also, and before all else, the cause of disorder—which was moral. With this in mind, she exercised her apostolate among the people as well as among the leaders. And among the people this apostolate was more fruitful. With the assistance of her nuns in Lucca, she induced innumerable souls to change their way of life, and her priest followers, Fathers Caffarini, Domenici, and Fra Tommaso delle Fonte, had to spend long hours hearing confessions. . . . There have come down to us a number of documents which show the enormous impression Catherine made—letters which she wrote in answer to various civic personalities, among them the elders of the city and various ladies." [11] "But in spite of all the respect and love which was shown to Catherine herself, the citizens of Lucca had, presumably, already decided that when it suited them, they would give up the pope's cause and attach themselves to Florence and the other rebellious republics." [13]

Catherine must have recognized this, for she was not persuaded to prolong her stay in Lucca. In the late fall she went on to Pisa, which she had been urged, again and again, to revisit, and occupied herself with new plans for a crusade against the infidels, only too well aware that they had little chance of fruition. As to Pisa itself, she "found the district seething. Influenced by the errors and crimes committed by the French ecclesiastics and functionaries, incapable of understanding the Italian mentality, little by little, not only Siena, Urbino, Todi and Forli, but more than eighty other cities in central Italy revolted against the pope; so that the Vicar of Christ upon earth was the object of fierce anti-clericism among whole populations." [11] The handwriting on the wall was only too plain: she might persuade them to remain neutral a little longer, but Pisa and Lucca would be the next to fall. Unless Gregory could be induced to return to Rome, all Italy would be lost to him. In her next letter to him, couched in even plainer language than ever before, Catherine tried to make this very clear.

She returned to Siena for Christmas, but with little heart for its celebration. One of the first sights that met her eyes as she came into the city was a flag, new to Siena, flying from the Mangia Tower—the same red flag, inscribed with the word LIBERTAS, that Florence had adopted earlier in the year; she knew this did not mean Liberty in any true sense of the word. It meant turmoil. And, on the twenty-first, Gregory had announced the appointment of nine new cardinals—only one an Italian. One of the others was a Spaniard and all the rest French, three among them relatives of the Pope.. Catherine could not count on any of these to counsel the Pope's return to Rome. She knew that, on the contrary, the full weight of the College of Cardinals would be thrown against such a movement. The favorite nephew, Gerald DuPuy, no longer an abbot, but a Prince of the Church, alone had enough power to keep his uncle among the fleshpots.

Temporarily, the new year was brightened for Catherine by an addition to her circle of friends in the person of Stefano Maconi, a young nobleman who had hitherto kept aloof. Since she seemed to have great gifts as a mediator, he had been persuaded that this extraordinary Mantellata might be helpful in freeing his powerful family from a feud in which it had become involved with two which were still more powerful—the Rinaldini and the Tolomei. Maconi himself reports that she received him "not shyly or fearfully like a young girl as I had expected, but like a loving sister whose brother has returned from a long journey." [13] It was the old story: her graciousness and loving-kindness drew him to her so quickly and so irresistibly that he was ready to listen to almost anything she might suggest, and her suggestions were sound and constructive. After negotiations had been settled to the satisfaction of all involved and there remained no real reason, as far as the rival families were concerned, why Stefano should continue to visit her, he found that he wanted nothing so much as to remain in her company always. Smiling, she added him to her secretarial staff.

There was plenty to write about. The Florentines were again engaged in active war against the Papacy and Catherine's enemies probably said that she was now the one who was playing both ends against the middle. Early in the new year, the Pope summoned all the members of the insurgent Florentine government to appear before him in Avignon, not later than the end of March, and threatened that, if they did not do so, he would proclaim an interdict. At the same time, he sent ambassadors to sue for peace, thus displaying a lack of savoir-faire and judgment similar to that which the papal legate, de Noellet, had shown when he simultaneously forbade the export of grain and demanded sixty thousand guilders of tribute money. Catherine's greatest friend in Florence, Niccolo di Soderini, was one of the officials so summoned and so threatened; and her passionate appeals to the Pope to show patience and leniency toward his children were unquestionably prompted by personal feeling, as well as a strong, but objective, yearning for peace. During the same period that she was writing these fervent appeals to Gregory, one of which, at least, she entrusted to Neri di Landoccio for delivery, she was writing to Soderini "tackling the problem from the other side." She exhorted the Florentine government to seek forgiveness from the Pope and to be reconciled with him at any price. It did not lie in their province, she said, to judge the bad shepherds —God would do that. And however corrupt they might be, they had been consecrated and alone could administer the Sacraments.

Her entreaties to Soderini might have carried more weight if, just at this time, the papal army had not committed such outrages that nothing could extenuate its crimes. Sir John Hawkwood was again in the hire of the papal legate, with the Florentines on the offensive. Probably this did not come as too much of a shock to Catherine. She was a mystic, but she was also a realist, in much the same way as Teresa of Avila, whom, as a matter of fact, she resembled in many respects, among them her personal charm and her adaptability when it came to travel. She could hardly have believed that her daring approach to Hawkwood and his surprising response to it meant more than a breathing space for Pisa; and she had been thankful enough to get that, even if she got nothing from him for any other city, and if his promise about the crusade had been words writ in water. But she could hardly have foreseen the slaughter at Cesena, which was allegedly in retaliation for the capture of Bologna by the anti-papal league, or the use of bloodhounds to supplement a mercenary army. In the face of such wanton wickedness and violence, there was nothing she could say to persuade the Florentine officials who had been summoned to Avignon that they should meekly go there. Messengers were dispatched to report, in the name of the republic, that the political leaders would not be able to appear. The Pope replied by making good his threat: Florence was put under an interdict and all members of the Eight of War and twenty-one other leaders, Soderini among them, were excommunicated—that is to say, all Florentine citizens were declared outlaws and their leaders were deprived of the Sacraments. Raimondo wrote Catherine that, wherever Florentines had business connections and were no longer protected by the law, they were subject to seizure and confiscation of their property by foreign governments. They would have to seek reconciliation with the Pope through the intervention of persons to whom he would listen.

There was no question as to whom Raimondo meant by this reference, and Catherine was ready and willing to undertake the mission. She began it, indirectly, by sending Raimondo and two other priests to Avignon with additional letters to the Pope, written in the same vein as those she had sent before: demands for reform within the Church, for a return of the Supreme Pontiff to Rome and for peace with the Christian rebels. Next, she wrote to Soderini and offered her services as an intermediary. These were enthusiastically accepted and she was urged to come back to Florence. Early in May of 1376, she and her usual companions reached there for the second time.

It was almost exactly two years since she had been there for the first time. Then, an obscure and defenseless young girl, she had come to appear before a great tribunal and answer grave charges against her character. Now, an important public figure, hailed as a mediatrix of extraordinary gifts, she had come at the urgent request of a great city. Before, she had shared the inadequate lodgings of her brothers, who had never prospered in their trade as dyers after their flight to Florence from Siena. Now she was the house guest of the Soderini in their palazzo. But even if her sudden rise to fame and power would have proved intoxicating, under normal circumstances, which is doubtful—since humility remained one of Catherine's outstanding characteristics—the conditions which awaited her were so appalling that all sense of exhilaration would have died a-borning. There were no Masses, and only a few priests were permitted, under exceptional circumstances, to baptize babies and administer the Last Rites to the dying. What the plague had been to the flesh, the interdict was to the spirit.

True, there were signs of religious awakening: flagellants scourged themselves, processions of penitents filed mournfully through the streets, brotherhoods were formed to help the poor. But none of these manifestations was coupled with unconditional surrender to the Pope. Until that happeend, the ban would not be lifted—unless a way could be found to bring about an armistice, if not an advantageous peace. Perhaps not many Florentines felt that Catherine could help them achieve this; but there were some, among these several important figures besides Soderini and certain of his fellow officials; the archbishop; the Vallombrosan monk, Giovanni delle Celle, who had delivered Catherine from the charge of witchcraft at her trial; Barduccio Canigiani, who was added to Catherine's ever-growing secretarial staff, and his brother Ristoro, both men of considerable influence; Benvenuto Minuccio and Buonaccorso di Lapo. Since all these were convinced of her efficacy, others decided that the experiment of having her go to Avignon was at least worth trying. They speeded her on her way, promising that official representatives would follow and that these would be guided by her advice.

12

THE EXPERIMENT was bold, but it was not as rash as might appear on the surface. The Florentines were not choosing Catherine as their emissary primarily because of her gifts as a mystic, but because of her proven powers as a mediator. Gregory himself had recognized these by ordering her to Lucca. Even before that, on the occasion of her first visit to Pisa, he had regarded her as a personage of such importance that he had commanded she should always be accompanied by three priests when she traveled and, since then, he had sent Alfonso de Vadaterra—a Spaniard who had been Bishop of Jaen, but was now a hermit of St. Augustine—all the way from Avignon to Siena to give her the papal blessing and to ask for her prayers. It was just as well to have a representative against whom the Pope was not prejudiced to begin with, as he would have been, almost instinctively, against any Florentine. He was in entire agreement with one of his predecessors, Boniface VIII, who had declared, "There are five elements: earth, water, fire, air and Florentines." He believed they would trick and deceive almost everybody, for sheer love of trickery and deceit and that no one could foresee what they would do next. He was less vehement in expressing himself about the Sienese in general, and on Catherine personally he was known to look not only with favor but with respect and, perhaps, even with a little awe. Lacking qualities of decisiveness and perseverance himself, he was, nevertheless, able to recognize and admire them in others.

Moreover, the secret of the stigmata, like most secrets, had undoubtedly leaked out; such a mark of Divine favor set its bearer apart from ordinary mortals and gave him supernal qualities which it was not wise to disregard.

It seems safe to assume that, from the beginning of her association with Fra Raimondo, Catherine had been privileged to envision many aspects of temporal, as well as spiritual, life of which she had hitherto been, at best, only vaguely aware and that, generally speaking, she was receptive to his teachings. But nothing that he may have said in explanation or excuse about the so-called Babylonian Captivity altered the steadfast belief she had persistently held that everything about it was evil. Probably the fact that she felt this way added force to her argument that Rome and only Rome was the suitable seat for the Holy See, that it always had been and always would be. A more dispassionate observer might have disagreed with her. When Benedict XI, an Italian and an ex-General of the Dominicans, died—very probably of poison—in Perugia, whither he had removed because of the Romans' "dark temper," the Eternal City "had reached the extremes of degradation and despair. Its broken thoroughfares were, for the most part, the uncontested property, filth littered and unsightly, of starved mongrels and lawless wretches. Those houses which remained occupied were fortified and barricaded and if their owners were not bandits they were forced to a self-reliant code which rendered possible their survival among bandits." [30] It took eleven months for the College of Cardinals, which also met in Perugia, to select another Pope and in 1305 the choice finally fell on Bertrand de Goth, Archbishop of Bordeaux and ex-Vicar General of Lyons, who took the name of Clement V.

Contrary to popular belief, he was by no means the first Frenchman to wear the triple crown: Sylvester II (999–1003), Urban II (1088–1099), Urban IV (1261–1264), Clement IV (1265–1268) and Martin IV (1281–1285) were all French; but all had accepted Rome without question as their capital. Apparently Clement V, who had never been there before his election, never seriously considered going there after it. Of the twenty-four cardinals he created between 1305 and 1314, twenty-three were French, and in this and in many other matters of policy he was greatly influenced by the French King, Philip IV, nicknamed the Fair, to whom he undoubtedly owed his election. It was at the latter's instigation that he dissolved the Order of

Knights Templars "a religious organization, with a strong military flavouring, which had been founded early in the twelfth century with the object of defending Jerusalem. The three vows of religion —poverty, chastity and obedience—were undertaken by the Knights, and skill in the military art was required as were also certain genealogical qualifications. Over 20,000 members of the Order had perished in battle in less than two centuries. Great properties were accumulated and such an organization, rich and armed, claiming indeed at certain times the prerogatives of a sovereign power, could not but be an affront to a monarch of the calibre of Philip. Heresy and sacrilege and the practice of unnatural lust was his cry and soon the loathsome glare of the dreaded stake was visible against the sky of many a city and castle as confessions, before the processes of rack and screw, came quick and bountiful." [30]

His culpable complacency as far as the wicked king was concerned is probably the most serious well-authenticated charge that can be made against Clement V. He had always been in the habit of spending a good deal of time at Pessac, the family domain, famous for its vineyards—indeed, the wine, still called Clement V, is probably the same which the pontiff most enjoyed. He was crowned at Lyons and then devoted several months traveling from one place to another, searching for a climate which might be better suited to his frail health than those in the regions where he had formerly lived. He reached Avignon in the spring, when the landscape of Provence is beautified by flowering almond and the silvery leaves of olive trees, and the loveliness of the scene may well have influenced his desire to linger there. But his eventual decision to make Avignon —which, though located in southeastern France, belonged to the kingdom of Naples—his headquarters seems to have been guided by the Cardinal of Prato, a Dominican, and the lodging that he found was in the Convent of the Frères Précheurs (Preaching Brothers), a modest establishment outside the city gates.

He made practically no changes in it. His requirements and his tastes were simple; and though he was a man of considerable wealth, he spent little on himself, limiting himself to private collections of precious stones and *orféverie*; aside from acquiring such masterpieces of the goldsmiths' and silversmiths' craft, he did not reveal himself as a patron of the arts, nor did he make any contribution to these which others might enjoy, with the result that he was characterized by his enemies as stingy. The Florentine historian, Villani, accused him of many other failings, some of them serious. Though Catherine was not born until more than thirty years after Clement's death, she probably heard and believed these charges, which included accusations of simony and nepotism and failed to mention great progress made in the propagation of the faith, which was this pope's most significant contribution to the Church. But though she longed and labored for reforms among the clergy, she was always insistent that human failings did not excuse disrespect for a great office; and it was the failure of a pope—any pope—to establish himself in Rome and to include more Italians in the College of Cardinals, rather than anything else he did or did not do, which most concerned her.

Throughout his pontificate, Clement V continued to spend as much time as his health would allow in journeys to the various places with which he had already been associated, both personally and officially, and toward which he never ceased to feel drawn. Evidently both he and the physicians with whom he was constantly surrounded overestimated his endurance; for it was in the course of one such trip, with Bordeaux as his intended destination, that mortal illness overcame him and he died, before he was fifty, at Roquemaure, in the chateau of his friend Raymond of Toulouse.

His successor, Jacques d'Euse, the member of a prosperous bourgeois family strongly rooted in Provence, took the name of John XXII. "He had a reputation for good judgment, learning and administrative ability"; [30] but his appearance was so unprepossessing that no contemporary chronicler failed to mention this handicap. He was apparently in much frailer health than Clement and he was seventy-two years old at the time of his election. However, he reigned for eighteen years and, throughout this entire period, engaged in varied and ceaseless activities. Though he conveyed the impression, doubtless with complete sincerity, that he intended to return to Rome "as soon as circumstances would permit," [31] he was the first pope who gave stability to a sojourn in Avignon. He had no idea of wandering around or of contenting himself with simple lodgings in a convent. He considered it more suitable to establish himself in the episcopal palace. As the French writer, Robert Brun, has wittily put it, "Formerly the pope was Bishop of Rome; this time the Bishop of Avignon became pope." [31]

In course of time, John XXII improved and enlarged the episcopal palace, which comprised four detached buildings opening on a central court and inadequately connected by a covered gallery. In front of it was a garden—on the site of the Court of Honor in the present palace—which was faced by such buildings as the almonry, the hospital and headquarters of the militant police. "We therefore wish," John XXII wrote in his Bull of December, 1318, "that the episcopal palace be enlarged in a way that seems to us worthy and suitable. We will therefore connect with the episcopal palace the almonry and the buildings of the new police headquarters which adjoin the church." [31] It was not yet a question of construction; it was a question of enlargement. The same document notes the acquisition of houses with their dependencies, porches and gardens.

For the most part, John XXII was able to pursue his policy of architectural expansion without much harassment and his boundless energy found various other outlets. He is said to have issued no less than sixty thousand official documents; and in the course of a raging controversy over heresy, when charges and countercharges were hurled about so recklessly that they included even the head of the Church "at the request of the University of Paris, he made a public profession of orthodoxy, saying 'the saints are in heaven where they see God face to face' "; but perhaps his greatest service, like that of his predecessor, was in the propagation of the faith. "John continued that policy of Clement which had given sturdy encouragement to the foreign missions, and Tartary and Turkestan were invaded by zealous monks whilst the established missions of Africa, Persia, and India were enlarged. Universities also profited by his interest and in 1321 he even gave some substance to the dream that never could really have been absent from the ambitions of a pope of those times. A crusade, very small but a fact, was formed and, consisting of a fleet of galleys, gained a few victories over the Turks. John's private life was void of scandal for he adhered, as much as his many administrative duties would allow, to the strict regime of a simple monk. His great fault was an unswerving belief that the papacy should remain in France." [30] But this, in itself, would have been enough to prejudice Catherine against him, even without the added insult represented by his choice of cardinals: twenty-three were French, one Spanish and only three Italian.

The first conclave held in Avignon took place after the death of John XXII. Twenty-four cardinals were present and the Count of

Noailles, representing the King of France, and the Seneschal of Provence were charged with the responsibility of seeing that these Princes of the Church had no opportunity to communicate with the outside world. The eminent Cardinal of Comminges represented the first choice of the conclave; but when he learned that his election was dependent on the condition that he would agree not to return the Holy See to Rome, he declined to accept it, "judging that at Avignon the papacy was in danger." The cardinals prevailed; the arrangement which had seemed temporary to Clement V and expedient to John XXII had become a pleasing fixation, as far as the electors were concerned; and, when they acted in unison, their power was greater than that of any one man, even a potential pope. They ended by electing "the humblest in their company," Jacques Fournier, who was the son of a baker and who had been a Cistercian monk. He took the name of Benedict XII.

A polychrome statue of him may still be seen in the crypt of the Vatican and there is also a cast of this at Avignon. He is revealed as a tall heavy man with ruddy color and is said to have had a compelling voice and forceful maner. He continued to wear the simple habit of a Cistercian and was affectionately known as "The White Monk." Even the venomous Villani found little to charge against him, except that he had bowed to the will of his fellow cardinals regarding the site of the Holy See. "After becoming pope, he made two attempts to go to Rome, but each time was thwarted, without any real opposition on his part." [30] So perhaps not only his wishes, but his determined purpose, were similar to those of the French cardinals. At all events, he bowed to them in no other respect. With prompt and unexpected firmness, he announced that the abuses connected with simony and nepotism, which had become more and more flourishing and extensive, must cease immediately; and he set the example for others by declaring that a pope should resemble Meschisedech—that is, he should have neither father nor mother nor genealogy. Then Benedict proceeded to practice what he preached. Not a single member of his family profited by his advancement. There is a rather touching story to the effect that his father, wishing to do him honor, outfitted himself with some handsome clothes, and stationed himself in the front row of the nobles who thronged the Consistory. The White Monk swept by him without a sign of recognition. The poor baker was completely crushed, believing that, despite his fine raiment, his son was ashamed of him. A friend suggested that he should return in his working clothes, coming straight from the shop without stopping to brush the flour from his garments. As soon as the Pope caught sight of him, Benedict rushed forward to embrace his father and then presented him with pride to the assembled cardinals.

Simple as were his personal tastes, it was not part of his plan to use the residence of a bishop as a papal palace. "The tranquillity of the Avignon landscape quickly vanished as a swarm of busy artisans built palaces not only for the pope but for each of his cardinals and their retinues. There was the construction necessary to house and feed and defend the great army required of any administrative center. Soldiers and priests, clerks and bureaucrats, lawyers and merchants, beggars and lackeys, jostled and shouted through thoroughfares that were no longer peaceful country lanes." [30] John XXII had encouraged his relatives to live near him and in considerable style; Benedict XII, who frowned on nepotism, made the prestige of the Church his first consideration. Though his kinsfolk were kept at a distance, anyone else who would add to this was made welcome. Scholars from all parts of the world were urged to establish themselves at his court, there to pursue their studies at their leisure and at his expense. Bankers, merchants and craftsmen of every description were assured of prosperity; and besides these permanent and semipermanent guests, princes and ambassadors from every part of the known world came and went on missions of ever-increasing significance.

In a Bull dated 1336, Benedict stated, "We have given careful consideration to the fact that it is very important for the Roman Church to have in the city of Avignon, where the Roman Court has resided for some time and where we reside with it, a special palace where the Pontiff can live whenever and for as long a time as it will seem to him necessary. We have also considered that John XXII, our predecessor of blessed memory, spent large sums from his treasure for the restoration and enlargement of the episcopal palace at Avignon, where he resided during his lifetime and where we ourselves reside, and also for the purchases of other houses near or adjacent to the palace; and that we ourselves should cause to be built sumptuous edifices on this same site and adjacent sites through our purchases in the name of the Roman Church." [31]

Aside from the papal palace itself, the establishments built for the cardinals were the most remarkable. They were known as *livrées* and apparently took their name from the fact that a cardinal's entire staff wore his special livery (*livrée*) and that the word, originally used to designate uniforms, came to mean the place where his retainers lived with him. Besides all those at Avignon itself, no fewer than fifteen *livrées* were erected in Villeneuve across the River Rhone; and some cardinals had two—one in the city and one in the suburbs. A nephew of John XXII, Armand de Via, was among those thus supplied. Some of these *livrées* are still in a state of preservation which permits a good idea of their original structure. "They were built with large inner courtyards, like the *atria* of the Romans and the patios of the Moors, and always fortified against surprise attacks, especially during the second half of the fourteenth century. The *livrée* presented to the street a strong proud front, with no windows below the second story. A watch tower, legacy of the seignorial *donjon,* guarded the entrance to the living quarters, which were reached through a vaulted corridor. The apartments of the cardinals and the dependencies, which were safe-guarded in this semi-fortress, opened on the aforementioned courtyard. In the case of a very large establishment, there was a second enclosure to provide for the staff of the cardinal, which included chancellors, chaplains, clerks, physicians, equerries, falconers, sergeants at arms, servants, couriers, grooms, cooks and cupbearers. Naturally, a vast amount of space was required for their headquarters." [32]

Many of the "sumptuous edifices" still stand and are still the object of mingled awe and admiration, as they were in Catherine's time; and though the question as to why a humble Cistercian should have wished to build on such a scale and with such ostentation has never, to my knowledge, been definitely answered, Robert Brun, a most perceptive authority, is among those who have pointed out that neither personal pride nor a challenge to the royal house of France could have been responsible. Benedict had no personal pride; and the relations between the Papal See and the Royal House of France, which was strongly and suitably established at Villeneuve on the opposite side of the Rhone, were at this time extremely cordial and co-operative. It seems probable that the reason Catherine assigned to it was the true one: namely, that he intended to establish the papacy firmly on French soil, and that he believed this was the way to do it.

Whatever his incentive may have been, his accomplishment, as we have already remarked, was astounding. The immense structure known as the "Old Palace," which is the part built by Benedict XII, encloses both a large and a small garden and a large courtyard and is surmounted by several towers; it comprises, among many other imposing apartments, a consistory, a conclave, a pontifical chapel and a mammoth kitchen; two private suites at the disposal of the Pope himself—in one of which was the room known as the *petit tinel,* where he received visitors informally; a separate suite at the disposition of his visitors; and a treasure room known as the *trésorerie basse* (lower treasury) to distinguish it from numerous other places where valuables were placed for safekeeping. It was to this room that Benedict ordered transported the famous treasure which John XXII had patiently accumulated during the eighteen years of his reign, and the exact amount of which he had kept secret. When he died, the cardinals ordered an inventory and, on a designated date, experts were called upon to examine the contents of the iron chests, in which were stored leather sacks crammed with gold pieces, and to determine their value. The chronicler Villani had a brother who was purveyor by appointment (*marchand fournisseur*) to the court and who was present on this exciting occasion. According to his testimony, eighteen million golden florins rolled out of their sacks, in addition to piles of precious stones and jeweled ornaments. But the Villani brothers were apparently given to exaggeration; the experts placed the value of the treasure at seven million florins.

Surely Benedict must have felt that such a habitation as he had built would suffice for all time. But his successor, Clement VI, had still more exalted ideas about a fitting residence for a pope—in fact, he is said to have remarked, rather condescendingly, that his predecessors did not know how to fill their office. The so-called New Palace, which he constructed and which forms a huge L-shaped addition to the Old Palace, enclosed a Court of Honor more than twice the size of the one flanked by Benedict's pontifical chapel, consistory and conclave; it was dominated by three additional towers; one arm of the L contained headquarters of the guard, the apartment where dignitaries waited to be received and the small audience chamber. The vast confines of the other wing were given over, in their entirety, to the great audience chamber.

But spaciousness was not Clement's only consideration as he

built; he was also concerned with luxury and beauty. The richest brocades and velvets, the finest tapestries, were used for hangings and upholstery. Master craftsmen of every kind—goldsmiths and silversmiths, painters and sculptors—were summoned to provide adornment. Clement came of a proud family, the Roger de Beaufort of Limousin, and he felt one to the manner born should keep greater state than the son of a *petit bourgeois* or a baker. "He had worn the Benedictine habit although it could not be said that his life was ever restrained to the monastic pattern. High birth and influence combined with intelligence and eloquence had previously won for him the rich sees of Arras, Sens and Rouen. Luxury and splendour had always characterized his career as a high prelate and the acquisition of the tiara was an opportunity he did not neglect to indulge these traits further. The papal court became the scene of lavish hospitality." [30]

It also became the capital of the Christian world. Clement gave even more conclusive proof than his predecessors of his conviction that the site of the Holy See should be permanently located in France. He purchased the sovereignty of Avignon from the Queen of Naples; from that time forth it no longer constituted part of her kingdom, but a papal state. Alphonse Daudet has painted a glowing picture of it. "For gaiety, for animation, for an endless succession of fetes, there never was such a city. From morning till night there were processions, pilgrimages, streets strewn with flowers and hung with tapestries, cardinals arriving by boat, their galleys dressed, their banners flying to windward, papal soldiers singing Latin songs in the public squares, mendicant friars rending the air with their harsh cries. The houses, clustered around the great papal palace like bees around their hive, hummed with activity. From them came the tick-tack of bobbins, the canticles of the warpers as they prepared the threads for the weavers; the shuttling of the looms; the rhythmic tapping of small hammers, the tuning of stringed instruments; and, rising from the bridge, the tinkle of tambourines. For, with us, when people are happy, they must dance and since, at this time, the streets were too narrow for the farandole, fifes and tambourines were taken to the bridge, where night and day there was dancing. What a wonderful epoch! What a fortunate city! Halberds which were only for show, prisons used only for the cooling of wines!"

This description is unquestionably so flamboyant in style as to lack realism; but French historians, no less than French romancers, give it authenticity. "The court of Clement VI," Brun tells us, "which was the most polished in Europe, had become the meeting place of exalted nobility. Balls, dramatic performances and tournaments provided constant entertainment for pleasure lovers, but papal Avignon was also frequented by the outstanding intellectuals of the period. Scholars, poets, men of letters, astronomers, were found there. Above all, artists of every nationality: sculptors from Paris, painters from Florence, Siena, Viterbo and Rome, goldsmiths from Limousin, illuminators from Toulouse, Flemish tapestry workers. There were also the gracious ladies of Avignon, without whom Petrarch [a voluntary exile from Florence] declared life would have been impossible for him, and who renewed the ancient traditions of the troubadours' courts of love." [31]

Admittedly, the composite picture is one of elegance, culture and romance, rather than of austerity and piety; but to those who can accept it as complete, it seems sophisticated rather than evil. Unfortunately, there were many who could not so accept it, and with reason; to these others—and Catherine's earliest informers were among them—it was a "hotbed of clerical decadence." That is the way she regarded it from her tenderest years.

To Clement's credit let it be said that he took time, amidst his pleasant worldly preoccupations, to receive with great courtesy a delegation from Rome. The Eternal City had now achieved some sort of order out of its chaos, in the form of a rather unsteady democracy, of which the famous Cola di Rienzi, who took part in the mission to Avignon, was the real ruler. Clement declined to consider the urgent request that he should return to Rome; by way of compensation for his absence, he promised his support to an official jubilee, to be held there at mid-century! It is doubtful if the delegation felt that its mission had been crowned with success.

"The greatest virtue possessed by Clement VI was his charity. This took on proportions equal to his usual sense of the magnificent, with the energetic measures he used to abate the miseries that followed in the wake of the Black Plague which devastated all Europe during his reign. Another aftermath of the dreaded epidemic was a wave of anti-semitism, for fanatics were hysterically accusing the Jews of spreading the disease by poisoning wells. The aptly named Pope fought the libel with vigour and announced that the Jews were under his protection. Consequently, at his death on the 6th December, 1352, there was not only the prescribed mourning in Christian churches but there was also sorrow in the synagogues of Israel." [30]

The successor of Clement VI, Stephen Aubert, Cardinal Bishop of Ostia, took the name of Innocent VI. He attempted some very radical reforms and some drastic economies. But his argument that all the prelates who had deserted their own sees and benefices should return thither, inevitably lost force because he himself showed no disposition to return to Rome! The Rienzi regime had collapsed and Rienzi himself had died a violent and untimely death; but the Spanish cardinal, Giles Albornoz, who had been dispatched to Rome by the Pope as his personal representative, accomplished such wonders that he was called "the Second Founder of the Papal States." [33] (The laws which Albornoz drew up for the Papal States, known as the "Aegidian Constitutions," remained in effect until 1816.) Innocent might well have considered the moment propitious for at least a visit; but he permitted the opportunity to escape him, and it was his successor, Urban V, who was the one who decided to take advantage of it several years later.

Outside of France, this decision was hailed with universal acclaim and even emperors came to render him homage. He was enthusiastically welcomed in Rome and, with a normal amount of cooperation, might well have considered his move a permanent one. But the gifted and militant Albornoz had died and no other powerful advocate for the end of the "exile" took his place. The French cardinals with whom the Pope was surrounded made no effort to suppress or overcome their mutinous discontent; and Rome was again in a state of turbulence. "Assassination, violence, robbery, crimes of every kind were the order of the day. Armed bands of mercenaries roamed the countryside and made the roads unsafe for pilgrims. The sacred shrines of the city were deserted." [33]

Urban was, in many ways, a very saintly man, but he was not a strong one. He did not know how to deal with such conditions himself and he could find nobody who would do it for him. Neither protests against his lack of perseverance nor prophecies of the disasters that would overcome him if he did not stand firm proved sufficiently powerful to bolster his wavering courage or calm his troubled mind. He followed the line of least resistance and went back to Avignon.

Horticulture, rather than architecture, had always been his favorite avocation; and, before his departure, he had greatly enlarged and beautified the gardens of his predecessors; this labor of love had marked an important contribution to the landscaping of the palace grounds. During his brief sojourn in Rome, one of his chief interests had centered in transforming the papal vineyard into an orchard, by planting fruit trees of every variety in it.[34] Now, on his return to his own "vine and fig tree," all he asked was to enjoy these in peace. Alas, in less than three months he gave truth to the prophecy that death would claim him if he deserted his post.

Catherine was one of the thousands who had rejoiced over Urban's return to Rome and who had grieved because he did not remain there. But, among those thousands, there were few, if any, whom his defection was to affect with such widespread results. She was now twenty-three years old and she had already been doing her own thinking and making her own decisions for more than a decade. In other words, though she would probably have accepted without question Fra Raimondo's and Vanni's reports on the pontificates of Clement V, John XXII and Benedict XII—all of which had ended before her birth—and also that of Clement VI, which ended when she was only five years old, she would have begun to make her own observations long before Innocent VI's ineffectual reign was over and Urban V would always have been very real to her—lamentably so. To the very end, she had hoped that he would somehow show himself strong after all. When she first heard that he had left Rome, she tried to convince herself and others that the news was only an idle rumor; when it was verified, her sorrow knew no bounds. But woe never crushed her. On the contrary, it served as an incentive to use every means in her power to rectify the conditions which had caused it. When she learned that Urban had died, her thoughts, her prayers and very soon her plans were all directed toward the possibility of a change of policy on the part of his successor, Gregory XI.

Unfortunately, nothing that she learned about him was calculated to make her feel that a new era of righteousness and glory had begun. The new Pope was the namesake and nephew of Clement VI and had been created a cardinal by his uncle when he was only eighteen years old. There could hardly have been a more flagrant example of nepotism's evils. Whatever the faults of his predecessors, most had possessed some significant qualities. Among them had been men of unblemished personal life, sometimes even bordering on the austere, and men outstanding as administrators and theologians. Several had been zealots in the propagation of the faith and, at the same time, liberal patrons of the secular arts. Two of them had been builders of such talent and vision that their architectural achievements were to become enduring monuments, perpetuating their fame. No such significant qualities could be attributed to the new Pope. In short, "Gregory was not a bad man but he was not remarkable for any talent and the best that could be said of him was that his nature was docile." [30]

It was on this docility that Catherine was counting when she left Florence for Avignon, with twenty-three companions, in the spring of 1376.

13

SHE CAME by boat, not, to be sure, like a cardinal with "galley dressed and banners flying to windward," but with the same privilege of beholding first from the river the magnificent sight of the papal palace looming against the blue Provençal sky, above the great rock of the Dom on which the city was built. Towers and spires surrounded it, but while these, too, achieved great heights, they lacked its majesty. It was an impregnable fortress, a superb abode, the greatest of all the "sumptuous edifices" of which Benedict had written with such pride of creation. All her life Catherine had lived in splendid cities; but not even lovely Lucca, engulfed by its sheltering walls; not even tawny Siena, with its sloping oval Piazza Populo del Campo; not even shining Pisa with its triumvirate of baptistry, cathedral and leaning tower provided such a sight as this.

Catherine had always been extremely sensitive to beauty in all its forms. Now, for the first time, she was unmoved by it. To her the proudly placed palace was only the prison of the pope who should have been in Rome. The fact that the prison was splendid and luxurious and that he was a willing prisoner only made matters worse in her eyes. She was happy to see Fra Raimondo, Fra Giovanni Tantucci and Neri di Landoccio, who were eagerly awaiting her arrival, but she was as brief as courtesy would permit with all the others who had come to meet her; and she expressed no pleasure at the arrangement which had been made for her lodging. According to some accounts, the *livrée* of a cardinal who had recently died was put at her disposal and that of her companions; according to others, she was conducted on arrival to the bishop's palace, there to be the guest of Archbishop Angelo Ricasoli. In any case, the habitation was certainly luxurious to the last degree and she would have preferred something simpler. She chose the most unpretentious room she could find, spent much of her time in an oratory and, as far as possible, remained secluded while awaiting the call to appear before His Holiness.

This was not long in coming. Gregory really wanted to see her. Within two days, she was summoned and received in conformity with the usage proper for visitors of ambassadorial rank—that is, in the Great Consistory of Benedict XII, for it was here that "it was customary to receive with great pomp sovereigns and their ambassadors. It was here that the papal nuncios came to make their reports and here that the pope proclaimed his selection of cardinals." [35] In every way, it provided a mise en scène worthy of such important events. Its beamed ceiling was decorated with taste and elegance; its walls were hung with priceless tapestries and superb paintings. At one end stood the throne on which the Pope was seated, and around this was grouped, in full regalia, his official family. Other persons, also magnificently attired, whose rank or duties entitled them to be present, were all provided with suitable places. Formality, coupled with splendor, was the order of the day.

As Catherine, accompanied by Fra Raimondo and announced by the Court Chamberlain, entered the Great Consistory, there was a sound of murmuring among the onlookers who had foregathered, whether because it was their function to be present at such a ceremony or because they were habitués privileged to satisfy their idle curiosity. Then, as a slight pale woman clad, like the priest who was with her, in the Dominican habit crossed the hall and knelt to kiss the Pope's ring, the silence became profound.

She was told to state her mission and rose to face the Pope with entire composure. Then she began to speak in the Tuscan dialect which came most naturally to her lips and in which she could best express herself, though she could now read Latin with ease and understood it when it was spoken by others. While Fra Raimondo acted as her interpreter, his was not a dual task; the Pope could not follow Catherine's remarks without help, but she could follow his;

and she was swift to recognize the genuine kindliness of his manner and the careful attention he paid to everything she said. Most of what she was telling him now, she had already written him; but her presence and her voice gave weight to the spoken words which the written ones had lacked. So did the fair-mindednes with which she had the courage to remind His Holiness that crimes had been committed against the Florentines no less than against the Papal State and that just grievances were not all on one side. She next proceeded to dwell on the Florentines' desire for reconciliation and the lengths to which they were now willing to go in order to do their share in bringing this about; and, as she did so, Gregory was persuaded that at least a truce, if not lasting peace, might well be in sight. Then, as she continued to speak with calmness and assurance, he became convinced that the negotiations for such a truce might safely be entrusted to this seemingly frail woman who was actually a vessel of preternatural strength.

She paused frequently, not only in order that Fra Raimondo might have time to translate, but that Gregory might have time to consider each point as she made it; and the Pope did not seize on any of these pauses as a pretext for interruption, much less for dismissal. He was, indeed, pondering, as she had hoped. When it was finally evident that she had come to the end of her exposition and her plea, he reminded her gently that, in any transactions which might take place between the Papal State and the excommunicated city, the honor and the dignity of the Church must be preserved. But what the details of these transactions should be, he was now willing to leave in her hands. With this startling statement and the expression of willingness to receive on its arrival the next Florentine mission, for which she had acted as precursor, he brought the audience to an end.

The same profound silence which had marked Catherine's presentation again fell on the Great Consistory as she left it. She did this as swiftly as she had entered, unconcerned by the knowledge that the reaction to this scene which had just taken place was sure to be vehement and might well be violent. She wanted to say a prayer of thanksgiving and she wanted to write a report to Florence; beyond that, she wanted nothing so much as to live in peace and seclusion until the official embassy arrived.

Of course, it was not possible for her to do the latter. Her presence in Avignon had aroused as much curiosity as antagonism and visitors of every sort and condition flocked to the palace where she and her companions were staying. She strove to be civil to these importunate strangers, but she found it impossible to be cordial, though graciousness had, hitherto, been one of her most outstanding characteristics. Quite possibly, her inability to speak and understand French at first added to her difficulties; but this was a difficulty which she must gradually have overcome. Five hundred years ago, Italian, French and Spanish—all three based on Latin, which was their common heritage—resembled each other much more closely than they do now, because there had been less time in which to establish differences; and Catherine would certainly have made a successful effort to surmount a linguistic handicap—indeed, we have proof that eventually she did so. Her greatest difficulty lay in the fact that now she saw no one whom she wanted for a friend and her chill civility discouraged friendly advances from others. Fra Raimondo tried to reason with her, begging her to temper the severity of her judgment with charity, but to no avail. "The stench of sin," which Catherine insisted she had been able to smell as far away as Siena, was so overpowering, in the case of many callers, that she could not endure it. For her the lovely ladies of Avignon, whom Petrarch had said he could not live without and whom the troubadours had idealized in song and story, were, to put it mildly, women of easy virtue, and Catherine did not always put it so mildly, in talking with her confessor or even with the Pope. As for the clergy who numbered so many "sisters" and "nieces" in their households, she had equally harsh words for them. Nepotism and simony were bad enough, without adding concubinage to other wrongdoings.

Several unfortunate experiences may well have been at least partially responsible for this uncompromising attitude. Among the young noblewomen whom Catherine had received with marked coolness was Alys de Beaufort Turenne, a kinswoman of the pope, who took umbrage at this lack of proper deference on the part of a social inferior and who, moreover, was sceptical on the subject of trances. She did not believe that the raptures into which Catherine fell upon receiving Holy Communion were anything but a form of play acting and she decided to prove this. The Sunday after she had come to this decision, which she confided to several friends, she knelt beside Catherine at the Communion rail and, drawing a long needle from a jeweled belt, drove it into Catherine's left foot. To her surprise and somewhat to her alarm, Catherine did not flinch or move, much less cry out; and Alys hastily left the church, swiftly followed by the friends whose curiosity had led them to accompany her, and who could not now be on their way fast enough to tell the news. A few minutes later, Catherine moaned as she recovered consciousness and Maconi, hastening to her side, discovered the injury and helped her home.

Some days elapsed before she could walk unaided and, meantime, she was subjected to another singularly trying experience of a different kind. Three clerical callers were announced and were admitted to Catherine's presence by the faithful Maconi. Their call, however, was not one of courtesy, but of inquisition; it had been instigated by powerful members of the French clergy who were determined to see Catherine discredited and had decided that this could best be done through tricky questioning. The visitors began by challenging her right to represent Florence at the Papal Court; quietly, but conclusively, she explained why she had been sent to do this and by whom. Finding that they were making no headway with the political aspects of the case, the visitors switched to its religious aspects; they wished her to account for her fasting, her trances and her visions. When she had done this, to their reluctant satisfaction, they turned to complicated theological subjects; for these too, she had a ready answer. The three prelates left her presence baffled and defeated. This woman's influence with the Pope might well be disastrous, as far as the interests of the French were concerned; not, however, because she was a witch or an impostor, but because she was honest, clever and determined.

As day after day went by and the Florentine mission, which was to have followed her closely, still failed to appear, Catherine found it increasingly hard to possess her soul in patience. True, during this period, Gregory sent for her several times and, instead of receiving her as an official ambassadress in formal audience, welcomed her in a friendly way as a valued adviser. She was able to converse with His Holiness candidly and expansively—and with little or no help from an interpreter, though Fra Raimondo remained available always—about many matters, among them the crusade Gregory had promised to call and the return to Rome which he was pledged to undertake. This pledge had been made privately long before, when

Gregory was still a cardinal; it was contingent upon his election to the papacy and, as far as he could recall, he had never spoken of it to anyone. But Catherine knew of it and, from the moment he found this out, he realized he would have to keep his vow. His conscience, so long dormant, had been awakened by her.

The mutual esteem and confidence between the pontiff and the Mantellata continued to increase and, at last, in September, the long-awaited mission from Florence arrived. But its arrival, instead of being a godsend, was a disaster. There had been a sudden change of government and the men who had speeded Catherine on her way were no longer in power. The emissaries, who were not the ones she had expected, promptly disowned her. They wanted none of her mediation; they and they alone would deal with the Pope and they had no intention of submitting to him.

Their arrogance and insubordination proved a boomerang; instead of injuring Catherine, to whom the Pope was turning more and more trustfully, they injured themselves and their city. Gregory refused to receive them or to lift the ban of excommunication on Florence. When they had left, humiliated, discredited and angry, the Pope began his own preparations for departure.

He did not make them without wavering. His family and his French friends besought him to stay where he was, where they could be with him, where he himself could be happy and safe. Some Spaniard, reported to be a saint, had been vouchsafed a vision in which he had been assured that Gregory would die in the course of his journey if he persisted in traveling to Rome. On hearing this rumor, Catherine immediately felt that it was a hoax and prayed that she might have Divine assurance as to the Pope's safety on his journey. She received this in a supernatural manner, satisfactory to her and to the Pope, whom she had asked to have delivered from all slavish fear. From another quarter came the prediction that, though the Pope would reach Rome safely, he might be poisoned there. This time, Catherine did not resort to prayer; she simply reminded the Pope, rather tartly, that there was likely to be as much poison in Avignon as in Rome. Now it was her hard common sense which prevailed. The interrupted preparations for departure were resumed.

Letters to Rome, long since drafted and then set aside, were put into finished form; they announced the Pope's impending departure from Avignon and his arrival in the Eternal City as soon thereafter as circumstances would permit. A governor was appointed for the city and the province. The Grand Master of the Order of St. John was instructed to ready the fleet to leave Marseilles for Genoa on October 1, and mule trains, laden with heavy ironbound chests, were started on their way to the coast. Six cardinals were given permission to remain in France; the others were instructed to accompany His Holiness or to follow close behind him. Leave-taking, even with those nearest and dearest, was curtailed and the Pope brought it arbitrarily to an end when his aged father knelt before him, imploring him to remain. There was only one way to answer this cry of despair without succumbing to it and this required an act of courage, the greatest in Gregory's life so far. He looked straight ahead of him and silently moved away.

"The Pope set out for Marseille to embark for Rome on September 13. That day marked the end of the exile at Avignon, which had lasted for seventy years. It marked one of the most important events of history, freighted with consequence—an event which for centuries has been discussed by students of history and politics, has been the subject of writers and artists. The hand of a simple virgin had removed barriers that seemed immovable, had done what neither writers nor diplomats nor rulers had been able to do." [11]

14

GREGORY HAD invited Catherine and her companions to travel in his suite, but she had asked to be excused; now that she had accomplished her purpose, by convincing him that he should return to Rome, she longed to retire as far as possible from the limelight and to resume her simple way of life. She did not leave Avignon by boat, as she had come; that mode of travel seemed to resemble too closely the pageantry of the popes. Instead, she and her faithful followers went on foot, like humble pilgrims, as far as Toulon. But her fame had preceded her; she was besieged by such crowds and received with such state by the archbishop that she could find no peace there; and she was so weary that she could not start walking again without a long rest. This would have meant an unwelcome delay, with a rough road stretching out interminably before her and further periods of enforced idleness when she resumed her journey.

Reluctantly, she agreed to continue her travels by sea, with Genoa as her first objective. The voyage was, however, of brief duration. The ship had skirted the coast no further than St. Tropez when a fierce storm forced it into the harbor and again the little band took to the road. But Catherine was no longer a prey to the complete exhaustion which had, at first, engulfed her after the strain of her stay in Avignon, and the crowds which welcomed her now did not overwhelm her like those in Toulon. She was slowly but surely approaching her own country, she would soon be among her own people.

When she reached Varezze, a town that had been decimated by the plague, her sympathy for its misfortunes was tempered by her pleasure in visiting the birthplace of the Blessed Jacopo de Voragine, the author of *The Golden Legend,* which had been one of her favorite books since childhood. Why, she inquired of the prominent citizens who waited on her in a delegation, did they not build a chapel in his honor? It would be a fitting place to pray for deliverance from the dread disease. When she left it was with the knowledge that her suggestion had found favor and, shortly thereafter, she learned that the plague had abated. It never returned.

A warm welcome was awaiting the travelers in Genoa and one of which they were happy to take advantage. A hospitable noblewoman by the name of Orietta Scotto received them as her guests and saw to it that they had the nourishing food and restful quarters of which they were so greatly in need after their long journey. Her home, though it was a palace, did not overwhelm them with its grandeur, like the *livrées* of Avignon. Its unpretentious entrance, modestly marked with the small carved escutcheon of an ancient Scottish family long domiciled in Genoa and related to such powerful Genoese as the Dorias and the Centurioni, was on the Via Canneto il Lungo, one of the innumerable winding streets with which Genoa is honeycombed; and none of the other buildings in the immediate neighborhood was palatial in type and size. But it stood on a corner and, in front, it faced the wharves, the harbor and the open sea, an ever-changing scene of activity and prosperity. All day long ships came into port while others went forth and disappeared, with swollen sails, on the horizon. Along the waterfront, hawkers peddled their wares, children darted among the crowds, soldiers marched and sailors rollicked, priests walked at a measured pace. In the evening, the sunset made the sky a panoply of glory and, soon thereafter, lights began to twinkle on both ships and shore and encircle with radiance the niches where holy images were enshrined on the façade of every house. Then there were moonlight and starlight streaming from the sky to the water and fading only when dawn came to herald another day.

Catherine, who had been unmoved by the splendor of the papal palace rising above the rocks of Avignon, looked out of her high window in the Palazzo Scotti with a prayer of thanksgiving and the joy of homecoming in her heart. No less than the sights she saw, the sounds she heard delighted her: the snatches of song that were as natural as breathing, the ringing of church bells above the clatter of carts, the rapid-fire, animated staccato voices, even the outcry of peddlers vaunting their wares. Once again she found the spirit and strength to receive her visitors cordially, to make visits herself, to resume her correspondence, to map out plans for the future.

But surrounded with comfort and care as she and her companions were, she was not free from anxiety. Stefano Maconi and Neri di Landoccio both fell ill; they required not only rest but medical attention; and though Monna Orietta immediately summoned the best physicians in Genoa to minister to their needs, their condition caused grave concern for some days before their eventual recovery seemed assured. Meanwhile, there had been no word of the Pope's arrival in Genoa; only the news that storms were raging all over the Ligurian Sea and rumors that the flotilla had been obliged to take refuge in one port after another. When Catherine finally learned that the fleet had reached Genoa, after a sixteen-day voyage and a narrow escape from shipwreck, these tidings were coupled with other information which was far from reassuring. Seasickness had taken heavy toll of almost everyone in the papal party, which had not been welcomed as warmly as Catherine and her friends; and, though it had been given hospitality in the palace of Pietro Fregoso, situated near the Church of St. Thomas, it was not as comfortably and pleasantly lodged as they were. The cardinals were all murmuring with dissatisfaction—in fact, there was a concerted movement on foot to convince Gregory that he should return to Avignon. Catherine had not forgotten the estimate of Gregory's character which reckoned docility as one of his best traits. It was on the accuracy of this estimate that she had based her willingness to undertake the mission to Avignon and she had benefited by it. But the cardinals might very well be the ones who would benefit by it now, as they had so often done in the past, before she interfered with their plans. If she had joined the Pope's suite, which she could so easily have done, she could still have pitted her arguments against theirs. But she had considered that her work was done, once she saw Gregory on his way to Marseilles. Now it might easily all be undone.

As she lingered in Genoa, impelled to stay where she was without understanding why, since she greatly longed to go home, she she could not dismiss these troubled thoughts from her mind, either during the activities of the day or the dark watches of the night. The latter she spent, for the most part, on her knees, for prayer was essential to her and it was only then that she could be confident of freedom from worldly intrusion on her communion with heaven. At such times, no one ventured to disturb her; all were concerned lest she should not have enough rest.

Therefore, a knock at the door, long after the palace was customarily sunk in slumber, alarmed her; her immediate thought was of some grave emergency. Neri or Stefano must have taken a turn for the worse; a physician should be summoned at once. But when she answered the knock, the night watchman who stood on the threshold, holding a lantern, told her he had been roused by a priest, who said he had known Sister Catherine in Avignon, and that it was essential he should see her at once. When the watchman had tried to close the door on the midnight intruder, the priest had exclaimed, imploringly, "My need is great. Admit me, in the name of Jesus Christ."

"Bring him to me at once," Catherine said breathlessly.

The watchman turned and went slowly down the long stone staircase that led to the entrance. Catherine remained in the open doorway, listening to his retreating footsteps and then for the sound that would be made by two men, instead of one, ascending the steep and narrow stairs. As these footsteps came nearer and approached the top, she could see by the flickering light of the lantern that the visitor beside the liveried guide was clad in a plain black cassock. Then a gleam fell on a great ring glittering in the gloom. As the watchman withdrew, Catherine fell on her knees before the Pope.

He had come to her in desperation, he told her as he gave her his hand, not only that she might kiss the ring, but that he might help her to rise. He seated himself, insisting that she should be seated too, and he then burst into vehement and desperate speech. Day after day he had listened to advisers who had urged his return to Avignon and their arguments seemed sound. Genoa had received them civilly, if coolly, but no one could tell how long this civility would last; it had a surface quality. Florence or one of its allies might seek, with success, to imprison them. As for Rome, that was in a state of revolution and no one was safe there, least of all the Pope and his princes. And so on and so on until finally there had been a Consistory and the majority of the cardinals had voted for the retreat.

Gregory had told them that he would carefully consider what they said and, when they left him, he did not think they had doubted that the next morning, he would consent to their importunities. To tell the truth, he himself thought this was what he would do—what he should do. But after he had gone to bed, after he was alone with his troubled thoughts—ah, Catherine knew all too well what that could mean!—he was not so sure. He tossed and turned and could not go to sleep. He became convinced that Catherine, and only Catherine, could help him and that he must not delay in seeking her help. So, finally, he rose and dressed, not in the regalia of a pope, but in the plainest of priestly garments. He was determined not to risk recognition and, as a matter of fact, he had experienced no difficulty in getting past the guards of the Fregoso palace. After all, priests came and went all the time; he looked to the watchmen just like any other humble member of the clergy; none of them had noticed the ring, which he had felt he had no right to remove. But crossing the city had been an ordeal. He had never been out in it alone, he did not know his way. And there were roisterers and evil looking men and painted women abroad—no one whom he could ask to direct him. But at last he had come to the cathedral square and he had heard that the Via Canneto il Lungo was not far from there. Then, fortunately, he met a patrol. And, thanks to their guidance, he had arrived.

What Gregory and Catherine said to each other in the next few hours, we do not know. Probably it does not matter, for we know that they understood each other, that there was no language barrier between them any more and, even if there had been, their spiritual harmony was now such that, somehow, they would have overcome it. Gregory himself said that he left Catherine's presence "strengthened and edified." *That* was what mattered. And it was, at last, clear to Catherine why she had felt impelled to remain in Genoa: her work with the Pope had not been done after all. He had come to depend on her while she was in Avignon and, when she was no longer available, he had missed her as a human being and felt lost without her moral support. But now that he had drawn on her strength all through the long night while they talked together, he would be able to resist temptation and prevail against hardship and danger. She could go home.[36]

Again it seemed best to travel by sea, so Catherine and her companions embarked for Leghorn, the port of Pisa, and again they were threatened with shipwreck. But they made harbor safely and found, as always, that their friends in Pisa were delighted to see them. It was pleasant to linger there for a while, without official responsibilities and, as Lapa and Tommaso had joined them, it was not necessary for Catherine to hurry back to Siena for a family reunion. Stefano Maconi went on ahead of them, to arrange a *ridotto*—a little room which could serve as a chapel for Catherine. The news from the Pope was good: he, too, had sailed from Genoa to Leghorn and from there he had gone to Coneto, which was in the Papal State, where he remained to celebrate Christmas. However, early in January, he continued on his way to Rome. None of the dire happenings which had been foretold by false prophets befell him. On the contrary, "the Supreme Pontiff, having arrived at Ostia, made solemn entrance into the city through the Porta San Paolo, riding a white mule, showered with confetti and flowers, amidst the delirious acclamations of the populace. The reception was so enthusiastic and spontaneous and colorful that the observant papal librarian, Pierre Ameilh, who was then compiling a poetic *Itinerarium Gregorii XI* was much impressed: 'Truly I should never have expected, in our time, to see with my own eyes such glory. . . .'

"The reinstatement of the papacy in its rightful place was not only an event, important though it was, in the history of the popes: it was an act that sent new energies flowing through the body of the Church. It was a renascence with consequences that were religious, moral, and political, with effects that were universal. With it began the second part of Catherine's program: the renascence of the Church through the reforms of its pastors. Many bishops, following the example of the Bishop of Rome, returned to their sees, too long vacant. The choice of cardinals and bishops was taken out of French politics and the papacy was liberated from vassalage to the French crown. The City of Rome, with its monuments both sacred and profane, with its relics and its landmarks, began to recover its vigor, despite turbulent and murderous factions, and to become once more the goal of pilgrimages and the common center of peoples: not the least evidence of that re-awakening of Catholicism, to which Catherine had given a decisive stimulus." [11]

15

AFTER HER return to Siena, early in 1377, Catherine continued to keep in touch with the Pope through correspondence with him personally and with general conditions in Florence and Rome through correspondence with numerous others. But she did not give all her time and thought to political matters, as she had for so long felt impelled to do; nor did she have as many family responsibilities as usual. Her mother was visiting at the Convent of Montepulciano, which two of Lapa's granddaughters—the children of Lisa and Bartolommeo—had entered as nuns. Catherine had introduced them to the Superior herself on the occasion of her second visit, which took place some time later than the first, when she went there to recover her strength after her ministrations during the plague, and which had also been marked by miraculous happenings. These, like the elevation of St. Agnes' foot, had been recorded by Fra Raimondo,[37] but conventual life soon resumed its usual peaceful pattern, the young girls progressed from novitiate to profession without any startling incidents, and Lapa was pleased and proud to be under the same roof with them. The long awaited moment, when Catherine could begin the restoration of the Castello Belcaro and prepare it to serve as a Dominican convent had at last apparently arrived.

Once her scruples about accepting so valuable a gift from the prominent financier, Nanni di Vanni Salvini, had been overcome by Fra Raimondo's sage advice, she had yearned to establish a Community there which would be worthy of the exalted name she had given it—Santa Maria degli Angeli; but over and over again she had postponed the establishment in favor of something that seemed to her even more urgent. Now she felt she could allow herself this respite and this reward.

Before the reward could become a fait accompli however, the respite ended; she was again called upon to act as an arbitrator, not between rival states this time, but between rival families, which, in their own way, were quite as powerful. There had been enmity between the Tolomei and the Salimbeni for generations and, more than once, it had taken a murderous turn; now they were at least disposed to call a truce, but they had been at war for so long that they were actually puzzled how to achieve any other state. The situation was further complicated by the fact that the two main branches of the Salimbeni family were at odds with each other and it was obviously necessary that they should become reconciled between themselves before they could hope to be reconciled with anyone else. Still another complication arose when Monna Rabe Tolomei, who had once besought Catherine's help in reforming her dissipated son and wayward daughters, became resentful because the Mantellata had so influenced the son, Matteo, that he had become a Dominican monk, and was in the group that had accompanied or followed Catherine to the remote Salimbeni castello, Rocca di Tentennano, in the Valle d'Orcia, when she went there to visit. Monna Rabe wrote angry letters, demanding Matteo's return and Matteo stubbornly remained in the mountain fortress. After all, he represented the Tolomei side of the ancient feud, which they all wanted to see brought to an end. Where could he operate as successfully as in the very stronghold of the enemy? This was his position, in which he was upheld by his hostess, Countess Bianchina, matriarch of the Salimbeni family.

At best, despite her lifelong devotion to the Salimbeni and theirs to her, Catherine could not have found the visit restful or even pleasant. Although she had never refused her help to anyone who was afflicted in body, mind or spirit, she had always shrunk, instinctively, from those in the second group. This was not from any lack of sympathy with them; it was because she felt that she was not equal to coping with them. Like most persons of her period, even the most learned, she attributed many forms of disaster to the work of demonaic forces—accidents, temptations, backsliding, cowardice, illness and, above all, insanity. Since she herself was "tortured" by demons in the form of temptation and illness, she believed she could not deliver others from "attacks" which took a different form. But when a "woman possessed," who was one of Bianchina's servants, was brought to her without warning, although she rebuked the countess, she took pity on the poor demented creature, as everyone had been sure she would; and after she had effected a cure in that quarter, she undertook others of similar character. Many of the insane were brought to her in fetters, and she always insisted that their chains must be unloosed. She sat quietly on the terrace of the fortress and when the captives had been released and brought to her, she had them kneel down so that they could put their heads in her lap. Holding them thus, one by one, she stroked their hair and their faces, spoke to them soothingly, prayed with them that they might be healed. No matter how filthy they were, she did not shrink away from them. No matter how violent they were at first, she calmed them. And she sent them away cured.

As we have already learned, she could do with very little sleep and, when she was ministering to the sick in hospitals, or presiding over the groups of *Caterinati* who met in her house, she was as active through the hours of the night as she was through the hours of the day. At the Rocca di Tentennano, however, the coming of darkness marked the end of the sessions with the afflicted on the terrace and participation in the gathering of nobles in the great hall. When she left, there was a general dispersal of the tumultuous company and, as she ascended the endless stone stairways and passed through the long dim corridors, her footsteps made the only sound; and when she reached her own small room, the silence and solitude which she so loved enfolded her. In this blessed quietude, if nowhere else, she could find peace.

One night she noticed, for the first time, that a small jar of pigment, with a quill and brushes beside it, lay on the table where she kept her crucifix and her books. Evidently, a well-trained servant had taken it for granted that she would want writing materials; and suddenly she decided that she did, though she had never in her life written anything with her own hand—all her voluminous correspondence had been transcribed by her secretaries, to whom she dictated with amazing ease and speed. Her maternal grandfather,

Nuccio Piacente, though only a humble quilt maker, had composed love lyrics of lofty sentiment. It had never occurred to her that she might have inherited his talent. Now she seated herself and, with comparable ease and speed, wrote a poem in the form of a prayer addressed to the Blessed Trinity:

Spirito Santo vieni nel mio core:
per la tua potenzia trailo a Te,
dammi carità con timore,
guardami, Cristo, da ogni male pensiero,
riscaldami del tuo santissimo amore,
si chè ogni pena mia paia leggiera,
Santo il mio Padre e dolce il mio Signore,
aiutami in ogni mio ministero
Cristo amore, Cristo amore.[38]

I believe that no one who reads her story could doubt that the help for which she asked in her ministry was granted her.[39]

16

CATHERINE'S LONG stay at the Rocca di Tentennano pleased no one besides herself and the Salimbeni. In the first place, it awakened uneasiness and distrust among the Defenders of the Sienese Government. "The Salimbenis had always been disturbers of the peace and time and time again had been at open war with the Republic"; what new political plots might not be hatching, far off in a castello which was also a fortress, situated at the top of an almost impregnable mountain, overlooking the wild and desolate Valle d'Orcia? Catherine replied to this charge indignantly: "The citizens of Siena should be thoroughly ashamed of themselves if they think we are staying with the Salimbeni to forge secret alliances." [13] Nevertheless, they continued to think so.

The Pope was equally displeased with her long period of seclusion on private property, not because he wanted her back in Siena, but because he wanted her back in Florence. In October of 1377, the Florentines had won a great victory over the Pope's mercenary army and, on the strength of it, decided to flout his authority. This attitude of defiance spread to the local clergy, who again began to say Mass quite openly, sometimes under civic compulsion, but sometimes of their own free will. The unhappy pontiff apparently had no power over them. He was, moreover, in great financial difficulties, which made his position all the more troublesome, since he could not resort to monetary persuasion. In his misery and bewilderment, he acted with characteristic lack of judgment, by trying to persuade Bernabò Visconti, of all men, to act as arbitrator in a situation for which that evil man's action had been, in no small degree, responsible. Fortunately, the Duke of Milan, whatever his lack of principle, was still too adroit a politician to become involved in a dispute, the outcome of which could not have possibly made him the gainer.

In response to the Pope's rebuke for her inaccessibility, Catherine wrote him more respectfully than she had the Defenders and entrusted the delivery of this letter to Fra Raimondo. Whether or not she would have done so if she had realized that, as soon as he returned to Rome, he would be reappointed Prior of Santa Maria sopra Minerva and that she would lose him as her confessor may be open to doubt. He had become extremely valuable to her in every way, and she may well have felt that since part of this value lay in the fact that she could share it with others she was entitled to it; at all events, she suffered very keenly at his loss.

While it may be presumed that he did, too, there were certainly compensations for him in the position that had been restored to him and, shortly after his return to Rome, he was summoned into the Pope's presence for a personal conference. It was rumored, Gregory said, that if Catherine would go back to Florence, the Florentines would make peace. Raimondo could not deny that there might well be some truth in the rumor; just before his departure from Siena, he had received a visit from Niccolo Soderini, who had intimated that the Florentines really did want peace, and who had mentioned several expedients which he thought might help to bring it about. Though Catherine's name did not arise in the course of conversation, it was there by inference. Raimondo did not feel happy at the prospect of sending her on what would probably be a dangerous mission, but he could not deny that it might also be an effective one. He was dismissed, only to be recalled soon thereafter and entrusted with credentials for Catherine. She was to proceed to Florence as the Pope's ambassador.

She now had no choice but to go there, just as she had had no choice but to go to Lucca when he ordered her there two years earlier. She took no priests with her this time, for she must appear to respect the interdict, even if the Florentines did not. However, as usual, the faithful Mantellate and Maconi and Neri accompanied her; so did the old hermit Santi, whom she had saved from the plague. Also as usual, she and her followers were invited to stay at the Palazzo Soderini. She appreciated the friendship of which this hospitality was a token; but increasingly she felt the need of solitary periods, on which she had always been dependent, and which were somehow harder to achieve in a nobleman's palace than they had been in the crowded household of a dyer. The weight of her responsibilities lay heavily upon her; she wanted and needed to be not only completely alone, but completely free from interruptions as she prayerfully thought over her problems and decided on her course of action. Recognizing this, her friends made a singularly gracious gesture: among Soderini's extensive holdings around the city were many hillside vineyards; he gave her a small parcel of land on one of these and had space cleared for a garden there; then, under the direction of the Canigiani, other members of the Guelph party contributed the money for the building of a little tower house. It contained only an oratory and a room which served both as a chamber and as a study. But that sufficed for all Catherine's needs. Gratefully, she withdrew to it whenever it was possible for her to do so. Like the biblical husbandman, she now had "a tower and a vineyard." They became not only her chosen headquarters, but her chosen refuge.[40]

The leaders among the Guelphs were not wholly disinterested in their satisfaction at having Catherine with them. Since she was the Pope's representative, her presence gave them an excuse for harsh measures against the so-called warmongers. But this time, the Florentines at least had more respect for the interdict than before the Pope's return from Avignon, and priests were not forced, against their consciences and their vows, to hold sacrilegeous services. Catherine believed this was the first sign that the citizens wished to return to grace and wrote diligently to all the monks and nuns of her acquaintance, asking for their prayers toward this end. Next, she succeeded in persuading the various powers to call a peace conference at Sarzana, a small city in northern Tuscany, to which the Pope sent three cardinals—all French—and Florence five ambassadors. Venice, France and Naples also sent emissaries and Bernabò Visconti represented Milan in person. There was every reason to expect promising results. But hardly were the meetings under way, when the sudden death of Gregory brought them to an abrupt end. The Cardinals departed for Rome to elect his successor; the ambassadors returned to their own countries; negotiations were, necessarily, at a standstill, awaiting instructions from the new Pope. It was a serious setback.

The reluctant choice of the Consistory fell upon the Archbishop of Bari, a Neapolitan by the name of Bartolommeo Prignano, who took the name of Urban VI. He was elected amidst scenes of great disorder, and there were even efforts to nullify the election, by forcing a miter on the head of the aged Cardinal Tebaldeschi and presenting him to the crowds, who were clamoring for a Roman pope, as the real choice of the Consistory. Tebaldeschi himself desired no part in this outrage and Prignano gave short shrift to the rebels; he pointed out that he had been chosen by the majority of votes, as decreed by the late Pope Gregory, and that his election was, therefore, valid.

In background, in character, in viewpoint and in methods, the new Pope was as different from his predecessor as was humanly possible. At Avignon, where he and Catherine had already met and become friends, he had been conspicuous for his austerity and integrity in a court otherwise luxury loving and corrupt. Furthermore, far from being indolent like his associates, he was a model of industry; as Vice-Chancellor of the late Pope, he had proven himself an able administrator. But he was severe, intolerant and unforgiving, both in his policies and in his manner of enforcing these. Though Catherine could count on him to begin the reforms with which Gregory had dallied so disastrously, she knew she could not depend on him to be patient with wrongdoers and merciful to them. He demanded of the Florentines not peace at any price, but peace at his price. The result, as might have been expected, was civil war.

After the failure of the conference at Sarzana, Catherine had decided that she should remain in Florence, awaiting developments. She was, of course, no longer an ambassador, since the Pope who had appointed her was dead and Urban had taken no official action, as far as she was concerned, though she had been in friendly communication with him. But she kept hoping that, in one way or another, she might prove her usefulness. However, as the Guelph patricians continued their policy of persecution, the resentment of the Ghibelline plebeians flared into rebellion and, presently, the whole city was the prey of mob violence as unreasoning as it was devastating. From her hillside retreat, Catherine could see the flames that devoured the homes of her friends and protectors and hear the shouts of the marauders and the screams of their victims. She knew it would not be long before the murderous mob reached the vineyard and she had no delusions as to her probable fate when it did. But the idea of flight never once entered her mind. When the raiders were so close that she could hear the raucous cries of "Catherine! Where is the damn witch?" she went quietly forward to meet them as they burst into the garden, carrying clubs, torches and bared swords. Then she fell quickly on her knees.

"I am Catherine," she said calmly. "If you have been appointed to kill me, do so."

The leader of the band, whose arm was already raised to strike her down, stammered and sheathed his sword, drawing away from her with the same haste that he had shown a moment earlier as he rushed forward. Then he turned and fled, his followers tearing after him. Something stronger than witchcraft was at work; they hastened to escape from it while there was yet time.

Catherine rose from her knees and again gazed sadly out at the burning city. She would have welcomed martyrdom. It was life, in a world of hatred and violence, that seemed unbearable to her.

However she may have felt about remaining where she was—and evidently that is what she wanted and intended to do—she was almost forcibly persuaded that she must not. Neither the Canigiani nor the Soderini could offer her hospitality now, for their palazzos were among those which had been burned. But the tailor, Francesco di Pippini, and his wife Agnese, who had been among Catherine's first friends in Florence, when she came to appear before the tribunal, had been left unmolested, and they now offered her asylum which she accepted. However, even their home did not assure her of safety, so she left Florence for a "woodland retreat." It is not certain whether this was on the heights of Vallombrosa or in the Casentino Valley; possibly she went to both; either would have been appropriate and would have had a great appeal to her. It will be recalled that her friend and advocate, Giovanni delle Celle, whose support had been so invaluable to her at the time of her trial, was a monk at Vallombrosa, which had a superb location and was equipped with a pleasant and commodious guest house. Moreover, it had a poignant history: it had been founded by a young nobleman, Giovanni Gualberto, who, realizing it was Good Friday, had spared the life of his most deadly enemy, when the man who had killed his brother was suddenly at his mercy. Then he had stolen into the church of the Benedictines "and prayed before the great Crucifix, begging God to pardon him; and while he prayed thus, the Christ miraculously bowed His head 'as it were to give him a token how acceptable was his sacrifice of his resentment.'" After that, Giovanni did not wish to leave and the monks readily received him as a novice. But when he had dwelt with them several years, he set out with one companion "to search for closer solitude" and, discovering it at Vallombrosa, founded a community of his own, with the doctrine of forgiveness for its Gospel.

This story would have been deeply moving to Catherine; she would have loved living where she would constantly be reminded of it. But she would also have thought of La Verna, in the Casentino Valley, as a hallowed spot, because there "in a lonely and stony place rises the strange rock, set with cypress and with fir, backed by marvelous great hills" where, on the Feast of the Exaltation of the Holy Cross, St. Francis of Assisi received the stigmata. At La Verna, Catherine would also have found comfort and quietude.

Nevertheless, she could not be content to remain long absent from what she considered her post of duty and, on her return to Florence, she wrote to Raimondo with an urgent message for the Pope. "'I must beg you to ask Christ on earth not to let peace be delayed because of what has happened. On the contrary—say to him that he must work even faster to bring about peace, so that he can be free to occupy himself with the great plans he has for the glory of God and the rebuilding of the Church. For these events have not altered anything, and the town is now quite calm. Tell him to hurry, in the name of mercy, for it is the only way that an end can be made to the innumerable offences which have been committed against God. Tell him that he must have mercy and sympathy for the souls which are in darkness. Tell him that he must free me from this prison, because if no peace is made I feel it impossible to leave the town, and I long to come away and taste the blood of the holy martyrs, to visit His Holiness and meet you again, so that I can tell you of the wonderful things God has done in these days to delight our souls, intoxicate our hearts and increase our hope in the light of our holy faith.'" [13]

Next, she wrote to Urban himself, over and over again. Her first letter was merely a plea for mercy—and still more mercy toward the wrongdoers who had incurred his wrath. In the next one, she begged him to be patient with those who had given him advice, assuring him that this was done only for his welfare, as a son would do if he were really fond of his father. " 'He cannot bear,' she continues, 'to see anything done which might bring shame or injustice on his father, and he watches zealously, for he knows that his father is only human, and has such a large family to look after that he himself cannot see everything. If his true-born sons do not watch over his honour he will often be betrayed. So it is with Your Holiness; you are father and lord of the whole of Christendom, Holy Father; we are all under your wings. You have authority over all things, but the range of your eye is limited as is all men's, and therefore it is necessary that your children keep watch with honesty and without slavish fear, and do all that can serve the glory of God and your honour, for the safety of the souls which are under your care. I know that Your Holiness deeply desires to find helpers who can serve you, but then it is necessary to be patient with them. . . .' " [13]

Other forces, besides that of Catherine's eloquence, were, undoubtedly, also at work. But whatever these were, they do not seem to have had the same power over the Pope as this rain of letters which appealed to his reason, as well as his heart. He was admittedly a stern man, even a vengeful one; but he was not immovable; in the end it was he who capitulated. On July 18, 1377, a messenger arrived in Florence from Rome, bearing an olive branch; on the 28th, a treaty of peace was signed. Two days later, Catherine left her tower and her vineyard never to see them again.

"After the return of the Pope to Rome, the pacification of Florence was her greatest triumph. She had labored for peace without counting danger and fatigue. And now she had completed her task; so at long last, as she had desired, she could leave Florence and return home." [11]

17

LISA COLOMBINI, Catherine's beloved sister-in-law, had inherited the Benincasa family farm near San Rocco a Pilli and it was there and not to Siena itself that Catherine went first. She had always loved it and she believed that if peace and quiet existed anywhere on earth, she should be able to find them here. But, apparently, they did not. She was almost immediately greeted with tidings that seemed to her even worse than any she had heard before. She was, of course, aware of the disgraceful rioting which had marred the Consistory when Bartolommeo Prignano received the majority of votes and took the name of Urban VI; but no one had then taken too seriously the bit of shameful play acting in which Cardinal Tebaldeschi had been forcefully mitered. Now one of the very men who had most warmly supported Urban at that time, namely Cardinal Robert of Geneva, was a ringleader in a revolt against him. Encouraged by Robert, thirteen cardinals declared that they had voted for Prignano only to avoid certain death at the hands of a mob which was clamoring for an Italian and that, as he was chosen under duress, the election was unlawful. These cardinals put themselves under the protection of Count Gaetano of Fondi, who had a grudge of his own against Urban, and foregathered in the city which he ruled. There they elected Robert as their "pope." He took the name of Clement VII and lost no time in hurrying off to Avignon. What was soon to be known as the Great Western Schism had begun. The terrible spectacle of a divided Christendom darkened the earth.

Why Catherine should have felt the least personal responsibility for this catastrophe may be somewhat puzzling to the modern mind. But the fact remains that she did. She believed that, if she had prayed more earnestly and practiced greater self-denial, if she had used her God-given eloquence to greater avail, it might have been averted. She felt weighted down with such a sense of inadequacy and unworthiness that she even hesitated to approach the altar rail. But fortunately for her—and for the world—her depression did not result in a state of desuetude, but in fresh firmness of purpose. She felt sure that the Pope—the real Pope—would send for her and that, when he did, she must go to Rome. She also felt sure that when she left home this time, it would be forever.

There was not much she needed to do, in a material way, to prepare for this permanent leave-taking. The Convent of St. Mary of the Angels, which she had established at Belcaro, would now have to pass out of her control, but that could not be helped; if it were the will of God that the community should flourish, it would go on without her. She visited it, of course, and satisfied herself that everything there was as it should be, for the time being. But she did not worry about it.[41] On the other hand, she felt a burning need to unburden her soul of much that she had still left unsaid, despite the hundreds of letters she had already written. In October, 1378, she left San Rocca a Pilli and sought out a solitary cell, long the habitat of her early friend and follower, Fra Santi, who gladly put it at her disposal. It was located, not far from other similar retreats, on the pleasant outskirts of Siena. There she spent some days in prayer and meditation. Then she sent for three of her faithful disciples, Barduccio, Stefano and Neri, and charged them to listen attentively and record carefully everything she was about to say. They promised to obey her faithfully and took turns in recording her words, though she went on and on, without stopping, for five days.

The result of this amazing feat, unparalleled in literature, was one of the most remarkable documents that has ever been given to mankind. In length, it is enormous. (In a modern edition it runs to over five hundred printed pages.) But its scope is by no means only that of size. As Fra Raimondo, her first biographer, says, it "is a book overflowing with deep life-giving thoughts, revealed to her by the

Lord." Catherine herself referred to it simply as "The Book" or "My Book"; it was Raimondo who gave it a title and called it "The Dialogue" because "the saint in the first thirteen chapters tells of making four requests of our Lord; the remainder of the book contains the responses of our Lord to her in the form of doctrinal exposition." The four "requests" are all supplications for mercy: "(1) for Catherine herself; (2) for the world; (3) for the Church; (4) for a particular case. But around these points Catherine develops and weaves in subjects of general interest. . . . In a period of bewilderment she gives anew a direction and a significance to existence: the direction of the divine and the significance of an ascent to God. She gives strength again to a people oppressed by fear, recalling all men to the beauty of sanctity, in which the soul, though existing in a mortal body, may even now taste immortality and, receiving everything from the hand of God, accepts tribulation along with consolation, life along with death; without being discouraged, always unafraid, founded upon a living rock. . . .

"In the *Dialogue,* therefore, we contemplate, in the divine sphere, the drama of the soul and of the Church in a critical hour of her history; something of the rapture of an apocalypse, reaching up to heaven for enlightenment and energy, and then taking up again on earth, with more force than ever, the perennial fight against the error of antichrist and his seizure of souls, to bring them back to the reality of the Redemption." [11]

When the book was finished, Catherine was ready to obey the expected summons from the Pope and go to Rome.

As usual, she was accompanied by a sizable group, which included most of her old friends; they traveled as beggars, asking for alms along the way and, when they reached Rome, they took humble lodgings on a street at the foot of the Pincio and continued to ask for alms. Evidently these were always forthcoming, since Catherine insisted on keeping open house, as far as her Sienese friends were concerned. Any and all of them who came to the Eternal City were her welcome guests, as long as they chose to remain, and were given ample opportunity to see all the great sights and undertake pilgrimages to holy places. In time, this expansive hospitality necessitated a move to a larger house in a different district, near the Church of Santa Maria sopra Minerva.

Catherine's own personal welcome in Rome had been all that she could possibly wish and, in the face of it, her shaken morale must almost certainly have taken a turn for the better. The Pope had not been able to move into the Vatican, as the Romans were besieging the nearby castle fortress of Sant' Angelo, which a French garrison was holding for Clement. Urban was living at the monastery adjoining the Church of Santa Maria in Trastevere. Joyfully, he received Catherine and asked her to address the assembled cardinals on the subject of this schism, now no longer a sad prospect but a still sadder fact. Her speech, in which she dwelt first on God's providence and then on the need of courage in times of adversity, was a tremendous success. When she finished, Urban exclaimed, "This little woman puts us all to shame by her calmness and her strength! In the face of them, how can the Vicar of Christ show fear and fail His Church even if the whole world seem against him?"

He dismissed her and her companions with his blessing and after that they continued to see each other often. As the Pope was still living in a state of siege, deserted even by many of those whom he had most reason to trust—among them three Italian cardinals—Catherine advised him to collect a bodyguard of faithful clerics, seeking them out wherever they happened to be stationed and bidding them come to Rome. Among those so summoned was Catherine's old friend, the Prior of the Carthusian Monastery at Gorgona, and she supplemented the Pope's letter with one of her own. He responded gladly, as did most of the others who were approached; the most notable among the exceptions was another old friend, William Flete, the English hermit of Lecceto. He declined to leave his solitary retreat, and Catherine's assurance that woods and solitude could be found in the vicinity of Rome, no less than in the vicinity of Siena, failed to move him. Her next letter to him was one of rebuke. "The glow of your faith cannot be very ardent if you risk losing it by changing your dwelling." [13]

By no means were all of Catherine's associations with the Pope formal and official in character. At Christmastime, she sent him five oranges, still something of a rarity in Italy at that time. St. Dominic, the founder of her Order, had brought the first orange tree from Spain and planted it in the cloistered garden of the Monastery of St. Sabina.[42] Doubtless it was from this tree that Catherine plucked the fruit which she candied and covered with gold leaf.

She accompanied her gift with a charming letter, in which she first told the Pope that she desired to free him from the bitter agony which raged in his soul and prayed that this agony might disappear, so that he might know nothing but the sweet pain which makes the soul strong and passionate. "It is the pain which springs from the love of God," she told him. "I mean the sorrow and pain caused by our own faults." She then developed the theme of the difference between bitter pain and sweet pain and accompanied her letter with a series of wise maxims and a recipe for transforming bitter oranges into a delectable sweetmeat, by soaking them in boiling water, substituting "good and nutritious things" for the tough membrane and finally gilding the outside in order that it might have appeal to the eye, as well as to the palate. "What has become of the bitterness that was so unpleasant to human taste?" she asked. "It is drawn out by the fire and the water. Most Holy Father, it is just the same with a soul which understands the need of virtue. The beginning seems bitter, for the soul is still imperfect, but if it uses the remedy, which is the blood of Christ Crucified, then the water of grace which is in the blood will draw out the physical bitterness which causes our dislike."

The following spring, the fortress of Sant' Angelo formally surrendered to the Romans and the Pope was able, at long last, to leave Santa Maria in Trastevere and take up his residence in the Vatican. According to Fra Raimondo, it was Catherine who advised Urban to go barefoot from the place where he had taken sanctuary to his rightful dwelling, as an outward and visible sign of his gratitude to God. "An enormous crowd of people, wild with joy, followed the thanksgiving procession. Many considered that they could thank the Seraphic Virgin from Siena for the victory. Like Moses in the Old Testament, she had plucked victory for her people from heaven, with her hands which she held up in ceaseless prayer." [13]

But she could not hold up those praying hands much longer. She was only thirty-three years old, but her fragile body was now held erect only by the force of an interior flame and this was beginning to flicker. She had said of herself, "Fire is my nature," and this was true; but the fire had ceased to burn brightly and she did not try to kindle it anew. She no longer took a morsel of food or even a drop of water. She lived only upon the Eucharistic Host, just as her soul lived only upon Christ. She still wrote on and on, she still remained accessible to her family and friends, she still went regularly to Mass, though the time came when she could no longer go to St. Peter's, as had been her wont, but only to the oratory in her own house.[43] And, until the last moment, she continued to pray with such intensity that her disciples said afterward they thought not only their hearts but the "very stones" would break. Everything and everyone she had loved was included in these fervent prayers. She had never known fear in her life and she did not know it now in the presence of death, only joy and thanksgiving. "Beloved, You call me and I come . . . Father, into Your hands I commit my spirit." She made the Sign of the Cross and then she folded her hands and they were still. She lay at rest and her face was radiant, like that of an angel.

Catherine was canonized in 1461 by Pope Pius II (Aeneas Piccolomini of Siena). He drew up her Office with his own hand and the ceremony of canonization forms the subject of one of the great paintings in the splendid library of the cathedral in Siena which bears his name.

The dyer's daughter, whose powers of public service to her people and her Church and of private communication with her Savior, had transcended her womanhood. She had sanctified all three.

That was her way of love.

NOTES AND REFERENCES

Saint Agnes of Rome

1. Helen Walker Homan, *Saints of the Canon.* (Washington: National Council of Catholic Women).
2. H. V. Morton, *A Traveller in Rome.* (London: Methuen & Co., Ltd.)
3. The members of this community are called Donna (Lady) and not Sister or Mother, a custom comparable to that of certain Religious of the Sacred Heart who are addressed as Madam.
4. This pope, Clement VII (Giulio di Medici), who ruled rightfully from 1523 to 1534, is not to be confused with the antipope Robert of Geneva, who had taken the same name in 1378 (see p. 260 of Part III, Catherine of Siena).
5. John Farrow, *Pageant of the Popes.* (New York: Sheed and Ward).
6. This may be freely translated, embodying two of the sayings of Damasus, as:

   "History relates that, when the trumpet of persecution sounded its mournful note, the instinct of the little virgin, despite her youth, enabled her to protect herself against the tyrant, inflamed with evil passion. She conquered the fears that threatened to overcome her and covered herself with her tresses [protecting her chastity under a golden veil] so that no mortal eye saw the body that was the temple of the Lord.

   "O venerable virgin, illustrious martyr! I pray that you may favorably regard the petition of Damasus and grant him the gift and ornament of modesty."
7. J. P. V. D. Balsdon, *Roman Women—Their History and Habits.* (London: The Bodley Head).
8. Stewart Perowne, *Caesars and Saints.* (London: Hodder and Stoughton).

9. John Dennie, *Rome of To-day and Yesterday—The Pagan City.* (New York: G. P. Putnam's Sons).
10. John Coulson, *The Saints—A Concise Biographical Dictionary.* (New York: Hawthorn Books, Inc.)
11. To be sure, Tennyson has mistakenly connected Agnes with a convent, but his poem is permeated with his feeling for her purity. Keats's "Eve of St. Agnes" is admittedly a chronicle of romantic love, but the opening lines, dwelling on the bitter cold, reveal his knowledge of her feast day's date—January 21—and the poem is one of the most beautiful in the English language.
12. Cecilia, though wedded, according to Roman law, to a nobleman by the name of Valerian, is always listed as a virgin, as well as a martyr, because her husband respected her private vow to become the bride of Christ and never exercised his marital rights.
13. Monsignor Pio Cenci, *S. Agnese.* (Rome: Edizioni Bibliotechina).
14. Hymn of Prudentius.

Santa Francesca Romana

1. Actually, Siena dresses in medieval costume twice a year, for the Palio takes place both on July 2 and August 16.
2. H. V. Morton, *A Traveller in Rome.* (London: Methuen & Co., Ltd.)
3. Literally, Pious House of the Broken Bridge and House of Spiritual Exercises. The name Ponterotto was formerly applied to an entire district, but now is only used in very old titles, except when it refers to the actual bridge which, in its shattered condition, still partially spans the Tiber.
4. This manger is made from part of a fourth-century tomb, very similar in design to those at the famous Aliscamps in Arles, France.
5. Poem by Marigold Hunt as quoted in *More Saints for Six O'Clock* by Joan Windham. (London: Sheed and Ward).
6. José Antonio del Busto D. *El Arcabucero Gaspar de Flores, Padre de Santa Rosa.* (Lima: *Revista Historica,* Vol. XXIII, 1960).
7. The heraldic bearings—two lions rampant, supporting a globe—on the stone which once marked the grave of Paolo di Bussi, preserved in the Convent of the Tor di Specchi, testify to his right to a coat of arms.
8. Rome was then, as it is still, divided into fourteen *rioni,* or wards: Monti, Trevi, Colonna, Campo Marzo, Ponte, Parione, Regola, Sant' Eustachio, Pigna, Campitelli, Sant' Angelo, Ripa, Trastevere and Borgo. Parione continued to be among the most elegant of these.

The Church of St. Agnes and, indeed, the entire Piazza Navona—built on the site of Domitian's race track—is now famous for the seventeenth-century Bernini fountains. These, and the unique celebration known as the Befana (which takes place on the Eve of Epiphany) are among its most famous sights. Others include Bramante's architectural masterpiece, the Palazzo della Cancelleria and Peruzzi's Palazzo Massimo.

"The Palace of the Massimo, once built to follow the curve of a narrow winding street, but now facing the same great thoroughfare as the Cancelleria, has something of the same quality, with a wholly different character. It is smaller and more gloomy, and its columns are almost black with age; it was here, in 1455, that Pannartz and Schweinheim, two of those nomadic German scholars who have not yet forgotten the road to Italy, established their printing-press in the house of Pietro de' Massimi, and here took place one of those many romantic tragedies which darkened the end of the sixteenth century. For a certain Signore Massimo, in the year 1585, had been married and had eight sons, mostly grown men, when he fell in love with a light-hearted lady of more wit than virtue, and announced that he would make her his wife, though his sons warned him that they would not bear the slight upon their mother's memory. The old man, infatuated and beside himself with love, would not listen to them, but published the banns, married the woman, and brought her home for his wife.

"One of the sons, the youngest, was too timid to join the rest; but on the next morning the seven others went to the bridal apartment, and killed their stepmother when their father was away. But he came back before she was quite dead, and he took the Crucifix from the wall by the bed and cursed his children. And the curse was fulfilled upon them.

"Parione is the heart of Mediaeval Rome, the very centre of that black cloud of mystery which hangs over the city of the Middle Age. A history might be composed out of Pasquin's sayings, volumes have been written about Cardinal Pompeo Colonna and the ruin he wrought, whole books have been filled with the life and teachings and miracles of Saint Philip Neri, who belonged to this quarter, erected here his great oratory, and is believed to have recalled from the dead a youth of the house of Massimo in that same gloomy palace.

"The story of Rome is a tale of murder and sudden death, varied, changing, never repeated in the same way; there is blood on every threshold; a tragedy lies buried in every church and chapel; and again we ask in vain wherein lies the magic of the city that has fed on terror and grown old in carnage, the charm that draws men to her, the power that holds, the magic that enthralls men soul and body, as Lady Venus cast her spells upon Tannhauser in her mountain of old. Yet none deny it, and as centuries roll on, the poets, the men of letters, the musicians, the artists of all ages, have come to her from far countries and have dwelt here while they might, some for long years, some for the few months they could spare; and all of them have left something, a verse, a line, a sketch, a song that breathes the threefold mystery of love, eternity and death." (*Ave Roma Immortalis Studies from the Chronicles of Rome* by Francis Marion Crawford, 2 vol. The Macmillan Company, New York).

9. Berthem-Bontoux, *Sainte Françoise Romaine et Son Temps* (1384-1440). (Paris: Librarie Bloud & Gay).
10. Lady Georgiana Fullerton, *The Life of St. Frances of Rome, of Blessed Lucy of Narni, of Dominica of Paradiso, and of Anne de Montmorency:* with an introductory essay on the miraculous life of the saints by J. M. Capes, Esq. (London: Burns and Lambert).
11. H. V. Morton, *A Traveller in Rome.* (London: Methuen & Co., Ltd.)
    Among the frescoes in the reception room which adjoins the superb Lancisiana Library on the second floor of the hospital is one showing the presentation of the dead babies to the Pope and one showing the foster mothers feeding the babies to the sound of music. From the library it is possible to look down on the immense Corsia Sistina from the window of a concealed alcove, originally constructed for the express purpose of permitting the Grand Master of the Hospital to observe the great ward at any time, day or night, without being seen himself, and assure himself that the four hundred patients installed there were having every care and attention.
12. John Farrow, *Pageant of the Popes.* (New York: Sheed and Ward).
13. *Arcispedale di Santo Spirito in Saxia.* Official brochure of the hospital.
14. Though the basic structure of the Ponziani palace remains unchanged and—as I said in Chapter 1—the cellar, the banqueting hall and the chamber where the saint died may still all be seen in their original size and shape, the loggias and balconies and part of the inner court have disappeared and, therefore cannot be described except in a general way. Berthem-Bontoux in her voluminous biography of the saint takes great pains to enlighten the reader as to what they probably looked like. She mentions the frescoes in the Campo Santo of Pisa as showing many types of loggias and draws special attention to a fresco representing a three-story house which she believes may have borne a strong resemblance to that of the Ponziani. She

draws attention to the different types of courtyards found in the palace of the Medici in Florence, the Bevillacqua in Bologna and the Cancelleria in Rome, any one of which she thinks the palace of the Ponziani may have resembled. She also points out two rather interesting details: first, that though the Romans so enthusiastically accepted loggias and balconies, they never cared for ornate exterior staircases; and second, that practically none of the Italian houses built during the Middle Ages and Renaissance had chimneys! Such heat as the Romans had at this period—and it must have been sadly inadequate—came from what was apparently a type of brazier, as she goes on to say, *"on y était dans-l'usage de faire du feu dans des caisses pleines de terre et au milieu des chambres. Le mot* caminata, *qui figure dans les écrits du temps, indiquait seulement le lieu où l'on allumait du feu. Le palais Ponziani était certainement dans ce cas, car nous verrons Françoise descendre maintes fois, de nuit, à la cuisine, pour y faire chauffer des linges destinés à son mari depuis longtemps malade; d'autre part, un tas de cendre, provenant sans doute de la caisse à feu, servira au démon pour persécuter la sainte en prière dans son oratoire."*

Curiously enough, Berthem-Bontoux does not mention the fact that a loggia, especially provided so that the young bachelors of a prominent family might entertain their friends without supervision, was occasionally located some distance from the parental palace, as a separate entity. An arresting example of this is the beautiful loggia in Siena, located behind the great Piccolomini palace on the Via Ricasole and known as the *Loggia del Papa* (the Pope's Loggia) because it was built by Aenas Piccolomini, who later became Pius II, for the diversion of his family. (This is the same Pope who canonized his fellow Sienese, Catherine.) This loggia was designed by Antonio Federighi and is large and imposing. Another Sienese example of the same type is called the *Loggia della Mercanzia* (the Market Loggia) and was designed by Sano di Matteo in 1416 and mainly executed by Pietro del Minella in 1438. This, as its description implies, was built primarily not for the use of young men of prominent families and their close friends, but for a group of young merchants; however, it fulfills the same general principle: that of serving as a "sort of outdoor club for the young men of the period."

It is interesting to speculate whether or not such separate loggias may not have been the Italian forerunners of the French *Maisons de bouteille,* also called *vide-bouteilles* (literally, bottle-houses or bottle-emptiers) later provided on the outskirts of cities so that gay young blades might pass convivial hours without supervision.

15. Modern readers, used to the present spacing of Jubilee Years, may be confused at a reference to those occurring as close together as 1390, 1400 and 1423. There was a special reason for this which is explained in *The Sublime City,* edited by Igino Cecchetti, in the following manner:

"After the great Jubilee of 1300, there came sad days in the history of the Church. Boniface died outraged, and the Apostolic See was transported to Avignon. In 1343, the Romans sent an Ambassador to Pope Clement VI begging him to return to Rome and proclaim the Great Jubilee. . . .

"But the Pope did not return for the Jubilee. Clement VI was too much bound to France. . . . The Holy Year was not the splendid and magnificent success people thought it would be, but it corresponded to the spiritual needs of the day, although it failed to remedy the evils created in Rome by the absence of the Papal Court. Many years were still to pass and innumerable miseries to visit Rome and Italy before the Pope returned to his See. When he did come back, his advent was accompanied by new evils caused by the lack of understanding between the court and the citizens. Rome could not do without a Pope. The city without the Pontiff was a ring without a jewel. But how many times was he not met with violence. And for reasons on which we cannot dwell here, when he did come back, a terrible schism broke out causing great harm to the Church.

"The third Jubilee was celebrated in the atmosphere of that schism. Despite his shortcomings, Urban VI was really a holy man. For him the Jubilee was the remedy for the scandal of the two Popes and the two obediences struggling with each other. For him it was also a cure for schism. Remembering Our Lord's death, he commanded that the Holy Year should take place every thirty-three years. The last had taken place in 1350, so the next should be proclaimed in 1383. But in 1383 Urban was constrained to leave Rome and wander far. In 1389, when he was at last able to return to his palace next to Saint Peter's, he hastened to proclaim the Jubilee which took place under his successor Boniface IX. It was one of the most glorious Jubilees in history. Before ten years had passed, people were already thinking of another Jubilee. The Romans remembered that Pope Clement VI had ordered the Jubilee to be celebrated every fifty years and fifty years were up in 1400. People began to remark that they were beginning a new century. What was going to be done about the Jubilee? The schism gave no signs of ceasing and Christendom merely tried to unite its scattered and disunited members.

"A wave of spirituality passed over Northern Italy in 1399. It was the movement of the 'WHITES,' people dressed in white who went from city to city, a cross in their hands praying and asking for peace and repentance. They moved towards Rome also and united themselves to the citizens demanding a Holy Year. This Jubilee therefore was celebrated at the instance of the people. The Pope hastened to make peace with Rome and the Romans hurried to make peace with him, renouncing certain privileges which they had enjoyed for a long time in order to put no obstacle in his way. The Pope returned to Rome, because of the Holy Year of Pardon, as he insisted on calling it."

Cecchetti further tells us that "among the pilgrims of the fourth Holy Year in 1400 was a young French peasant girl named Isabell, who on January 6, 1412 was to give birth to Saint Joan of Arc, the second patron saint of France. There was also Duccio Corsini, ancestor of Saint Andrew Corsini, and Blessed John Dominici who was to have so influential a part in the schism of Avignon and the conversion of the Hussites. The most remarkable feature of this Jubilee was however a mass pilgrimage known as the 'FLAGELLANTI.' They wore a white cloak with a red cross and went about chanting sacred hymns and in the intervals scourging themselves."

16. This child, like his young cousins, is buried in the family chapel of the Ponziani in St. Cecilia's Church.
17. Paolo di Bussi was buried in the vault of the Church of St. Agnes on the Piazza Navona, with which the family already had such close associations. The slab which once marked his tomb, adorned with his coat of arms, was moved from the Church of St. Agnes to the Tor di Specchi when the former was reconstructed.
18. Indeed, some of Francesca's biographers have made the same sad mistake. Lady Georgiana Fullerton says, "He [Ladislas] was continually looking out for occasions to persecute those Roman nobles who remained faithful to the cause of the Church. He was abetted in this by the faction of the Colonnas, and some other powerful families, who supported the pretensions of the anti-popes Gregory XII. and Benedict XIII. against the legitimate pontiff Alexander V., recently elected by the Council of Pisa."
19. This is one of the apartments which can still be seen and is, indeed, used as the dining room for the "guests" of the Pia Casa di Ponterotto.
20. The bowl in which Francesca compounded these miraculous remedies is preserved in the Tor di Specchi and, during the novena which marks the saint's feast—March 9—it is filled with flowers, from which visitors are permitted to carry away blossoms.

21. Matthew 9:18-34; Mark 5:22-43; Luke 8:41-56.
22. The question inevitably arises in the inquiring mind as to why she did not baptize the baby herself, since this would, of course have been permissible under the circumstances. But very probably she thought such an emergency measure would make a less lasting impression on a woman, who had been so remiss in the matter of Baptism, than a ceremony performed by a priest.
23. According to Berthem-Bontoux, he was a doctor of Toulouse, but Collison-Morley, in his history, *Naples Through the Centuries,* designates him as a Florentine.
24. Domenico Grandi and Antonio Galli, *The Story of the Church.* Translated and edited by John Chapin. (Garden City, New York: Hanover House. A division of Doubleday & Company, Inc.)
25. Berthem-Bontoux dates her adoption of this from the period at which we have now arrived, and quotes the archives of the Tor di Specchi for authority. This, however, would nullify Lorenzo's attitude after the first miracle—see Fullerton, p. 36—and the general belief that Francesca's simple and unchanging dress had made her a familiar figure in the streets of Rome. Moreover, sumptuous clothing would surely have been most unsuitable for her labors in the vineyard, as well as her nursing. Modern authorities I have consulted prefer the version I have used.
26. Reformers were especially loud in their denunciation of the *cyprienne* which, apparently, took its designation from the bad name given, at the time, to the inhabitants of Cyprus, who, rightly or wrongly, were condemned as a dissolute lot. Larousse defines a *cyprienne* as a "long dress worn by Italian women in the fourteenth century, made without folds and with a deep square-cut décolletage and big sleeves. A long line of buttons extended down the front from top to bottom of the dress." He then goes on to say, "Preachers frequently attacked the décolleté and the luxury and extraordinary richness of the buttons."
27. R. P. Dom J. Rabory, *Vie de Sainte Françoise Romaine Fondatrice des Oblates de Tor di Specchi.* (Paris: Librairie Catholique Internationale de L'Oeuvre de Saint-Paul).
28. Some authorities give the date of Bernardine's visit as two years later, but I believe the explanation of this is that he came twice.
29. "In the Name of Our Lord Jesus Christ, I, Sister Frances, daughter of Paul Bussa, offer myself to God Almighty, to the Most Glorious Virgin Mary, to our Blessed Father Benedict, and to this venerable Monastery of Santa Maria Nova in Rome, which belongs to the Order of Monte Oliveto, in the presence of all the Saints whose relics are in this place, in the presence of the Reverend Brother Hippolyte

of Rome, Prior of the above mentioned Monastery, who, in the name, and by the authority of the Most Reverend Abbot General of the above mentioned Order, Brother Jerome of Perugia, will receive me as Oblate in this monastery and I promise perpetual stability of my oblation, the conversion of my ways and obedience.

"I have written this letter in faith, by my own hand and have subscribed to it with my own signature.

"In the year of the Incarnation of the Lord, 1425, the fifteenth day of August, in Rome, in the above mentioned Church of Santa Maria Nova.

"I, Sister Frances Bussa de Pontianis."

30. Two authorities question this trip. Maria Castiglione Humani, a modern biographer of Francesca, questions the authenticity of this trip and gives as her authority, P. Lugano, another biographer whose work I have not seen, but which is included among the documents at the Vatican Library. However, except by these two authors, the authenticity of the trip does not seem to have been questioned and I have followed the authorities who accept it.
31. Maria Castiglione Humani, *S. Francesca Romana La Santa Dei Ponziani.* (Bari: Edizioni Paoline).
32. In Santa Francesca's day and at the present time there are only thirteen Oblates at the Tor di Specchi.
33. It is interesting to note how often there is a reference to Francesca as "The Strong Woman"—a title also proudly associated, to this day, with the Venerable María Vela, a sixteenth-century Spanish nun of the Cistercian Order, in the Convent of Santa Ana in Avila.

Saint Catherine of Siena

1. Edmund G. Gardner, *Florence and Its Story,* Mediaeval Towns Series. (London: J. M. Dent & Sons, Limited).
2. Piero Misciattelli, *The Mystics of Siena.* English version by M. Peters-Roberts. (New York: D. Appleton and Company).
3. There is still a district in the city known as Castelsieno.
4. Contrary to the general impression, the famous horse race known as the Palio, which is still celebrated with medieval pageantry twice a year—on July 2 and August 16—was not run in St. Catherine's time. The first race took place in 1656.
5. The Fonte Gaia, or Gay Fountain, in the Campo, which is the one with which present-day travelers are the most familiar and which is uncovered, is not numbered among these. It was not built until the

fifteenth century, whereas the others are of much earlier construction.

6. These fountains are still in use, though not for so many purposes as originally. A modern swimming pool adjoins the Fontebranda, the successor to one of primitive type, dating from about the seventeenth century. It was and is largely patronized.
7. Blessed Raymond of Capua, Confessor to the Saint, *The Life of St. Catherine of Siena,* translated by George Lamb. (New York: P. J. Kenedy & Sons).
8. Piero Misciattelli, *The Mystics of Siena.* English version by M. Peters-Roberts. (New York: D. Appleton and Company).

   In a niche on the wall of the warehouse which has since been built on the site of the Benincasas' dwelling is a charming bust of the saint, made of glazed terracotta in delicate colors. On the base is inscribed the following verse:

   Santa Caterina da Siena Virgine
   Tu che questo suolo un giorno
   Possedendo calcasti, ora dal cielo
   Rendilo pur d'ogni dovizia adorno.

   This may be freely translated as:

   "St. Catherine, Virgin of Siena
   Who once didst tread this very ground,
   Look down from Heaven with favour on it,
   With richest gifts let it be crowned."

9. Among the numerous references to visions in the Bible, the following may be mentioned: "The word of the Lord came to Abram by a vision, saying: Fear not, Abram, I am thy protector, and thy reward exceeding great." (Genesis 15:1). . . . "The Lord came down in a pillar of the cloud, and stood in the entry of the tabernacle calling to Aaron and Mary. And when they were come, He said to them: Hear my words: if there be among you a prophet of the Lord, I will appear to him in a vision, or I will speak to him in a dream." (Numbers 12:5 & 6). . . . Peter, quoting from the prophet Joel, told his fellow apostles, "And it shall come to pass, in the last days, (saith the Lord,) I will pour out of my Spirit upon all flesh: and your sons and your daughters shall prophesy, and your young men shall see visions, and your old men shall dream dreams." (Acts 2:17). . . . Adam and Eve "heard the voice of the Lord God walking in paradise at the afternoon air." (Genesis 3:8). . . . Moses heard the voice again and again; all the Mosaic laws were given in this way, and it was the voice of the Lord that led Joshua to victory. . . . Jacob "saw in his sleep a ladder standing upon the earth, and the top thereof touching heaven: the

angels also of God ascending and descending by it." (Genesis 28:12). . . . Pharao said to Joseph, "I have dreamed dreams, and there is no one that can expound them: now I have heard that thou art very wise at interpreting them. Joseph answered: Without me, God shall give Pharao a prosperous answer." (Genesis 41:15 & 16). . . . Stephen "being full of the Holy Ghost, looking up steadfastly to heaven, saw the glory of God, and Jesus standing on the right hand of God. And he said: Behold, I see the heavens opened, and the Son of man standing on the right hand of God." (Acts 7:55). . . . As Saul "went on his journey, it came to pass that he drew nigh to Damascus; and suddenly a light from heaven shined round about him. And falling on the ground, he heard a voice saying to him: Saul, Saul, why persecutest thou me?" (Acts 9:3). . . . "And a great sign appeared in heaven: A woman clothed with the sun, and the moon under her feet, and on her head a crown of twelve stars." (Apocalypse 12:1.)

10. These springs, now generally called the Bagno Vignoni, are still held in high regard and are much frequented. They have kept much of their medieval character and atmosphere. Several of the buildings which surround the reservoir where Catherine bathed are virtually unchanged, as is the great pool itself; and the scalding water, enveloped in mists of steam, still comes bubbling up at one end. Leading from this main reservoir to smaller pools are open conduits through which the warm water flows freely and anyone who wishes may sit on the brinks of these conduits to bathe feet and legs. On the day we visited the springs, several women and children and one or two men were doing so—people apparently of peasant stock, but all clean, all orderly and all friendly. For more prosperous patrons, besides the dressing rooms adjoining the reservoir, there are two inns near the plaza, one flanked by a pleasant garden with a grape arbor and, lately, an annex has been built to this one, because of the great demand for rooms. We were invited to look at these and found them acceptable according to modern standards of simple comfort—not luxury—and the inn's cuisine has been highly praised to us.
11. Igino Giordani, *Catherine of Siena—Fire and Blood.* Translated from the Italian by Thomas J. Tobin. (Milwaukee: The Bruce Publishing Company).
12. Even the mastery of foreign languages often proceeds in much the same way as the mastery of the printed word in one's own language. I have often heard this difficult process compared to climbing a high hill, so slowly and laboriously that it seemed as if the top could never be reached. Then, all at once, there you are at the summit and you can go racing down again whenever you choose! This is particularly true, of course, in the case of a foreign language learned by an adult;

a child, given half a chance, learns a foreign language with no struggle at all.

It may also be noted, for the benefit of those who never heard of this method or have not approved of it, that some forty or fifty years ago many American children were very generally taught words before they were taught separate letters. I must confess that I was one of the mothers who failed to approve: not because a child did not learn to *read* quickly in this way, but because, when he needed to begin using a dictionary, he was quite helpless until he *had* learned the alphabet! That Catherine could read with ease and fluency, recognizing words but not individual letters until much later, does not seem to me in the least phenomenal.

13. Sigrid Undset, *Catherine of Siena.* Translated by Kate Austin-Lund. (New York: Sheed and Ward).
14. Monteoliveto Maggiore is a celebrated Benedictine Abbey about twenty-one miles from Siena. It is the Motherhouse of the Olivetan Monks, founded and dedicated to St. Scolastica in 1313, when the Sienese nobleman, Bernardo Tolomei, and other Sienese patricians retired there to lead hermits' lives. "Based on the Rule of St. Benedict, in 1319 it became the Congregation of Santa Maria di Monteoliveto, a Rule which has contributed much to the fields of science and art and is considered one of the greatest monasteries in Italy." (Aldo Lusini and Sandro Chierichetti, *Siena—An Illustrated Guide Book.* Siena: Stefano Venturini).
15. Latin inscriptions on marble plaques, placed near the entrance of the convent, recall the visits of Catherine, as well as the sojourn of St. Augustine, and the occurrence of a miracle. They also admonish the visitor—with blessings on his comings and goings—to remember that this is a holy place. Seminarians from Siena spend their summer retreats here; but, aside from this, the monastery is, alas, deserted, except for a family of peasants who act as caretakers. Structurally, the building is still sound and though the frescoes are in a deplorable condition, it is easy to see how beautiful they once were.
16. Psalms 50:12.
17. This Order, also called the Order of Girolamo, whose members had established themselves in the Valle d'Orcia, becoming devoted servants of God and consecrating themselves to the saving of souls, should not be confused—though they often are—with the *Gesuiti* (Jesuits) whose Order was founded by Ignatius Loyola more than two centuries later. The Order of Gesuati was abolished by Clement IX in 1668.
18. Sigrid Undset puts Lisa's departure earlier and says Lisa took the children with her when she went; though, at another point, she says, "some of the children were left with Lapa" and, all things being equal,

that would seem the safest place for all of them. Wohl—alone among authorities I have consulted—calls Lisa "a relative of Lapa" and not the wife of Bartolommeo. Of course, Lisa is a fairly common name and Catherine had an elder sister, who was also called Lisa, of whom very little is known, except that she was unmarried and that she died of the plague; but the combination of Lisa with Colombini provides more identification. After carefully sifting all available evidence, I have decided that the sources which designate Lisa Colombini as Bartolommeo's wife are the most convincing; I have also accepted the time of her departure for Florence as the one which seems most plausible.

19. These were painted in the fifteenth century by Paolo Uccello and were typical of the scenes from Scripture which constituted what were then known as poor men's Bibles. Most of the populace was still illiterate, but it was devout; and those who were unable to read the printed page were glad to learn Bible stories from painted walls. The frescoes of the Green Cloister began with the Creation of the Animals and Adam and continued as far as the Crucifixion. These frescoes finally deteriorated to such a degree through exposure that it was necessary to remove many of them in order to preserve them; but the preparatory drawings, called *sinopi,* can still be seen and the general effect is still one of soft and restful color.

It should also be noted that the name by which the Chapter House itself is now most generously known, *Capella degli Spagnoli* (Spanish Chapel) was not given it until 1540—that is, nearly two hundred years after Catherine's appearance there. Eleonora da Toledo, wife of Grand Duke Cosimo I de Medici, assigned it to the Spanish dignitaries in her suite, as a gathering place for ceremonials of religious nature. "Thus the unsuitable name of the *Spanish Chapel* came to be used instead of the former name of Chapter House which had a very different meaning. It would be no bad thing to revive the earlier name, especially as the allegorical pictures painted for the Chapter House have never been in any way connected with the manners and customs of a princely court." (Piero Bargellini, *The Cloisters of Santa Maria Novella and the Spanish Chapel.* Florence: Arnaud).

20. Most references that I have found to the origin and growth of these two political parties are both dull and confusing. The following, gleaned from *Daily Life in Florence in the Time of the Medici* by J. Lucas-Dubreton, who, in turn, acknowledges his indebtedness to a *novelliere* of the fourteenth century, *Ser* Giovanni Fiorentino, seems to me delightful:

"Two German lords, one named Guelf and the other Gibelin, were close friends, but one day when returning from the hunt they quarrelled about a bitch and became mortal enemies, so that the barons and lords of Germany were also divided, some siding with Guelf and others with Gibelin. Now, as the latter felt they were the weaker party, they appealed to the Emperor Henry I; their adversaries then appealed to Pope Honorius III, who was at odds with the Emperor, and all because of a wretched bitch.

"Now it came to pass in the year 1215 that this evil strife invaded Italy, and in the following manner. There dwelt in the house of the Buondelmonti in Florence a wealthy and valiant knight who had pledged his troth to a daughter of the Amidei. As he was passing the house of the Donati one day, a lady called to him and said:

" 'Messer, I am astonished that you should have a leaning for one who would be scarce fit to unloose your shoes. I had been reserving my daughter for you. I desire that you see her.'

"And she forthwith called the girl, whose name was Ciulla, fairer and more pleasant than any other maiden in Florence. 'Here,' she said, 'is the bride I reserved for you.'

"Buondelmonte fell in love at first sight.

" 'Madam, I am ready to do as you wish.' And before leaving he chose Ciulla for wife and gave her his ring.

"When they heard that Buondelmonte had taken a different wife, the Amidei and their friends swore to take vengeance. Each man was giving his opinion when one said: '*Cosa fatta è fatta*,' which means that 'a dead man never makes war.' " (According to most authorities, the correct quotation is, "*Cosa fatta, capo ha.*" At all events, that is the way present day Florentines use the expression—see Gardner's *Florence and Its Story;* Gardner also gives the name of Ciulla's mother as Gualdrada.)

"On Easter morning Buondelmonte was on his way back from breakfast on the far bank of the Arno. Wearing a white gown and mounted on a snow-white palfrey, he was at the lower end of the Ponte Vecchio by the statue of Mars which the Florentines used to worship when they were pagans and where fish is sold now, when a band of men rushed out, pulled him from his horse and killed him.

"Florence was in an uproar, and this man's death led to a cleavage among the nobility: the Buondelmonti became leaders of the Guelphs and the Amidei of the Ghibellines. Next, the seeds of evil faction were sown all over Italy, and lords and peoples separated into two camps. Thus the Guelph and Ghibelline parties sprang up in Germany on acount of a bitch and in Italy on account of a woman."

Mr. Lucas-Dubreton further notes: "This classification was not destined to remain rigid. In the course of time and under the pressure of circumstances, it was to break down. Sometimes there were

Guelphs who favored the Emperors and Ghibellines who sided with the Pope."

21. In 1215, the war between the Guelphs and Ghibellines came to a head, but it existed before then. The "Ciompi" (those who wore sabots), the lowest class of the Florentine people, rose, headed by a certain Michele di Lando, on July 20, 1278 and demanded the right to have some say in the Florentine government. Michele di Lando died in 1301.
22. This room is now an oratory and still contains the stone slab, set in a slight declivity, on which she slept.
23. "Matteo di Cenni di Fazio was a Sienese nobleman of signal virtue and for that reason very dear to the holy virgin. He was made Rector of the Misericordia on September 1st, 1373." (Blessed Raymond of Capua, *The Life of St. Catherine of Siena,* translated by George Lamb. New York: P. J. Kenedy & Sons).
24. This miracle forms the subject of one of the superb paintings in the famous Piccolomini Library of the Cathedral of Siena and various other works of art. Though the convent which Agnes founded and the adjoining church, which now bears her name and where she is buried under the high altar, have not been preserved in their entirety, the room where she died and other portions of the original structure have been carefully kept and the modern additions have been tastefully made. Her tomb and the many relics preserved in the death chamber are still objects of constant and devout veneration. About a hundred years ago, the Dominican Nuns left this convent to join Sienese communities and it became a Dominican monastery. It now maintains a fine educational institution, which provides for studies all the way from primary grades to post-graduate work.
25. For some years, Siena had been in a state of political upheaval. In 1368, when Catherine's brothers, who had both held government positions, were obliged to flee to Florence, the Council of Twelve Members—*Le Dodici*—was composed entirely of commoners. Later, after much turmoil and bloodshed, in the course of which a visit from the Emperor, Charles IV, resulted in fresh disturbances, a new Government of Twelve was set up; but this time the officials called themselves by another name—*Difensori del Popolo Sienese*—Defenders of the Sienese People—and this group was made up of the *Popolo Minuti* —or working classes—who had five representatives; the gentry who had four; and the nobility who had three. Nevertheless, despite this apparent minority, the nobles had more political power than before, especially the great family of the Salimbeni, who had always been customers and patrons of the Benincasas. They were given "citizenship"—that is to say, they were henceforth to be eligible to hold

political positions, whatever party was in power, and they were accorded the right to maintain, in their own name, five fortresses outside the city of Siena. Catherine often visited them in these *castellos* and several of them became closely identified with her story.

26. The Palazzo Buonconti, which was imposingly situated beside the Church of Santa Cristina on the southern bank of the Arno, was destroyed by a bomb in the second World War. A marble plaque on the rear wall of the church verifies this sad destruction and identifies the exact location of the palazzo, of which only part of a crumbling façade remains. However, the Palazzo Gambacorti on the Corso Italia —the principal street of Pisa—which belongs to the same period, happily escaped; and though part of the interior has been converted into offices, the façade and patio give a very good idea of the architecture of the times as favored by wealthy noblemen and prominent officials. The Medici palace, likewise still standing, belongs to a slightly later period, but also helps to do the same thing.
27. Like several others of Catherine's associates and converts, she achieved sanctity. Pius VIII canonized her.
28. Blessed Raymond of Capua, Confessor to the Saint, *The Life of St. Catherine of Siena,* translated by George Lamb. (New York: P. J. Kenedy & Sons).

    The miraculous occurrence at the Church of Santa Cristina in Pisa on Laetare Sunday is the one generally accepted as marking Catherine's reception of the stigmata and is the one invariably represented in paintings. However, according to many authorities, there had been a similar, though less comprehensive, experience in Siena before she began her work of public ministry. Giordani refers to it in the following words: "Once when she had asked of Jesus a sign that her prayers were being heard, He made her hold out her hand, the palm of which He pierced with a nail. It was the beginning of the stigmata, later on made complete in 1375 in the chapel of St. Cristian at Pisa."
29. Caffarini, like Fra Raimondo, wrote a biography of Catherine from the vantage point of a contemporary.
30. John Farrow, *The Pageant of the Popes.* (New York: Sheed and Ward).
31. Robert Brun, *Avignon au Temps des Papes.* (Paris: Librairie Armand Colin).
32. Fernand Benoit, *Villeneuve-lez-Avignon.* (Paris: Henri Laurens, Editeur).
33. Domenico Grandi and Antonio Galli, *The Story of the Church.* Translated and edited by John Chapin. (Garden City, New York: Hanover House. A Division of Doubleday & Company, Inc.)

34. According to Robert Brun, this orchard, which reminded Urban V of the one he had in Avignon, forms the basis for the present Vatican garden.
35. Dr. Gabriel Colombe, *Le Palais des Papes d'Avignon.* (Paris: Henri Laurens, Editeur).

    There seems to be a general impression that Catherine was received in the Great Audience chamber, built by Clement VI; but as M. Sylvain Gagnière, present Director of the Papal Palace, pointed out to me and as Dr. Colombe makes clear in his book, this was used as a Tribunal, the seat of the Rota, and not as a diplomatic reception room. Catherine was not on trial, as she had been in Florence; she was an accredited ambassador and there was no reason why she should have been summoned to appear before a court of justice. Quite probably the feeling that her visit should be regarded as being of great importance is responsible for the inclination to place the scene of one of the most dramatic episodes in history where it would appear most impressive; and unquestionably the Great Audience, with its double row of Gothic columns, which give it two naves, and its immense height and length, is one of the most awe-inspiring apartments in the world, even in its present denuded and empty state. When it was enriched with paintings and tapestries and peopled by an enthroned pope, red-robed cardinals and all those summoned to appear before them, either to assist in their deliberations or for trial, it must have been overpowering in its splendor.
36. The Scotti palace still stands, structurally sound, though it is now a tenement and the section of the city where it stands has become a rough one. There is a large marble plaque on the side near the door which bears the following inscription:

NEL MCCCLXXVI
GIUNGEVA IN GENOVA REDUCE DA AVIGNONE
NUNZIA DI PACE ALLA CHIESA E ALL'ITALIA
E OSPITATA IN QUESTA CASA
DA MADONNA ORIETTA SCOTTO
DIMORAVA PIU' GIORNI
SANTA CATERINA DA SIENA
QUI IN PONTEFICE GREGORIO XI
NEL RICONDURRE A ROMA LA SEDIA PONTIFICALE
TRAEVA A PRENDER LENA
DALLA PAROLA INSPIRATA DI LEI
E QUI LA SANTA
CONSOLAVA DI PRODIGIOSA GUARIGIONE
STEFANO MACONI E NERI DI LANDOCCIO

DE'PAGLIARESI
PERCHE' DI SI'EGREGI FATTI DURASSE PERENNE
LA MEMORIA
ALCUNI CITTADINI PONEVANO QUESTA LAPIDE
MDCCCLXXX

This may be freely translated as:

"In 1376, St. Catherine of Siena, ambassador of peace to the Church and to Italy, arrived in Genoa from Avignon. She was hospitably received in this house by Madonna Orietta Scotto and remained here for several days.

"Here Pope Gregory XI was inspired by her noble words to return the Papacy to Rome.

"Here the Saint nursed Stefano Maconi and Neri di Landuccio di Pagliaresi back to health, comforting and sustaining them.

"This plaque has been placed here by citizens of the town so that these remarkable events may always be commemorated.

1880"

37. "On this second visit to blessed Agnes's body, another miracle happened that is worth recording.

"As soon as she arrived at the convent, then, and set foot inside it, her first thought was to go and venerate the body of the blessed Agnes, followed by her companions and some of the nuns. When she came into the presence of the corpse she did not go towards the feet this time, but, radiant with joy, went up to the head. Perhaps in her humility she wanted to avoid any second miraculous elevation of the foot, or she may have remembered the Magdalene, who first anointed the Saviour's feet with ointment when He was sitting at table and then sprinkled it on His head. Bending down, she lowered her face close to Agnes's, which was wrapped in a silk cloth threaded with gold, and remained in that position.

"A long time passed, and then she turned to her companion and sister-in-law Lisa, the mother of the two girls she had brought to the convent, and said to her, joyfully, 'Can't you see the gift she has sent us from heaven? Why are you so ungrateful?' At these words Lisa and the others, raising their eyes, saw very fine, perfectly white manna coming down like rain, in such abundance that it made Agnes's body and Catherine herself, and all the other people there, quite white, and Lisa was able to collect handfuls of the grains.

"Not without reason did this appear in this place, for the miracle of the manna had been very common with Agnes, especially when she prayed. I remember describing in my life of her how the daughters she was instructing in the ways of the Lord, ignorant of what was happening, saw her get up from prayer with her cloak all white and tried to shake it off until she gently stopped them.

"Agnes, knowing that Catherine was one day to be her companion in heaven, through this her accustomed miracle was beginning to accompany her and honour her on earth. Quite rightly, too, for this manna, with its whiteness and the fineness of its grains, represents to those who understand these things purity and virgins. All this I know from these two lives, and not through any merit of my own have I recorded it, but by the Saviour's mercy.

"Witnesses of this miracle were Catherine's companions, including Lisa, who is still alive, and many nuns belonging to the convent, who stated on their honour to me and the Friars that this was how the thing happened, describing it and assuring us that they had seen it all with their own eyes. Many of them have now passed on to the next life, but their testimony I can well remember, as can the Friars who were with me at the time. Lisa, indeed, showed a number of people the manna she had collected, and made a present of it to them.

"In truth, infinite are the amazing things that God revealed through His bride Catherine whilst she was amongst us, and not all are set down in this book. Those that can read here have been written to the honour and glory of the Divine Name and for the good of souls, and also that I may not be found ungrateful for the gift given me from heaven. May God keep me from burying the talent that is meant to be used profitably, and enable me to return it to Him with some increase—the fruit of gratitude." (Blessed Raymond of Capua, *The Life of St. Catherine of Siena,* translated by George Lamb. New York: P. J. Kenedy & Sons).

38.

"O Holy Ghost
O Deity Eternal
Christ-Love, come into my heart.

By Thy power allure me to Thee, my God,
and grant me charity with fear.
Guard me, O Love unspeakable,
from every evil thought;
warm me and fire me
with Thy sweetest love,
that all pain may seem slight to me,
my Holy Father, my sweet Lord.
Help me now in my every service.

Christ-Love! Christ-Love!"

Translation by Sister Madeleva, C.S.C., St. Mary's College, Notre Dame, Indiana, as given by Igino Giordani in *Catherine of Siena—Fire and Blood.*

39. Some of Catherine's biographers have questioned the authenticity of this beautiful story because no copy of the poem or anything else she penned herself is still extant. I see no reason for doing so. After all, the remarkable aspect of the case lies in the fact that nearly six hundred years after her death so many of her writings—four hundred letters and *The Dialogue*—are still available, not that some are missing. Catherine herself said, in a letter to Fra Raimondo, that she suddenly discovered she could write, through divine inspiration when she was in a state of rapture and places the time definitely at the Rocca, in connection with this poem! Moreover, Tommaso Caffarini also tells the story in the *Leggenda Minore,* saying that this gift (of writing) had been bestowed on her as a consolation at a time when she had many difficulties and trials, which was certainly true of her stay with the Salimbeni. Sigrid Undset interprets the episode very practically: "It does not seem unlikely that Catherine one day discovered that she herself could do what others do every day, nor that she received this ability as a special gift from God."

    The pigment used at that time, both for ordinary writing and for the more elaborate drawing of capital letters, was what we have come to call sienna—spelled, for some unknown reason, with two n's instead of one. *The American College Dictionary* (New York: Random House) defines it as: "a ferruginous earth used as a yellowish-brown pigment (raw sienna) or, after roasting in a furnace, as a reddish brown pigment (burnt sienna)."
40. This tower house, incorporated in a larger one, is still intact and is still standing in the erstwhile vineyard, which is now a charming residential section, known as the Costa San Giorgio (St. George's Hill). The frescoes in the oratory belong to the eighteenth century, but structurally it is exactly as when St. Catherine used it. This and the study bedroom form part of a property belonging to Miss Dorothy Good, whose help has been so invaluable to me in writing about St. Catherine.
41. As a matter of fact, Belcaro again became a private residence not long after her death and still remains one. It is in excellent condition and can be visited.
42. This tree may still be seen there.
43. This oratory may still be seen. It adjoins the Church of Santa Maria sopra Minerva, where Catherine is buried.

BIBLIOGRAPHY

Saint Agnes of Rome

Balsdon, J. P. V. D., *Roman Women—Their History and Habits.* London: The Bodley Head.

Cenci, Monsignor Pio, *S. Agnese.* Rome: Edizioni Bibliotechina.

Coulson, John, *The Saints—A Concise Biographical Dictionary.* New York: Hawthorn Books, Inc.

Dennie, John, *Rome of To-Day and Yesterday—The Pagan City.* New York: G. P. Putnam's Sons.

Farrow, John, *Pageant of the Popes.* New York: Sheed and Ward.

Homan, Helen Walker, *Saints of the Canon.* Washington: National Council of Catholic Women.

Horgan, Paul, *Rome Eternal.* New York: Farrar, Straus & Cudahy.

Jameson, Anna, *Sacred and Legendary Art.* (2 vols.) Boston and New York: Houghton Mifflin and Company.

Michelin Guide to Italy. London: The Dickens Press.

Morton, H. V., *A Traveller in Rome.* London: Methuen & Co., Ltd.

Muirhead, L. Russell, *Rome and Central Italy.* The Blue Guides. London: Ernest Benn Limited.

Perowne, Stewart, *Caesars and Saints.* London: Hodder and Stoughton.

Wiseman, Nicholas Cardinal (Retold by Eddie Doherty), *Fabiola.* New York: P. J. Kenedy & Sons.

Santa Francesca Romana

Arcispedale di Santo Spirito in Saxia. Official booklet of the Hospital.

Armellini, Mariano, *Le Chiese di Roma dal Secolo IV al XIX* (Vol. I). Rome: Edizioni R.O.R.E. di Nicola Ruffolo.

Berthem-Bontoux, *Sainte Françoise Romaine et Son Temps* (1384–1440). Paris: Librairie Bloud & Gay.

Cali, Francois, *Dictionnaire Pittoresque de la France.* France: Arthaud.

Cecchetti, Igino, *The Sublime City.* Published for the Catholic War Veterans of U.S.A., Washington, D.C. by Edizioni Arte e Scienza, Roma, Piazza Pio XII 3.

Collison-Morley, Lacy, *Naples Through the Centuries.* London: Methuen & Co., Ltd.

Crawford, Francis Marion, *Ave Roma Immortalis—Studies from the Chronicles of Rome.* (2 vols.) New York: The Macmillan Company.

de Angelis, Pietro, *L'Ospedale Apostolico di Santo Spirito in Saxia Nella Mente e Nel Cuore dei Papi.* Rome.

Musica e Musicisti Nell'Arcispedale di Santo Spirito in Saxia. Rome.

de Angelis, Salvatore, *Glorie della Madonna di Ponterotto.* Tivoli: Stabilimento Tipografico Mantero.

del Busto D., José Antonio, *El Arcabucero Gaspar de Flores, Padre de Santa Rosa.* Lima: *Revista Historica,* Vol. XXIII, 1960.

Farrow, John, *Pageant of the Popes.* New York: Sheed and Ward.

Fullerton, Lady Georgiana. *The Life of St. Frances of Rome, of Blessed Lucy of Narni, of Dominica of Paradiso, and of Anne de Montmorency with an Introductory Essay on the Miraculous Life of the Saints* by J. M. Capes, Esq. London: Burns and Lambert.

Grandi, Domenico and Galli, Antonio, *The Story of the Church.* Translated and edited by John Chapin. Garden City, New York: Hanover House, a division of Doubleday & Company, Inc.

Horgan, Paul, *Rome Eternal.* New York: Farrar, Straus & Cudahy.

Humani, Maria Castiglione, *S. Francesca Romana La Santa dei Ponziani.* Bari: Edizioni Paoline.

Keyes, Frances Parkinson, *The Rose and the Lily.* New York: Hawthorn Books, Inc.

Kittler, Glenn D., *The Papal Princes—A History of the Sacred College of Cardinals*. New York: Funk & Wagnalls.

Michelin Guide to Italy. London: The Dickens Press.

Morton, H. V., *A Traveller in Rome*. London: Methuen & Co., Ltd.

Muirhead, L. Russell, *Rome and Central Italy*. The Blue Guides. London: Ernest Benn, Limited.

Pastor, Dr. L., *The History of the Popes*. St. Louis: Herder Book Co.

Rabory, R. P. Dom J., *Vie de Sainte Françoise Romaine Fondatrice des Oblates de Tor de' Specchi*. Paris: Librairie Catholique Internationale de L'Oeuvre de Saint-Paul.

Sheed, Maisie Ward, *St. Frances of Rome*. Washington: National Council of Catholic Women.

Windham, Joan, *More Saints for Six O'Clock*. London: Sheed and Ward.

Through the cooperation of John Howard, I have found twenty additional books, pamphlets and articles about Santa Francesca Romana in the Vatican Library. These works are available to any serious student for consultation.

Saint Catherine of Siena

Benoit, Fernand, *Villeneuve-lez-Avignon*. Paris: Henri Laurens, Éditeur.

Brion, Marcel, *La Provence*. Paris: B. Arthaud.

Brun, Robert, *Avignon au Temps des Papes*. Paris: Librairie Armand Colin.

Burton, Katherine, *Saint Catherine of Siena*. Washington: National Council of Catholic Women.

Caffarini, Fr. Tommaso, *Leggenda Minore*.

Capua, *Beato* Raimondo *da, Vita di Santa Caterina da Siena*. Siena: Ezio Cantagalli.

——— Blessed Raymond of (Confessor to the Saint), *The Life of St. Catherine of Siena*. Translated by George Lamb. New York: P. J. Kenedy & Sons.

Cecchini, Giovanni, *The Piccolomini Library in Siena Cathedral*. Siena: The Opera Metropolitana of Siena.

Chierichetti, Sandro, *Pisa—An Artistic and Illustrated Guide*. Milan: Industrie Grafiche N. Moneta.

Colombe, Dr. Gabriel, *Le Palais des Papes d'Avignon*. Paris: Henri Laurens, Éditeur.

de Wohl, Louis, *Lay Siege to Heaven, A Novel of St. Catherine of Siena*. Philadelphia and New York: J. B. Lippincott Company.

Farrow, John, *Pageant of the Popes*. New York: Sheed and Ward.

Gardner, Edmund G., *Florence and Its Story*. (Mediaeval Towns Series) London: J. M. Dent & Sons, Ltd.

——— *The Story of Siena and San Gimignano*. (Mediaeval Towns Series) London: J. M. Dent & Sons, Ltd.

Giordani, Igino, *Catherine of Siena—Fire and Blood*. Translated from the Italian by Thomas J. Tobin. Milwaukee: The Bruce Publishing Company.

Grandi, Domenico and Galli, Antonio, *The Story of the Church*. Translated and edited by John Chapin. Garden City, New York: Hanover House, a division of Doubleday & Company, Inc.

Horgan, Paul, *Rome Eternal*. New York: Farrar, Straus & Cudahy.

Kaftal, George, *St. Catherine in Tuscan Painting*. Oxford: Blackfriars.

Kittler, Glenn D., *The Papal Princes—A History of the Sacred College of Cardinals*. New York: Funk & Wagnalls.

Lacombe, Noël, *Villeneuve-les-Avignon*. Nimes: Louis Salle, Éditeur.

Lucas-Dubreton, J., *Daily Life in Florence in the Time of the Medici*. Translated from the French by A. Lytton Sells. London: Ruskin House, George Allen and Unwin Ltd.

Lusini, Aldo and Chierichetti, Sandro, *Siena—An Illustrated Guide Book*. Siena: Stefano Venturini.

Machiavelli, Niccolo, *History of Florence and of the Affairs of Italy*. New York: Harper & Brothers.

Michelin Guide to Italy. London: The Dickens Press.

Misciattelli, Piero, *The Mystics of Siena*. English version by M. Peters-Roberts. New York: D. Appleton and Company.

Mollat, G., *Les Papes d'Avignon* 1305–1378. Paris: Letouzey & Ané.

Origo, Iris, *The Merchant of Prato*. London: Jonathan Cape.

Ross, Janet and Erichsen, Nelly, *The Story of Lucca*. (Mediaeval Towns Series) London: J. M. Dent & Sons, Ltd.

St. Catherine of Siena, *Dialogos de Santa Catalina de Sena*. Madrid: D. Pedro Julian Pereyra—1797.

Undset, Sigrid, *Catherine of Siena.* Translated by Kate Austin-Lund. New York: Sheed and Ward.

Young, G. F., *The Medici.* New York: The Modern Library.

Through the cooperation of the Marchesa Dottoressa Olga Campanari and John Howard, I have found no fewer than one hundred thirty-three books, pamphlets and articles about St. Catherine listed in the Vatican Library. These works are available to any serious student for consultation.

INDEX

Q

R

T

THE AUTHOR AND HER BOOK

FRANCES PARKINSON KEYES, *whose books have been best-sellers almost every year since 1936 and are published simultaneously in England and the United States and in as many as twelve foreign languages, was born at the University of Virginia, where her father, John Henry Wheeler, a Bostonian transplanted to the South, was head of the Greek department. Her mother was Louise Fuller Johnson, a New Yorker who had earlier moved to Newbury, Vermont. After Dr. Wheeler's death, Frances and her mother spent their summers in Newbury, Vermont, and their winters in Boston, a city which was to become the scene of* Joy Street *(Messner, 1950), a best-seller of 1950-51. As a girl, she studied in Geneva and Berlin, as well as Boston, and with a governess. She speaks four languages and even today spends much time in travel. She was married at eighteen to Henry Wilder Keyes, whose home, Pine Grove Farm, near Haverhill, New Hampshire, was just across the river from Newbury, Vermont. In 1917 he became governor of New Hampshire. In 1919 he was elected to the United States Senate and served three terms, during which Mrs. Keyes divided her time between her family of three sons and the beginning of a literary career, initiated with articles in the Atlantic Monthly and a novel,* The Old Gray Homestead *(Houghton Mifflin, 1919). Her interest in her husband's Washington career led her to depict Washington political life in a series of letters to American women which became a Good Housekeeping running feature entitled* The Letters from a Senator's Wife *and was later published in book form by Appleton in 1924. In 1923 she began a novel set in Washington which appeared in 1930 as* Queen Anne's Lace *(Liveright, 1930). From 1923 to 1935 she was an associate editor of Good Housekeeping and from 1937 to 1939 editor of the National Historical Magazine. Mrs. Keyes has spent much time in France, which led to the biography of St. Therese,* Written in Heaven *(Messner, 1937) and the life of St. Bernadette of Lourdes,* The Sublime Shepherdess *(Messner, 1940), and a more personal record,* Along a Little Way *(new and revised edition, Hawthorn, 1962). In 1940 she visited Mexico to write* The Grace of Guadalupe *(Messner, 1941). Mrs. Keyes holds degrees of Litt. D. from Bates College and George Washington University, and in 1951 received the degree of Doctor of Humane Letters from the University of New Hampshire "as a distinguished author, ambassador of good will, and interpreter of American life." In 1946 she received the Siena Medal awarded annually to "the outstanding Catholic woman in the United States"; in 1950 the Silver Medal of French Recognition for her aid in reconstructing the Abbaye of the Benedictines at Lisieux; and in 1959 she was decorated with the Order of Isabella the Catholic in recognition of her work in Spain; and in 1962 the Legion of Honour in additional recognition of her work in France. She still retains her ownership of the Oxbow, her ancestral homestead at Newbury, Vermont, and her legal residence is still at Pine Grove Farm, the Keyes' family home at North Haverhill, New Hampshire; but in the winter she uses the historic Beauregard House in New Orleans, which she has restored, as her writing center. Among her books besides those previously mentioned are:* The Career of David Noble *(Frederick Stokes, 1921),* Silver Seas and Golden Cities *(Liveright, 1931),* Lady Blanche Farm *(Liveright, 1931),* The Safe Bridge *(Messner, 1934),* Senator Marlowe's Daughter *(Messner, 1935),* The Happy Wanderer *(Messner, 1935),* Honor Bright *(Messner, 1936),* Capital Kaleidoscope *(1937),* Parts Unknown *(Messner, 1938),* The Great Tradition *(Messner, 1939),* Fielding's Folly *(Messner, 1940),* All That Glitters *(Messner, 1941),* Crescent Carnival *(Messner, 1942),* Also the Hills *(Messner, 1942),* The River Road *(Messner, 1945),* Once on Esplanade *(Dodd, Mead, 1947),* Came a Cavalier *(Messner, 1947),* Dinner at Antoine's *(Messner, 1948),* All This Is Louisiana *(Harper*

Bros., 1950), The Cost of a Best-Seller *(Messner, 1950),* Steamboat Gothic *(Messner, 1952),* Bernadette of Lourdes *(Messner, 1953),* The Royal Box *(Messner, 1954),* The Frances Parkinson Keyes Cookbook *(Doubleday, 1955),* Blue Camellia *(Messner, 1957),* The Land of Stones and Saints *(Doubleday, 1957),* Victorine *(Messner, 1958),* Station Wagon in Spain *(Farrar, Straus & Cudahy, 1959),* Frances Parkinson Keyes' Christmas Gift *(Hawthorn, 1959),* Mother Cabrini: Missionary to the World *(Vision Books, 1959),* The Third Mystic of Avila *(Farrar, Straus & Cudahy, 1960),* Roses in December *(Doubleday & Co., 1960),* The Chess Players *(Farrar, Straus & Cudahy, 1960),* The Rose and the Lily *(Hawthorn, 1961),* Madame Castel's Lodger *(Farrar, Straus, 1962),* Therese: Saint of a Little Way *(Hawthorn, 1962),* St. Anne, Grandmother of Our Saviour *(new and revised edition, Hawthorn, 1962),* The Restless Lady *(Liveright, 1963)* and A Treasury of Favorite Poems *(Hawthorn, 1963).*

Daughters of St. Paul